The Gandhi Reader

A Source Book
Of His Life
And Writings

Edited by Homer A. Jack

Grove Press, Inc. • New York

First Evergreen Edition published in 1961
ISBN: 0-394-62472-6
Library of Congress Catalog Card Number: 83-80414

Manufactured in the United States of America

GROVE PRESS, INC., 196 West Houston Street, New York, N.Y. 10014

9 8 7 6 5 4 3 2

GROVE PRESS EASTERN PHILOSOPHY AND LITERATURE SERIES   EDITED BY HANNELORE ROSSET

INTRODUCTION

Mohandas K. Gandhi was one of the great men not only of our time, but of all history. Greatness is an elusive quality: a conqueror who wins great victories may scarcely be remembered in the next century; a saint who remains unknown to his countrymen may be worshiped by another generation. Gandhi's greatness, which was widely recognized during his lifetime, has not diminished and indeed is likely to increase. He lived in the first half of the twentieth century, when inventors and rulers captured men's imaginations and souls: Edison, Ford, and Marconi; Lenin, Hitler, and Stalin. Gandhi shares contemporary regard with statesmen like Churchill and Roosevelt as well as with creative thinkers like Einstein and Schweitzer. Yet when the history of this era is written in perspective, Gandhi will stand securely beside Einstein and Schweitzer as one of the truly great creative personalities of our age. He is certainly the most important figure produced in centuries by a non-Western civilization.

Although Gandhi was revered by millions in the East, he was widely known and admired in the West. He was perhaps most commonly thought of as the little brown man in a white loincloth who successfully twisted the tail of the British lion. However, the writings of Gandhi are but little known, at least in the United States—much less than those of his Indian contemporaries, Nehru and Tagore, or his intellectual peers, Einstein and Schweitzer.

Gandhi left much to posterity. His legacy consisted not of personal possessions, but of a dramatic life and penetrating ethical insights. There is an embarrassing divergence between the lives and the doctrines of many world leaders. With Gandhi, his life and his teachings were one. The best exposition of his message was his own biography, much of which, fortunately, he has related himself.

Perhaps the most important single volume written by Gandhi was his autobiography, characteristically subtitled "The Story of My Experiments with Truth." This long work was written in the Gujarati language and later translated into English. It was first published serially in *Young India*, beginning in 1925. One of its limitations is its incomplete description of Gandhi's first experiments with *satyagraha* (non-violent direct action) during the twenty years he was in South Africa. This is provided in a second, less-known autobiographical volume—composed when Gandhi was in prison—entitled *Satyagraha in South Africa* and published in 1928.

Gandhi's autobiography terminates in 1920, when Gandhi had almost three decades of intense activity before him. He never had the time or inclination to write further autobiographical volumes, but certain works officially compiled by his close associates describe some of the climactic events in his life. These include the "great trial" of 1921, the midnight operation in 1924, the "great fast" of 1924, the London Round Table Conference in 1931, the "epic fast" in 1932, Gandhi's activity during World War II, his conferences with Jinnah over Pakistan, and his pilgrimages to Noakhali and Calcutta in 1946–47.

The great bulk of Gandhi's writings was in the form of editorials or short essays for his weekly newspapers. In 1903, in South Africa, he launched the English and Gujarati weekly newspaper, *Indian Opinion*. He soon found the newspaper to be an indispensable political tool. In India, in 1919, he helped establish the English-language *Young India* and its Gujarati edition, *Navajivan*. In 1933 *Young India* became *Harijan*—Gandhi's word for the untouchables. Some of his editorials and articles had tremendous political influence. In the 1940s, for example, *Harijan* was issued in a total of twelve editions in nine languages and, in addition, Gandhi's most important articles were reprinted the next day in all the newspapers of India. In his last years his own writings appeared less frequently; in their place were summaries of his speeches and talks after prayers, and descriptions of his activities by other persons.

Gandhi's writings in these newspapers have been reprinted in a number of "authorized" collections. These are available on such subjects as self-restraint, Christian missions, non-violence in war and peace, Hindu-Moslem communal unity, Hinduism, village industries, diet and diet reform, women and social injustice, and students. These collections constitute the great bulk of Gandhi's writings and comprise many thousands of pages of fascinating reading. No subject was too large for a Gandhi editorial, and none was too small. In his writings and in his talks after prayers, Gandhi delighted in the juxtaposition of the sublime with the familiar; to him anything was sublime which helped the people, even if it dealt with traditionally forbidden or unpleasant subjects.

In addition to his autobiographical and editorial writings, Gandhi was the author of a number of important miscellaneous works. In 1909, while on a voyage from London to South Africa, he composed the pamphlet *Hind Swaraj* or *Indian Home Rule*. In a sense this is Gandhi's *Mein Kampf*, for much of his later political philosophy may be found in this early pamphlet. In 1941 he published another significant pamphlet entitled *Constructive Programme: Its Meaning and Place*. This is a matured estimate of his total domestic "platform." Also in this miscellaneous category should be mentioned *Songs from Prison*, the translations that Gandhi made in prison in 1930 from the Upanishads and other Indian discourses. In 1946 the English translation of Gandhi's version of the Bhagavad Gita was issued as *The Gita According to Gandhi*.

Of the rich biographical material about Gandhi, the earliest book is Joseph J. Doke's *An Indian Patriot in South Africa*, published in 1909. The most widely known early biography was Romain Rolland's *Mahatma Gandhi* (1924). The best biography published to date is undoubtedly Louis Fischer's *The Life of Mahatma Gandhi* (1950); the longest is D. G. Tendulkar's eight-volume *Mahatma* (1951–1954). A number of other biographies have appeared in recent years, including several written especially for high school children.

A whole field of literature has developed explaining Gandhi's philosophy, beginning with C. F. Andrews' important volume, *Mahatma Gandhi's Ideas* (1929). Two historic volumes appeared in 1939 and 1944 on the occasion of Gandhi's seventieth and seventy-fifth birthdays. Finally, a number of pamphlets and books have appeared dealing with the period just before and after Gandhi's death.

Not many will now agree with Winston Churchill, who once tried to dismiss Gandhi as a "seditious fakir." Yet not all will agree as to whether Gandhi was primarily a saint or a politician. Gandhi himself said that "people describe me as a saint trying to be a politician, but the truth is the other way around." Trained in the law rather than in religion or philosophy, Gandhi nevertheless had a consuming interest in religion and sought to live a truly religious life. He not only succeeded as few men have done, but he devised a new religious approach to the problem of combating evil. Yet Gandhi was also a politician. His religion was of the market place, seldom above it. Both in South Africa and in India his efforts were unambiguously political. As Horace Alexander wisely observed, Gandhi's whole life was "a kind of dialectic," first preparing his people for freedom and then helping them to attain it.

Gandhi's patient efforts to prepare the Indian people for freedom have been called "the constructive program." This dealt at various times with a wide range of domestic reforms: Hindu-Moslem communal unity, elimination of untouchability, prohibition, home spinning, village industries, village sanitation, basic education, adult education, emancipation of women, education in health and hygiene, and other topics. Some of Gandhi's prescriptions were somewhat provincial in that they were not completely relevant to other cultures. Other aspects of his constructive program had and have universal significance.

Gandhi's greatest contribution was in the field of methodology. With the help of Hindu and Christian scriptures and insights from Henry D. Thoreau and Count Leo Tolstoy, he devised a new method of warfare—one which large or small groups, or even whole nations, could use against the greatest manifestations of evil: racism, imperialism, and war. The term *satyagraha* was coined by Gandhi as a more satisfactory phrase than "passive resistance" or "civil disobedience," and the method of *satyagraha* was evolved by him through long experimentation first in South Africa and later in India.

Here is truly an epochal social invention. Gandhi said that *satyagraha* is meant for the common people, not merely for saints. It is war without violence. It is based on love, not on hate: on loving one's opponents and suffering to convert them. It differentiates between the sin and the sinner, between the evil and the evil-doer. It is the weapon of the brave, not of the weak. It demands discipline and may entail self-sacrifice, suffering, fasting, imprisonment, and death, yet it has the supreme virtue of providing means consonant with the highest ends.

In this anthology Gandhi is first presented through his biography—the drama of his life—and only secondarily through his message. Wherever possible, Gandhi speaks for himself. Where this has not been possible, the writings of those who knew him well have been used for the most part. Much has necessarily had to be omitted. Yet the range is wide enough to give the reader a fair sample of Gandhi's many interests as well as of the major events in his life.

This book is not meant to be a substitute for a good biography of Gandhi or for the detailed study of his writings. After reading these articles by and about him, perhaps the reader will be induced to delve further into Gandhi's life and to take to heart his life and message. Gandhi himself would wish us to devote our energies not to forming a cult in his honor, but to achieving international and domestic peace with justice by non-violent means.

HOMER A. JACK

Evanston, Illinois
October 2, 1955

CONTENTS

Chapter 10. The Salt March (1930)

Chapter 11. The Round Table Conference (1931)

GLOSSARY OF INDIAN TERMS

Ahimsa	Non-violence (a, privative; himsa, violence). This is an ancient Hindu precept, proclaimed by Buddha, by disciples of Vishnu, and by Mahavira, founder of Jainism.
Ashram	Religious community or institution or school; place of discipline and service.
Ba	Familiar title for mother in Gujarati. Used as a title of respect for Mrs. Gandhi.
Bai, behn	A kindly way of addressing a woman.
Bapu	Familiar title for father in Gujarati. Used throughout India as a title of respect for Gandhi.
Bhagavad Gita	The Song of the Divine Lord. This is a poem of 700 stanzas, part of the Mahabharata.
Bhajan	Hymn.
Brahmacharya	Continence, sexual self-restraint; literally, conduct that leads one to God.
Brahman	The essence of the godhead.
Brahmin	The highest caste in Hinduism—those who have knowledge; often, though incorrectly, spelled Brahman.
Charkha	The hand spinning wheel.
Congress	The Indian National Congress, an unofficial political organization.
Crore	100 lakhs, or 10,000,000.
Darshan	A form of spiritual happiness induced by being in the presence of a cherished person, place, or thing.
Dharma	Religion or religious duty.
Dhoti	The loincloth worn by Hindu men, usually a long piece with ornamental borders that is tucked in at the waist.
Gandhiji	A title of respect for Gandhi, the ji a common suffix of respect corresponding to sir or mister. Sometimes the suffix was used after Mahatma—Mahatmaji.
Ghee, ghi	Clarified butter; it is boiled and the watery particles and the curds are skimmed off.
Gita	Song. See Bhagavad Gita.
Goondas	Rowdies.
Gujarati	Language spoken in the province of Gujarat, India, where Gandhi was born.

Guru	Spiritual guide.
Harijans	A term given by Gandhi to the untouchables (*hari,* God's; *jan,* people). See Untouchables.
Hartal	Cessation of work; a form of non-violent demonstration in which all work ceases, shops are closed, etc.
Haveli	A temple for those of the Vaishnava faith.
Hindi	The language of northern India, with Sanskrit roots.
Hindu Mabasabha	A political party of orthodox Hindus.
Hindustani	A language based on Hindi but containing many Arabic and Persian words.
Khaddar (khadi)	Hand-spun or homespun cloth.
Khan	A common suffix to the names of Moslems of all ranks.
Khilafat	A Pan-Islamic movement in India in response to the deposal of the Sultan of Turkey (who was Caliph of Islam) as a result of Turkey's defeat in World War I.
Kshattriya	The second caste in Hinduism—those who rule.
Lakh	100,000.
Lathi	A long stick, usually made of bamboo, tipped with brass or iron, often 6 to 8 feet long.
Mahabharata	The national epic of which Krishna is the divine hero. The Bhagavad Gita is part of the Mahabharata.
Mahasabha	See Hindu Mahasabha.
Mahatma	Great soul (*maha,* great; *atma,* soul).
Mantra	Magic name of God; an incantation or formula of prayer sacred to any deity.
Manusmriti	Laws of Manu, a Hindu law-giver; an ancient religious code upholding the caste system and containing accounts of creation.
Maulana	A religious teacher of Islam; man of erudition; an honorific term.
Moksha	Freedom from the cycle of death and rebirth; salvation.
Muslim	Belonging to Islam; frequent Indian spelling of Moslem.
Mussulman	Follower of Islam; frequent Indian spelling of Mohammedan. Spelled variously.
Pandit	A learned man or teacher, especially a Brahmin, in Hindu religion, law, and science.
Parsi	A Zoroastrian of India descended from Persian refugees.
Pathans	A Mohammedan Afghan people of India's northwest frontier.
Puranas	Sacred Hindu legends.
Ram Raksha	A recitation of sacred texts asking for the protection of Rama.

Rama	The divine incarnation of the Supreme Being in human form as described in the epic, Ramayana.
Ramanama	The word used for the constant repetition of the name, Rama, as an act of devotion to the Lord.
Ramayana	The sacred epic of north India.
Rupee (Rs.)	The monetary unit of India; present value about 21 cents. Three pies equal one pice; four pice equal one anna; sixteen annas equal one rupee.
Sahib	Mr. or Master; often used in speaking of or addressing Europeans.
Sanatani	An orthodox Hindu.
Sardar	A title meaning leader.
Sari	The principal garment of an Indian woman, being a long piece of cloth wrapped around the waist, a portion covering the bosom and the head.
Satyagraha	Truth-force or soul-force (sat, truth; agraha, firmness); non-violent direct action; passive resistance; civil disobedience; non-violent non-cooperation.
Satyagrahi	One who practices satyagraha.
Shastras	Scriptures.
Sheth	Master, a name given to Hindus of importance in Sind and other parts of West India.
Shrijut (Sjt.)	A common title equivalent to esquire; often Shri or Srj.
Shrimati	A common title for women.
Shudra	The fourth (and lowest) caste of Hinduism—those who labor.
Sikh	A member of a religious sect founded about 1500 A.D. in the Punjab.
Siva (Shiva)	A god of the Hindu triad, typifying destruction and reproduction.
Swadeshi	Belonging to, or made in, one's own country (swa, self; deshi, country); applied to movement for boycott of foreign goods.
Swaraj	Self-government (swa, self; raj, government); independence.
Tamil	A language spoken in southern India and Ceylon.
Telugu	The largest division of the Dravidian dialects in southern India.
Untouchables	Castes or communities which, through ancestry, profession, or custom, are looked upon as impure by orthodox Hindus. Also called Scheduled Castes, Depressed Classes, Pariahs, and Harijans.
Upanishads	Hindu religious philosophical discourses.
Urdu	A Persianized Moslem form of Hindustani.

Vaishnava   A sect of Hindus worshiping Vishnu as the one su-
                     preme God.
Vaishya   The third caste in Hinduism—those who trade and
                     farm.
Varna   Caste.
Varnashrama dharma   Religion of caste (varna, color; ashrama, place of
                     discipline).
Vedanta   An important Hindu philosophical system.
Vedas   Earliest Hindu religious hymns.
Vishnu   The second god of the Hindu triad; the preserver.
                     The other gods are Brahma, the creator, and Siva,
                     the destroyer and regenerator.

PRINCIPAL CHARACTERS IN THE BOOK

Alexander, Horace G. (1889–   ). An English Quaker who taught at Birmingham for twenty years, visited India several times, and returned there in 1946 at Gandhi's request.

Ali, Mohammed (1878–1930?). Prominent Moslem leader and close friend of Gandhi. His older brother was Shuakat Ali.

Ambedkar, Bhimrao Ramji (1893–   ). The leader of the untouchables of India. For a time he was Minister of Law in the Government of India.

Andrews, Charles Freer (1871–1940). An itinerant British missionary who first met Gandhi in South Africa in 1914 and was on intimate terms with him for the next quarter century. He was given the title *"Deenabandhu,"* meaning "The Friend or Brother of Those who Deserve Compassion."

Banker, Shankarlal G. (1889–   ). The publisher of *Young India* who was tried and sentenced with Gandhi in 1922.

Besant, Mrs. Annie (1847–1933). A British theosophist who went to India to live. She became active in Indian politics and was president of the Indian National Congress in 1917. She founded the Central Hindu College at Benares.

Cripps, Sir Stafford (1889–1952). A wealthy lawyer and Labor Member of Parliament, who was sent to India in March 1942 by Prime Minister Winston Churchill with proposals on the postwar status of India. He was later Chancellor of the Exchequer in the Labor Government from 1947 to 1950.

Das, Chittaranjan R. (1870–1925). A leader of the Indian nationalist movement from Bengal. He was called *"Deshbandhu,"* meaning "Friend of the Country."

Desai, Mahadev (1892–1942). For more than twenty-four years he was Gandhi's personal secretary and chronicler.

Doke, Rev. Joseph J. (1861–1913). A Baptist missionary in South Africa who befriended Gandhi and was his first biographer.

Gandhi, Devadas (1900–   ). Gandhi's fourth son, now managing editor of *The Hindustan Times* in New Delhi. He is married to Lakshmi, daughter of C. Rajagopalachari.

Gandhi, Harilal (1888–1948). Gandhi's eldest son, who died in a tuberculosis hospital.

Gandhi, Karamchand (1823–86). Gandhi's father, who was for a time Prime Minister of a small state in western India.

Gandhi, Kasturba[i] (1869–1942). Gandhi's wife, whom he married in 1882 and who was the mother of their four sons.

Gandhi, Maganlal (1883–1928). Gandhi's second cousin who lived with him in South Africa. He suggested the root of the term, satyagraha, and managed Gandhi's ashram in India.

Gandhi, Manilal (1892–   ). Gandhi's second son, who for many years continued his interests in South Africa, including the editorship of Indian Opinion at Phoenix, Natal.

Gandhi, Putlibai (1841–91). Gandhi's mother.

Gandhi, Ramdas (1897–   ). Gandhi's third son, now living in Nagpur, India.

Gokhale, Gopal Krishna (1866–1915). President of the Indian National Congress in 1905 and founder of the Servants of India Society, he was Gandhi's political mentor.

Jinnah, Mohammed Ali (Qaid-i-Azam) (1876–1948). A wealthy Bombay lawyer who organized the Moslem League in 1934. He was the father of Pakistan and its first Governor-General.

Kallenbach, Herman (1871–1945). An architect in South Africa, of German nationality, who became a close associate of Gandhi during the decade ending 1914.

Malaviya, Pandit Madan Mohan (1861–1946). A distinguished Brahmin leader of orthodox Hinduism who for many years worked closely with Gandhi.

Mirabehn (Madeleine Slade) (1892–   ). The daughter of a British admiral who joined Gandhi's ashram in 1925 and was associated with his work in India until his death.

Naidu, Mrs. Sarojini (1879–1949). An Indian nationalist leader and poetess who was closely associated with Gandhi. She was president of the Indian National Congress in 1925 and Governor of the United Provinces at the time of her death.

Nayyar, Dr. Sushila (1916–   ). A woman physician who attended Kasturba Gandhi in her later years and also Mahatma Gandhi. She is the sister of Pyarelal.

Nehru, Jawaharlal (1889–   ). He worked closely with Gandhi in the Indian National Congress after first meeting him in 1916. He was president of the Congress in 1936, 1937, and 1946 and was named first Prime Minister of independent India.

Nehru, Motilal (1861–1931). The father of Jawaharlal. A Kashmir Brahmin, he abandoned his wealthy law practice and became a leader of the Indian National Congress. He was a close associate of Gandhi.

Patel, Sardar Vallabhbhai (1875–1951). A lawyer in Ahmedabad, he first became associated with Gandhi in 1916 and was a leading official of the Congress after that time. He was Deputy Prime Minister of India at the time of his death.

Polak, Henry S. L. (1882–   ). An Englishman who became a close associate of Gandhi in South Africa from 1904 to 1914. He later was a lawyer and journalist in England.

Prasad, Rajendra (1884–   ). He first met Gandhi in Champaran in 1917 and was an official of the Congress and associate of Gandhi after that time. In 1950 he became the first President of India.

Pyarelal (Nayyar) (1899–   ). A secretary on Gandhi's staff who succeeded Mahadev Desai as personal secretary after Desai's death in 1942.

Rai, Lajpat (Lalaji) (1864–1928). A nationalist leader from the Punjab who was mortally wounded in a political demonstration.

Rajagopalachari, Chakravarti (1879–   ). After joining the *satyagraha* campaign in 1919, he became closely associated with Gandhi and his daughter married Gandhi's son, Devadas. He was Governor-General of India from 1948 to 1950.

Rolland, Romain (1866–1944). French author who received the Nobel Prize for literature in 1915 and wrote the first widely read biography of Gandhi.

Smuts, Jan Christiaan (1870–1951). South African statesman and general who opposed Gandhi during the *satyagraha* campaigns culminating in the Smuts-Gandhi pact in 1914.

Tagore, Rabindranath (1861–1941). Indian poet and author who was awarded the Nobel Prize for literature in 1913.

Tilak, Bal Gangadhar (1856–1920). A Brahmin scholar and mathematician who was a leader of the nationalist movement. He was called "*Lokamanya*," meaning "Beloved of the People."

PART ONE 1869-1914

1 THE EARLY YEARS (1869–1892)

BIRTH AND PARENTAGE
by M. K. Gandhi

This is the first chapter of Gandhi's well-known autobiography, entitled An Autobiography, or The Story of My Experiments with Truth. It was written in Gujarati and translated into English by Mahadev Desai, Gandhi's secretary. Begun while Gandhi was in prison in 1922, it first appeared serially in Gandhi's newspaper, Navajivan, and in English in Young India, beginning in December 1925; in America it appeared in Unity magazine. The full autobiography was first published in book form in a two-volume Indian edition, the first volume in 1927 and the second in 1929. The book is aptly named, since it very frankly reveals Gandhi's experiments in living. It is one of the most candid autobiographies ever written. Because of this, C. F. Andrews felt that "it greatly needs editing for the West," and an abridgment under his editorship was published in London in 1930 with the title His Own Story. The complete autobiography was not published in America until 1948, under the title Gandhi's Autobiography.

THE GANDHIS belong to the Bania caste and seem to have been originally grocers. But for three generations, from my grandfather,

• Reprinted with permission from *Gandhi's Autobiography* (Washington: Public Affairs Press, 1948), Part I, Chapter I, pp. 11-14.

they have been Prime Ministers in several Kathiawad [1] States. Uttamchand Gandhi, alias Ota Gandhi, my grandfather, must have been a man of principle. State intrigues compelled him to leave Porbandar, where he was Diwan,[2] and to seek refuge in Junagadh. There he saluted the Nawab [3] with the left hand. Someone, noting the apparent discourtesy, asked for an explanation, which was given thus: "The right hand is already pledged to Porbandar."

Ota Gandhi married a second time, having lost his first wife. He had four sons by his first wife and two by his second wife. I do not think that in my childhood I ever felt or knew that these sons of Ota Gandhi were not all of the same mother. The fifth of these six brothers was Karamchand Gandhi, alias Kaba Gandhi, and the sixth was Tulsidas Gandhi. Both these brothers were Prime Ministers in Porbandar, one after the other. Kaba Gandhi was my father. He was a member of the Rajasthanik Court. It is now extinct, but in those days it was a very influential body for settling disputes between the chiefs and their fellow clansmen. He was for some time Prime Minister in Rajkot and then in Vankaner. He was a pensioner of the Rajkot State when he died.

Kaba Gandhi married four times in succession, having lost his wife each time by death. He had two daughters by his first and second marriages. His last wife, Putlibai, bore him a daughter and three sons, I being the youngest.

My father was a lover of his clan, truthful, brave and generous, but short-tempered. To a certain extent he might have been even given to carnal pleasures. For he married for the fourth time when he was over forty. But he was incorruptible and had earned a name for strict impartiality in his family as well as outside. His loyalty to the state was well known. An Assistant Political Agent spoke insultingly of the Rajkot Thakore Saheb, his chief, and he stood up to the insult. The Agent was angry and asked Kaba Gandhi to apologize. This he refused to do and was therefore kept under detention for a few hours. But when the Agent saw that Kaba Gandhi was adamant, he ordered him to be released.

My father never had any ambition to accumulate riches and left us very little property.

He had no education, save that of experience. At best, he might be said to have read up to the fifth Gujarati standard. Of history and geography he was innocent. But his rich experience of practical affairs stood him in good stead in the solution of the most intricate questions and in managing hundreds of men. Of religious training he had very little, but he had that kind of religious culture which frequent visits to temples and listening to religious discourses make available to many Hindus. In his last days he began reading the Gita at the instance of a learned Brahman friend of the family, and he used to repeat aloud some verses every day at the time of worship.

The outstanding impression my mother has left on my memory is that of saintliness. She was deeply religious. She would not think of taking her meals without her daily prayers. Going to *Haveli*—the Vaishnava temple—was one of her daily duties. As far as my memory can go back, I do not remember her having ever missed the *Chaturmas*.[4] She would take the hardest vows and keep them without flinching. Illness was no excuse for relaxing them. I can recall her once falling ill when she was observing the *Chandrayana*[5] vow, but the illness was not allowed to interrupt the observance. To keep two or three consecutive fasts was nothing to her. Living on one meal a day during *Chaturmas* was a habit with her. Not content with that she fasted every alternate day during one *Chaturmas*. During another *Chaturmas* she vowed not to have food without seeing the sun. We children on those days would stand, staring at the sky, waiting to announce the appearance of the sun to our mother. Everyone knows that at the height of the rainy season the sun often does not condescend to show his face. And I remember days when, at his sudden appearance, we would rush and announce it to her. She would run out to see with her own eyes, but by that time the fugitive sun would be gone, thus depriving her of her meal. "That does not matter," she would say cheerfully, "God did not want me to eat today." And then she would return to her round of duties.

My mother had strong commonsense. She was well informed about all matters of state, and ladies of the court thought highly of her intelligence. Often I would accompany her, exercising the privilege of childhood, and I still remember many lively discussions she had with the widowed mother of the Thakore Saheb.

Of these parents I was born at Porbandar, otherwise known as Sudamapuri, on the 2nd October 1869. I passed my childhood in Porbandar. I recollect having been put to school. It was with some difficulty that I got through the multiplication tables. The fact that I recollect nothing more of those days than having learnt, in company with other boys, to call our teacher all kinds of names, would strongly suggest that my intellect must have been sluggish, and my memory raw.

CHILD MARRIAGE
by M. K. Gandhi

MUCH AS I WISH that I had not to write this chapter, I know that I shall have to swallow many such bitter draughts in the course of this narrative. And I cannot do otherwise, if I claim to be a worshipper of Truth. It is my painful duty to have to record here my marriage at the age of thirteen. As I see the youngsters of the same age about me who are under my care, and think of my own marriage, I am inclined to pity myself and to congratulate them on having escaped my lot. I can see no moral argument in support of such a preposterously early marriage.

Let the reader make no mistake. I was married, not betrothed. For in Kathiawad there are two distinct rites—betrothal and marriage. Betrothal is a preliminary promise on the part of the parents

• Reprinted with permission from Gandhi's Autobiography (Washington: Public Affairs Press, 1948), Part I, Chapter III, pp. 18-21.

of the boy and the girl to join them in marriage, and it is not inviolable. The death of the boy entails no widowhood on the girl. It is an agreement purely between the parents, and the children have no concern with it. Often they are not even informed of it. It appears that I was betrothed thrice, though without my knowledge. I was told that two girls chosen for me had died in turn, and therefore I infer that I was betrothed three times. I have a faint recollection, however, that the third betrothal took place in my seventh year. But I do not recollect having been informed about it. In the present chapter I am talking about my marriage, of which I have the clearest recollection.

It will be remembered that we were three brothers. The first was already married. The elders decided to marry my second brother, who was two or three years my senior, a cousin, possibly a year older, and me, all at the same time. In doing so there was no thought of our welfare, much less our wishes. It was purely a question of their own convenience and economy.

Marriage among Hindus is no simple matter. The parents of the bride and the bridegroom often bring themselves to ruin over it. They waste their substance, they waste their time. Months are taken up over the preparations—in making clothes and ornaments and in preparing budgets for dinners. Each tries to outdo the other in the number and variety of courses to be prepared. Women, whether they have a voice or no, sing themselves hoarse, even get ill, and disturb the peace of their neighbors. These in their turn quietly put up with all the turmoil and bustle, all the dirt and filth, representing the remains of the feasts, because they know that a time will come when they also will be behaving in the same manner.

It would be better, thought my elders, to have all this bother over at one and the same time. Less expense and greater éclat. For money could be freely spent if it had only to be spent once instead of thrice. My father and my uncle were both old, and we were the last children they had to marry. It is likely that they wanted to have the last best time of their lives. In view of all these considerations, a triple wedding was decided upon, and as I have said before, months were taken up in preparation for it.

It was only through these preparations that we got warning of the coming event. I do not think it meant to me anything more than the prospect of good clothes to wear, drum beating, marriage processions, rich dinners and a strange girl to play with. The carnal desire came later. I propose to draw the curtain over my shame, except for a few details worth recording. To these I shall come later. But even they have little to do with the central idea I have kept before me in writing this story.

So my brother and I were both taken to Porbandar from Rajkot. There are some amusing details of the preliminaries to the final drama—e.g. smearing our bodies all over with turmeric paste—but I must omit them.

My father was a Diwan, but nevertheless a servant, and all the more so because he was in favor with the Thakore Saheb. The latter would not let him go until the last moment. And when he did so, he ordered for my father special stage coaches, reducing the journey by two days. But the fates had willed otherwise. Porbandar is 120 miles from Rajkot,—a cart journey of five days. My father did the distance in three, but the coach toppled over in the third stage, and he sustained severe injuries. He arrived bandaged all over. Both his and our interest in the coming event was half destroyed, but the ceremony had to be gone through. For how could the marriage dates be changed? However, I forgot my grief over my father's injuries in the childish amusement of the wedding.

I was devoted to my parents. But no less was I devoted to the passions that flesh is heir to. I had yet to learn that all happiness and pleasure should be sacrificed in devoted service to my parents. And yet, as though by way of punishment for my desire for pleasures, an incident happened, which has ever since rankled in my mind and which I will relate later.[6] Nishkulanand[7] sings: "Renunciation of objects, without the renunciation of desires, is shortlived, however hard you may try." Whenever I sing this song or hear it sung, this bitter untoward incident rushes to my memory and fills me with shame.

My father put on a brave face in spite of his injuries, and took full part in the wedding. As I think of it, I can even today call before my mind's eye the places where he sat as he went through the different details of the ceremony. Little did I dream then that one day I should severely criticize my father for having married me as a child. Everything on that day seemed to me right and proper and pleasing. There was also my own eagerness to get married. And as everything that my father did then struck me as beyond reproach, the recollection of those things is fresh in my memory. I can picture to myself, even today, how we sat on our wedding dais, how we performed the *Saptapadi*,[8] how we, the newly wedded husband and wife, put the sweet *Kansar* [9] into each other's mouth, and how we began to live together. And oh! that first night. Two innocent children all unwittingly hurled themselves into the ocean of life. My brother's wife had thoroughly coached me about my behavior on the first night. I do not know who had coached my wife. I have never asked her about it, nor am I inclined to do so now. The reader may be sure that we were too nervous to face each other. We were certainly too shy. How was I to talk to her, and what was I to say? The coaching could not carry me far. But no coaching is really necessary in such matters. The impressions of the former birth are potent enough to make all coaching superfluous. We gradually began to know each other, and to speak freely together. We were the same age. But I took no time in assuming the authority of a husband.

EATING FORBIDDEN MEAT

by M. K. Gandhi

... [A] FRIEND ... informed me that many of our teachers were secretly taking meat and wine. He also named many well-known people of Rajkot as belonging to the same company. There were also, I was told, some high-school boys among them.

I was surprised and pained. I asked my friend the reason and he explained it thus: "We are a weak people because we do not eat meat. The English are able to rule over us, because they are meat-eaters. You know how hardy I am, and how great a runner too. It is because I am a meat-eater. Meat-eaters do not have boils or tumors, and even if they sometimes happen to have any, these heal quickly. Our teachers and other distinguished people who eat meat are no fools. They know its virtues. You should do likewise. There is nothing like trying. Try, and see what strength it gives."

All these pleas on behalf of meat-eating were not advanced at a single sitting. They represent the substance of a long and elaborate argument which my friend was trying to impress upon me from time to time. My elder brother had already fallen. He therefore supported my friend's argument. I certainly looked feeble-bodied by the side of my brother and this friend. They were both hardier, physically stronger, and more daring. This friend's exploits cast a spell over me. He could run long distances and extraordinarily fast. He was an adept in high and long jumping. He could put up with any amount of corporal punishment. He would often display his exploits to me and, as one is always dazzled when he sees in others the qualities that he lacks himself, I was dazzled by this friend's exploits. This was followed by a strong desire to be

• Reprinted with permission from *Gandhi's Autobiography* (Washington: Public Affairs Press, 1948), Part I, Chapters VI and VII, pp. 32-36.

like him. I could hardly jump or run. Why should not I also be as strong as he?

Moreover, I was a coward. I used to be haunted by the fear of thieves, ghosts, and serpents. I did not dare to stir out of doors at night. Darkness was a terror to me. It was almost impossible for me to sleep in the dark, as I would imagine ghosts coming from one direction, thieves from another and serpents from a third. I could not therefore bear to sleep without a light in the room. How could I disclose my fears to my wife, no child, but already at the threshold of youth, sleeping by my side? I knew that she had more courage than I, and I felt ashamed of myself. She knew no fear of serpents and ghosts. She could go out anywhere in the dark. My friend knew all these weaknesses of mine. He would tell me that he could hold in his hand live serpents, could defy thieves, and did not believe in ghosts. And all this was, of course, the result of eating meat.

A doggerel of the Gujarati poet Narmad was in vogue amongst us schoolboys, as follows:

> Behold the mighty Englishman
> He rules the Indian small,
> Because being a meat-eater
> He is five cubits tall.

All this had its due effect on me. I was beaten. It began to grow on me that meat-eating was good, that it would make me strong and daring, and that, if the whole country took to meat-eating, the English could be overcome.

A day was thereupon fixed for beginning the experiment. It had to be conducted in secret. The Gandhis were Vaishnavas.[10] My parents were particularly staunch Vaishnavas. They would regularly visit the *Haveli*.[11] The family had even its own temples. Jainism was strong in Gujarat, and its influence was felt everywhere and on all occasions. The opposition to and abhorrence of meat-eating that existed in Gujarat among the Jains and Vaishnavas were to be seen nowhere else in India or outside in such strength. These were the traditions in which I was born and bred.

And I was extremely devoted to my parents. I knew that the moment they came to know of my having eaten meat, they would be shocked to death. Moreover, my love of truth made me extra cautious. I cannot say that I did not know then that I should have to deceive my parents if I began eating meat. But my mind was bent on the "reform." It was not a question of pleasing the palate. I did not know that it had a particularly good relish. I wished to be strong and daring and wanted my countrymen also to be such, so that we might defeat the English and make India free. The word "Swaraj" I had not yet heard. But I knew what freedom meant. The frenzy of the "reform" blinded me. And having ensured secrecy, I persuaded myself that mere hiding the deed from parents was no departure from truth.

So the day came. It is difficult fully to describe my condition. There were, on the one hand, the zeal for "reform," and the novelty of making a momentous departure in life. There was, on the other, the shame of hiding like a thief to do this very thing. I cannot say which of the two swayed me more. We went in search of a lonely spot by the river, and there I saw, for the first time in my life—meat. There was baker's bread also. I relished neither. The goat's meat was as tough as leather. I simply could not eat it. I was sick and had to leave off eating.

I had a very bad night afterwards. A horrible nightmare haunted me. Every time I dropped off to sleep it would seem as though a live goat were bleating inside me, and I would jump up full of remorse. But then I would remind myself that meat-eating was a duty and so become more cheerful.

My friend was not a man to give in easily. He now began to cook various delicacies with meat, and dress them neatly. And for dining, no longer was the secluded spot on the river chosen, but a State house, with its dining hall, and tables and chairs, about which my friend had made arrangements in collusion with the chief cook there.

This bait had its effect. I got over my dislike for bread, forswore my compassion for the goats, and became a relisher of meat-dishes, if not of meat itself. This went on for about a year. But not more than half a dozen meat-feasts were enjoyed in all; because the State house was not available every day, and there was the obvious difficulty about frequently preparing expensive savory meat-dishes. I had no money to pay for this "reform." My friend had therefore always to find the wherewithal. I had no knowledge where he found it. But find it he did, because he was bent on turning me into a meat-eater. But even his means must have been limited, and hence these feasts had necessarily to be few and far between.

Whenever I had occasion to indulge in these surreptitious feasts, dinner at home was out of the question. My mother would naturally ask me to come and take my food and want to know the reason why I did not wish to eat. I would say to her, "I have no appetite today; there is something wrong with my digestion." It was not without compunction that I devised these pretexts. I knew I was lying, and lying to my mother. I also knew that, if my mother and father came to know of my having become a meat-eater, they would be deeply shocked. This knowledge was gnawing at my heart.

Therefore I said to myself: "Though it is essential to eat meat, and also essential to take up food 'reform' in the country, yet deceiving and lying to one's father and mother is worse than not eating meat. In their lifetime, therefore, meat-eating must be out of the question. When they are no more and I have found my freedom, I will eat meat openly, but until that moment arrives I will abstain from it."

This decision I communicated to my friend, and I have never since gone back to meat. My parents never knew that two of their sons had become meat-eaters.

EARLY GLIMPSES OF RELIGION
by M. K. Gandhi

FROM MY SIXTH or seventh year up to my sixteenth I was at school, being taught all sorts of things except religion. I may say that I failed to get from the teachers what they could have given me without any effort on their part. And yet I kept on picking up things here and there from my surroundings. The term "religion" I am using in its broadest sense, meaning thereby self-realization or knowledge of self.

Being born in the Vaishnava faith, I had often to go to the Haveli. But it never appealed to me. I did not like its glitter and pomp. Also I heard rumors of immorality being practised there, and lost all interest in it. Hence I could gain nothing from the Haveli.

But what I failed to get there I obtained from my nurse, an old servant of the family, whose affection for me I still recall. I have said before that there was in me a fear of ghosts and spirits. Rambha, for that was her name, suggested, as a remedy for this fear, the repetition of Ramanama.[12] I had more faith in her than in her remedy, and so at a tender age I began repeating Ramanama to cure my fear of ghosts and spirits. This was of course short-lived, but the good seed sown in childhood was not sown in vain. I think it is due to the seed sown by that good woman Rambha that today Ramanama is an infallible remedy for me.

Just about this time, a cousin of mine who was a devotee of the Ramayana [13] arranged for my second brother and me to learn Ram Raksha.[14] We got it by heart, and made it a rule to recite it every morning after the bath. The practice was kept up as long

• Reprinted with permission from Gandhi's Autobiography (Washington: Public Affairs Press, 1948), Part I, Chapter X, pp. 47-51.

as we were in Porbandar. As soon as we reached Rajkot, it was forgotten. For I had not much belief in it. I recited it partly because of my pride in being able to recite *Ram Raksha* with correct pronunciation.

What, however, left a deep impression on me was the reading of the *Ramayana* before my father. During part of his illness my father was in Porbandar. There every evening he used to listen to the *Ramayana*. The reader was a great devotee of Rama—Ladha Maharaj of Bileshvar. It was said of him that he cured himself of his leprosy not by any medicine, but by applying to the affected parts *bilva* leaves which had been cast away after being offered to the image of Mahadeva [15] in Bileshvar temple, and by the regular repetition of *Ramanama*. His faith, it was said, had made him whole. This may or may not be true. We at any rate believed the story. And it is a fact that when Ladha Maharaj began his reading of the *Ramayana* his body was entirely free from leprosy. He had a melodious voice. He would sing the *Dohas* (couplets) and *Chopais* (quatrains), and explain them, losing himself in the discourse and carrying his listeners along with him. I must have been thirteen at that time, but I quite remember being enraptured by his reading. That laid the foundation of my deep devotion to the *Ramayana*. Today I regard the *Ramayana* of Tulasidas [16] as the greatest book in all devotional literature.

A few months after this we came to Rajkot. There was no *Ramayana* reading there. The *Bhagavat*,[17] however, used to be read on every *Ekadashi* [18] day. Sometimes I attended the reading, but the reciter was uninspiring. Today I see that the *Bhagavat* is a book which can evoke religious fervor. I have read it in Gujarati with intense interest. But when I heard portions of the original read by Pandit Madan Mohan Malaviya during my twenty-one days' fast, I wished I had heard it in my childhood from such a devotee as he is, so that I could have formed a liking for it at an early age. Impressions formed at that age strike roots deep down into one's nature, and it is my perpetual regret that I was not fortunate enough to hear more good books of this kind read during that period.

In Rajkot, however, I got an early grounding in toleration for all branches of Hinduism and sister religions. For my father and mother would visit the *Haveli* as also Shiva's and Rama's temples, and would take or send us youngsters there. Jain monks also would pay frequent visits to my father, and would even go out of their way to accept food from us—non-Jains. They would have talks with my father on subjects religious and mundane.

He had, besides, Musalman and Parsi friends, who would talk to him about their own faiths, and he would listen to them always with respect, and often with interest. Being his nurse, I often had a chance to be present at these talks. These many things combined to inculcate in me a toleration for all faiths.

Only Christianity was at the time an exception. I developed a sort of dislike for it. And for a reason. In those days Christian missionaries used to stand in a corner near the high school and hold forth, pouring abuse on Hindus and their gods. I could not endure this. I must have stood there to hear them once only, but that was enough to dissuade me from repeating the experiment. About the same time, I heard of a well known Hindu having been converted to Christianity. It was the talk of the town that, when he was baptized, he had to eat beef and drink liquor, that he also had to change his clothes, and that thenceforth he began to go about in European costume including a hat. These things got on my nerves. Surely, thought I, a religion that compelled one to eat beef, drink liquor, and change one's own clothes did not deserve the name. I also heard that the new convert had already begun abusing the religion of his ancestors, their customs and their country. All these things created in me a dislike for Christianity.

But the fact that I had learnt to be tolerant to other religions did not mean that I had any living faith in God. I happened, about this time, to come across *Manusmriti* [19] which was amongst my father's collection. The story of the creation and similar things in it did not impress me very much, but on the contrary made me incline somewhat towards atheism.

There was a cousin of mine, still alive, for whose intellect I had great regard. To him I turned with my doubts. But he could not resolve them. He sent me away with this answer: "When you grow up, you will be able to solve these doubts yourself. These questions ought not to be raised at your age." I was silenced, but was not comforted. Chapters about diet and the like in *Manusmriti* seemed to me to run contrary to daily practice. To my doubts as to this also, I got the same answer. "With intellect more developed and with more reading I shall understand it better," I said to myself.

Manusmriti at any rate did not then teach me *ahimsa*.[20] I have told the story of my meat-eating. *Manusmriti* seemed to support it. I also felt that it was quite moral to kill serpents, bugs, and the like. I remember to have killed at that age bugs and such other insects, regarding it as a duty.

But one thing took deep root in me—the conviction that morality is the basis of things, and that truth is the substance of all morality. Truth became my sole objective. It began to grow in magnitude every day, and my definition of it also has been ever widening.

A Gujarati didactic stanza likewise gripped my mind and heart. Its precept—return good for evil—became my guiding principle. It became such a passion with me that I began numerous experiments in it. Here are those (for me) wonderful lines:

> For a bowl of water give a goodly meal;
> For a kindly greeting bow thou down with zeal;
> For a simple penny pay thou back with gold;
> If thy life be rescued, life do not withhold.
> Thus the words and actions of the wise regard;
> Every little service tenfold they reward.
> But the truly noble know all men as one,
> And return with gladness good for evil done.

PLAYING THE ENGLISH GENTLEMAN
by M. K. Gandhi

Gandhi graduated from high school in 1887 and enrolled in Samaldas College in his home province. He disliked this school and fell in with the suggestion that he study law in England. With some difficulty he secured the blessings of his wife, mother, and brother, but he reaped the opprobrium of his caste in Bombay. On September 4, 1888 he sailed alone from Bombay and arrived in Southampton about three weeks later. After several shifts, he roomed in the house of a widow in West Kensington. He had some difficulty in adjusting himself to the new culture and climate, as this excerpt shows.

I HAD NOT YET started upon my regular studies. I had just begun reading newspapers, thanks to Sjt. Shukla.[21] In India I had never read a newspaper. But here I succeeded in cultivating a liking for them by regular reading. I always glanced over *The Daily News, The Daily Telegraph,* and *The Pall Mall Gazette.* This took me hardly an hour. I therefore began to wander about. I launched out in search of a vegetarian restaurant. The landlady had told me that there were such places in the city. I would trot ten or twelve miles each day, go into a cheap restaurant and eat my fill of bread, but would never be satisfied. During these wanderings I once hit on a vegetarian restaurant in Farringdon Street. The sight of it filled me with the same joy that a child feels on getting a thing after its own heart. Before I entered I noticed books for sale exhibited under a glass window near the door. I saw among them Salt's *Plea for Vegetarianism.* This I purchased for a shilling and

• Reprinted with permission from *Gandhi's Autobiography* (Washington: Public Affairs Press, 1948), Part I, Chapters XIV and XV, pp. 66-67, 69-71.

went straight to the dining room. This was my first hearty meal since my arrival in England. God had come to my aid.

I read Salt's book from cover to cover and was very much impressed by it. From the date of reading this book, I may claim to have become a vegetarian by choice. I blessed the day on which I had taken the vow before my mother. I had all along abstained from meat in the interests of truth and of the vow I had taken, but had wished at the same time that every Indian should be a meat-eater, and had looked forward to being one myself freely and openly some day, and to enlisting others in the cause. The choice was now made in favor of vegetarianism, the spread of which henceforward became my mission. . . .

I decided . . . to become polished and make up for my vegetarianism by cultivating other accomplishments which fitted one for polite society. And for this purpose I undertook the all too impossible task of becoming an English gentleman.

The clothes after the Bombay cut that I was wearing were, I thought, unsuitable for English society, and I got new ones at the Army and Navy Stores. I also went in for a chimney-pot hat costing nineteen shillings—an excessive price in those days. Not content with this, I wasted ten pounds on an evening suit made in Bond Street, the centre of fashionable life in London; and got my good and noble-hearted brother to send me a double watch-chain of gold. It was not correct to wear a ready-made tie and I learnt the art of tying one for myself. While in India, the mirror had been a luxury permitted on the days when the family barber gave me a shave. Here I wasted ten minutes every day before a huge mirror, watching myself arranging my tie and parting my hair in the correct fashion. My hair was by no means soft, and every day it meant a regular struggle with the brush to keep it in position. Each time the hat was put on and off, the hand would automatically move towards the head to adjust the hair, not to mention the other civilized habit of the hand every now and then operating for the same purpose when sitting in polished society.

As if all this were not enough to make me look the thing, I directed my attention to other details that were supposed to go towards the making of an English gentleman. I was told it was necessary for me to take lessons in dancing, French and elocution. French was not only the language of neighboring France, but it was the *lingua franca* of the Continent over which I had a desire to travel. I decided to take dancing lessons at a class and paid down £3 as fees for a term. I must have taken about six lessons in three weeks. But it was beyond me to achieve anything like rhythmic motion. I could not follow the piano and hence found it impossible to keep time. What then was I to do? The recluse in the fable kept a cat to keep off the rats, and then a cow to feed the cat with milk, and a man to keep the cow and so on. My ambitions also grew like the family of the recluse. I thought I should learn to play the violin in order to cultivate an ear for Western music. So I invested £3 in a violin and something more in fees. I sought a third teacher to give me lessons in elocution and paid him a preliminary fee of a guinea. He recommended Bell's *Standard Elocutionist* as the text-book, which I purchased. And I began with a speech of Pitt's.

But Mr. Bell rang the bell of alarm in my ear and I awoke.

I had not to spend a lifetime in England, I said to myself. What then was the use of learning elocution? And how could dancing make a gentleman of me? The violin I could learn even in India. I was a student and ought to go on with my studies. I should qualify myself to join the Inns of Court.[22] If my character made a gentleman of me, so much the better. Otherwise I should forego the ambition.

RELIGIOUS STUDIES
by M. K. Gandhi

After a number of experiments in English living, Gandhi settled down to the frugal life of a student. He took his own rooms, and improved his weak English. He studied Latin, French, chemistry, and other subjects in a private class and passed the London matriculation examinations. In the meantime, he joined a vegetarian society and was appointed to its executive committee.

TOWARDS THE END of my second year in England I came across two Theosophists,[23] brothers, and both unmarried. They talked to me about the *Gita*. They were reading Sir Edwin Arnold's translation —*The Song Celestial*—and they invited me to read the original with them. I felt ashamed, as I had read the divine poem neither in Sanskrit nor in Gujarati. I was constrained to tell them that I had not read the *Gita*, but that I would gladly read it with them, and that though my knowledge of Sanskrit was meagre, still I hoped to be able to understand the original to the extent of telling where the translation failed to bring out the meaning. I began reading the *Gita* with them. The verses in the second chapter

> If one
> Ponders on objects of the sense, there springs
> Attraction; from attraction grows desire,
> Desire flames to fierce passion, passion breeds
> Recklessness; then the memory—all betrayed—
> Lets noble purpose go, and saps the mind,
> Till purpose, mind, and man are all undone.

• Reprinted with permission from *Gandhi's Autobiography* (Washington: Public Affairs Press, 1948), Part I, Chapter XX, pp. 90-92.

made a deep impression on my mind, and they still ring in my ears. The book struck me as one of priceless worth. The impression has ever since been growing on me with the result that I regard it today as the book par excellence for the knowledge of Truth. It has afforded me invaluable help in my moments of gloom. I have read almost all the English translations of it, and I regard Sir Edwin Arnold's as the best. He has been faithful to the text, and yet it does not read like a translation. Though I read the Gita with these friends, I cannot pretend to have studied it then. It was only after some years that it became a book of daily reading.

The brothers also recommended The Light of Asia by Sir Edwin Arnold, whom I knew till then as the author only of The Song Celestial, and I read it with even greater interest than I did the Bhagavadgita. Once I had begun it I could not leave off. They also took me on one occasion to the Blavatsky Lodge and introduced me to Madame Blavatsky and Mrs. Besant. The latter had just then joined the Theosophical Society, and I was following with great interest the controversy about her conversion. The friends advised me to join the Society, but I politely declined saying, "With my meagre knowledge of my own religion I do not want to belong to any religious body." I recall having read, at the brothers' instance, Madame Blavatsky's Key to Theosophy. This book stimulated in me the desire to read books on Hinduism, and disabused me of the notion fostered by the missionaries that Hinduism was rife with superstition.

About the same time I met a good Christian from Manchester in a vegetarian boarding house. He talked to me about Christianity. I narrated to him my Rajkot recollections. He was pained to hear them. He said, "I am a vegetarian. I do not drink. Many Christians are meat-eaters and drink, no doubt; but neither meat-eating nor drinking is enjoined by Scripture. Do please read the Bible." I accepted his advice, and he got me a copy. I have a faint recollection that he himself used to sell copies of the Bible, and I purchased from him an edition containing maps, concordance, and other aids. I began reading it, but I could not possibly read through the Old Testament. I read the book of Genesis, and the chapters that followed invariably sent me to sleep. But just for the sake of being able to say that I had read it, I plodded through the other books with much difficulty and without the least interest or understanding. I disliked reading the book of Numbers.

But the New Testament produced a different impression, especially the Sermon on the Mount which went straight to my heart. I compared it with the *Gita*. The verses, "But I say unto you, that ye resist not evil: but whosoever shall smite thee on thy right cheek, turn to him the other also. And if any man take away thy coat let him have thy cloke too," delighted me beyond measure and put me in mind of Shamal Bhatt's [24] "For a bowl of water, give a goodly meal" etc. My young mind tried to unify the teaching of the *Gita*, the *Light of Asia* and the Sermon on the Mount. That renunciation was the highest form of religion appealed to me greatly.

This reading whetted my appetite for studying the lives of other religious teachers. A friend recommended Carlyle's *Heroes and Hero-Worship*. I read the chapter on the Hero as a prophet and learnt of the Prophet's [25] greatness and bravery and austere living.

Beyond this acquaintance with religion I could not go at the moment, as reading for the examination left me scarcely any time for outside subjects. But I took mental note of the fact that I should read more religious books and acquaint myself with all the principal religions.

And how could I help knowing something of atheism too? Every Indian knew Bradlaugh's [26] name and his so-called atheism. I read some book about it, the name of which I forget. It had no effect on me, for I had already crossed the Sahara of atheism. Mrs. Besant, who was then very much in the limelight, had turned to theism from atheism, and that fact also strengthened my aversion to atheism. I had read her book *How I Became a Theosophist*.

BEGINNING LIFE AS A LAWYER
by M. K. Gandhi

Gandhi made a brief trip to Paris to visit the Exhibition in 1890. He studied for his bar examinations, spending "nine months of fairly hard labor to read through the Common Law of England." Having passed his examinations, he was called to the bar on June 10, 1891, enrolled in the High Court on June 11, and sailed for India on June 12. He was met at Bombay by his elder brother, and told that his mother had died while he was in England. The news had been withheld to spare him the blow in a foreign land. Gandhi wrote, "My grief was even greater than over my father's death; most of my cherished hopes were shattered." His brother had, however, made plans for him to practice law.

MY ELDER BROTHER had built high hopes on me. The desire for wealth and name and fame was great in him. He had a big heart, generous to a fault. This, combined with his simple nature, had attracted to him many friends, and through them he expected to get me briefs. He had also assumed that I should have a swinging practice and had, in that expectation, allowed the household expenses to become top-heavy. He had also left no stone unturned in preparing the field for my practice.

The storm in my caste over my foreign voyage was still brewing. It had divided the caste into two camps, one of which immediately readmitted me, while the other was bent on keeping me out. To please the former my brother took me to Nasik before going to Rajkot, gave me a bath in the sacred river and, on reaching Rajkot, gave a caste dinner. I did not like all this. But my brother's love

• Reprinted with permission from *Gandhi's Autobiography* (Washington: Public Affairs Press, 1948), Part II, pp. 115, 116, 117, 119-20, 121, 123, 128-29.

for me was boundless, and my devotion to him was in proportion to it, and so I mechanically acted as he wished, taking his will to be law. The trouble about readmission to the caste was thus practically over. . . .

My relations with my wife were still not as I desired. Even my stay in England had not cured me of jealousy. I continued my squeamishness and suspiciousness in respect of every little thing, and hence all my cherished desires remained unfulfilled. I had decided that my wife should learn reading and writing and that I should help her in her studies, but my lust came in the way and she had to suffer for my own shortcoming. Once I went the length of sending her away to her father's house, and consented to receive her back only after I had made her thoroughly miserable. I saw later that all this was pure folly on my part.

I had planned reform in the education of children. My brother had children, and my own child which I had left at home when I went to England was now a boy of nearly four. It was my desire to teach these little ones physical exercise and make them hardy, and also to give them the benefit of my personal guidance. In this I had my brother's support and I succeeded in my efforts more or less. I very much liked the company of children, and the habit of playing and joking with them has stayed with me till today. I have ever since thought that I should make a good teacher of children. . . .

Expenses thus went up. New things were added every day. We had succeeded in tying a white elephant at our door. But how was the wherewithal to be found? To start practice in Rajkot would have meant sure ridicule. I had hardly the knowledge of a qualified vakil [27] and yet I expected to be paid ten times his fee! No client would be fool enough to engage me. And even if such a one was to be found, should I add arrogance and fraud to my ignorance, and increase the burden of debt I owed to the world?

Friends advised me to go to Bombay for some time in order to gain experience of the High Court, to study Indian law and to try to get what briefs I could. I took up the suggestion and went. . . .

Whilst in Bombay, I began, on the one hand, my study of Indian law and, on the other, my experiments in dietetics in which Virchand Gandhi, a friend, joined me. My brother, for his part, was trying his best to get me briefs.

The study of Indian law was a tedious business. The Civil Procedure Code I could in no way get on with. Not so, however, with the Evidence Act. Virchand Gandhi was reading for the Solicitor's Examination and would tell me all sorts of stories about barristers and vakils. "Sir Pherozeshah's ability," he would say, "lies in his profound knowledge of law. He has the Evidence Act by heart and knows all the cases on the thirty-second section. Badruddin Tyabji's wonderful power of argument inspires the judges with awe."

The stories of stalwarts such as these would unnerve me.

"It is not unusual," he would add, "for a barrister to vegetate for five or seven years. That's why I have signed the articles for solicitorship.[28] You should count yourself lucky if you can paddle your own canoe in three years' time."

Expenses were mounting up every month. To have a barrister's board outside the house, whilst still preparing for the barrister's profession inside, was a thing to which I could not reconcile myself. Hence I could not give undivided attention to my studies. I developed some liking for the Evidence Act and read Mayne's *Hindu Law* with deep interest, but I had not the courage to conduct a case. I was helpless beyond words, even as the bride come fresh to her father-in-law's house!

About this time, I took up the case of one Mamibai. It was a "small cause." "You will have to pay some commission to the tout," I was told. I emphatically declined.

"But even that great criminal lawyer Mr. So-and-So, who makes three to four thousand a month, pays commission!"

"I do not need to emulate him," I rejoined. "I should be content with Rs. 300 a month. Father did not get more."

"But those days are gone. Expenses in Bombay have gone up frightfully. You must be businesslike."

I was adamant. I gave no commission, but got Mamibai's case

all the same. It was an easy case. I charged Rs. 30 for my fees. The case was not likely to last longer than a day.

This was my debut in the Small Causes Court. I appeared for the defendant and had thus to cross-examine the plaintiff's witnesses. I stood up, but my heart sank into my boots. My head was reeling and I felt as though the whole court was doing likewise. I could think of no question to ask. The judge must have laughed, and the vakils no doubt enjoyed the spectacle. But I was past seeing anything. I sat down and told the agent that I could not conduct the case, that he had better engage Patel and have the fee back from me. Mr. Patel was duly engaged for Rs. 51. To him, of course, the case was child's play.

I hastened from the Court, not knowing whether my client won or lost her case, but I was ashamed of myself, and decided not to take up any more cases until I had courage enough to conduct them. Indeed I did not go to Court again until I went to South Africa. There was no virtue in my decision. I had simply made a virtue of necessity. There would be no one so foolish as to entrust his case to me, only to lose it!

. . . I wrung my hands in despair. My brother also felt much worried. We both came to the conclusion that it was no use spending more time in Bombay. I should settle in Rajkot where my brother, himself a petty pleader, could give me some work in the shape of drafting applications and memorials. And then as there was already a household at Rajkot, the breaking up of the one at Bombay meant a considerable saving. I liked the suggestion. My little establishment was thus closed after a stay of six months in Bombay. . . .

Disappointed, I left Bombay and went to Rajkot where I set up my own office. Here I got along moderately well. Drafting applications and memorials brought me in, on an average, Rs. 300 a month. For this work I had to thank influence rather than my own ability, for my brother's partner had a settled practice. All applications etc. which were, really or to his mind, of an important character, he sent to big barristers. To my lot fell the applications to be drafted on behalf of his poor clients. . . .

In the meantime a Meman [29] firm from Porbandar wrote to my brother making the following offer: "We have business in South Africa. Ours is a big firm, and we have a big case there in the Court, our claim being £40,000. It has been going on for a long time. We have engaged the services of the best vakils and barristers. If you sent your brother there, he would be useful to us and also to himself. He would be able to instruct our counsel better than ourselves. And he would have the advantage of seeing a new part of the world, and of making new acquaintances."

My brother discussed the proposition with me. I could not clearly make out whether I had simply to instruct the counsel or to appear in court. But I was tempted.

My brother introduced me to the late Sheth Abdul Karim Jhaveri, a partner of Dada Abdulla and Co., the firm in question. "It won't be a difficult job," the Sheth assured me. "We have big Europeans as our friends, whose acquaintance you will make. You can be useful to us in our shop. Much of our correspondence is in English and you can help us with that too. You will, of course, be our guest and hence will have no expense whatever."

"How long do you require my services?" I asked. "And what will be the payment?"

"Not more than a year. We will pay you a first class return fare and a sum of £105, all around."

This was hardly going there as a barrister. It was going as a servant of the firm. But I wanted somehow to leave India. There was also the tempting opportunity of seeing a new country, and of having new experience. Also I could send £105 to my brother and help in the expenses of the household. I closed with the offer without any higgling, and got ready to go to South Africa.

2 FIRST YEARS IN AFRICA (1893-1904)

ON THE WAY TO PRETORIA
by M. K. Gandhi

Gandhi sailed for South Africa without his family in April 1893. He reached Durban toward the end of May and was met by his employer, Abdulla Sheth, a Moslem who, although unlettered, was one of the most affluent Indian businessmen in Natal. Gandhi soon left for Pretoria, capital of the Transvaal, where his presence was required in connection with the lawsuit for which he had been brought from India. The following incidents of the journey left an indelible impression in his memory.

ON THE SEVENTH or eighth day after my arrival, I left Durban. A first class seat was booked for me. It was usual there to pay five shillings extra, if one needed a bedding. Abdulla Sheth insisted that I should book one bedding but, out of obstinacy and pride and with a view to saving five shillings, I declined. Abdulla Sheth warned me. "Look, now," said he, "this is a different country from India. Thank God, we have enough and to spare. Please do not stint yourself in anything that you may need."

I thanked him and asked him not to be anxious.

The train reached Maritzburg, the capital of Natal, at about

• Reprinted with permission from *Gandhi's Autobiography* (Washington: Public Affairs Press, 1948), Part II, pp. 140-46.

9 P.M. Beddings used to be provided at this station. A railway servant came and asked me if I wanted one. "No," said I. "I have one with me." He went away. But a passenger came next, and looked me up and down. He saw that I was a "colored" man. This disturbed him. Out he went and came in again with one or two officials. They all kept quiet, when another official came to me and said, "Come along, you must go to the van compartment."

"But I have a first class ticket," said I.

"That doesn't matter," rejoined the other. "I tell you, you must go to the van compartment."

"I tell you, I was permitted to travel in this compartment at Durban, and I insist on going on in it."

"No, you won't," said the official. "You must leave this compartment, or else I shall have to call a police constable to push you out."

"Yes, you may. I refuse to get out voluntarily."

The constable came. He took me by the hand and pushed me out. My luggage was also taken out. I refused to go to the other compartment and the train steamed away. I went and sat in the waiting room, keeping my hand-bag with me, and leaving the other luggage where it was. The railway authorities had taken charge of it.

It was winter, and winter in the higher regions of South Africa is severely cold. Maritzburg being at a high altitude, the cold was extremely bitter. My overcoat was in my luggage, but I did not dare to ask for it lest I should be insulted again, so I sat and shivered. There was no light in the room. A passenger came in at about midnight and possibly wanted to talk to me. But I was in no mood to talk.

I began to think of my duty. Should I fight for my rights or go back to India, or should I go on to Pretoria without minding the insults, and return to India after finishing the case? It would be cowardice to run back to India without fulfilling my obligation. The hardship to which I was subjected was superficial—only a symptom of the deep disease of color prejudice. I should try, if possible, to root out the disease and suffer hardships in the process.

Redress for wrongs I should seek only to the extent that would be necessary for the removal of the color prejudice.

So I decided to take the next available train to Pretoria.

The following morning I sent a long telegram to the General Manager of the Railway and also informed Abdulla Sheth, who immediately met the General Manager. The Manager justified the conduct of the railway authorities, but informed him that he had already instructed the Station Master to see that I reached my destination safely. Abdulla Sheth wired to the Indian merchants in Maritzburg and to friends in other places to meet me and look after me. The merchants came to see me at the station and tried to comfort me by narrating their own hardships and explaining that what had happened to me was nothing unusual. They also said that Indians traveling first or second class had to expect trouble from railway officials and white passengers. The day was thus spent in listening to these tales of woe. The evening train arrived. There was a reserved berth for me. I now purchased at Maritzburg the bedding ticket I had refused to book at Durban.

The train reached Charlestown in the morning. There was no railway, in those days, between Charlestown and Johannesburg, but only a stage-coach, which halted at Standerton for the night en route. I possessed a ticket for the coach, which was not cancelled by the break of the journey at Maritzburg for a day; besides, Abdulla Sheth had sent a wire to the coach agent at Charlestown.

But the agent only needed a pretext for putting me off, and so, when he discovered me to be a stranger, he said, "Your ticket is cancelled." I gave him the proper reply. The reason at the back of his mind was not want of accommodation, but quite another. Passengers had to be accommodated inside the coach, but as I was regarded as a "coolie" and looked a stranger, it would be proper, thought the "leader," as the white man in charge of the coach was called, not to seat me with the white passengers. There were seats on either side of the coachbox. The leader sat on one of these as a rule. Today he sat inside and gave me his seat. I knew it was sheer injustice and an insult, but I thought it better to pocket it. I could not have forced myself inside, and if I had raised a protest, the coach would have gone off without me. This would have meant the loss of another day, and Heaven only knows what would have happened the next day. So, much as I fretted within myself, I prudently sat next the coachman.

At about three o'clock the coach reached Pardekoph. Now the leader desired to sit where I was seated, as he wanted to smoke and possibly to have some fresh air. So he took a piece of dirty sack-cloth from the driver, spread it on the footboard and, addressing me said, "Sami, you sit on this, I want to sit near the driver." The insult was more than I could bear. In fear and trembling I said to him, "It was you who seated me here, though I should have been accommodated inside. I put up with the insult. Now that you want to sit outside and smoke, you would have me sit at your feet. I will not do so, but I am prepared to sit inside."

As I was struggling through these sentences, the man came down upon me and began heavily to box my ears. He seized me by the arm and tried to drag me down. I clung to the brass rails of the coachbox and was determined to keep my hold even at the risk of breaking my wristbones. The passengers were witnessing the scene—the man swearing at me, dragging and belaboring me, and I remaining still. He was strong and I was weak. Some of the passengers were moved to pity and exclaimed: "Man, let him alone. Don't beat him. He is not to blame. He is right. If he can't stay there, let him come and sit with us." "No fear," cried the man, but he seemed somewhat crestfallen and stopped beating me. He let go my arm, swore at me a little more, and asking the Hottentot servant who was sitting on the other side of the coachbox to sit on the footboard, took the seat so vacated.

The passengers took their seats and, the whistle given, the coach rattled away. My heart was beating fast within my breast, and I was wondering whether I should ever reach my destination alive. The man cast an angry look at me now and then and, pointing his finger at me, growled: "Take care, let me once get to Standerton and I shall show you what I do." I sat speechless and prayed to God to help me.

After dark we reached Standerton and I heaved a sigh of relief on seeing some Indian faces. As soon as I got down, these friends said: "We are here to receive you and take you to Isa Sheth's shop. We have had a telegram from Dada Abdulla." I was very glad, and we went to Sheth Isa Haji Sumar's shop. The Sheth and his clerks gathered around me. I told them all that I had gone through. They were very sorry to hear it and comforted me by relating to me their own bitter experiences.

I wanted to inform the agent of the Coach Company of the whole affair. So I wrote him a letter, narrating everything that had happened, and drawing his attention to the threat his man had held out. I also asked for an assurance that he would accommodate me with the other passengers inside the coach when we started the next morning. To which the agent replied to this effect: "From Standerton we have a bigger coach with different men in charge. The man complained of will not be there tomorrow, and you will have a seat with the other passengers." This somewhat relieved me. I had, of course, no intention of proceeding against the man who had assaulted me, and so the chapter of the assault closed there.

In the morning Isa Sheth's man took me to the coach. I got a good seat and reached Johannesburg quite safely that night.

Standerton is a small village and Johannesburg a big city. Abdulla Sheth had wired to Johannesburg also, and given me the name and address of Muhammad Kasam Kamruddin's firm there. Their man had come to receive me at the stage, but neither did I see him nor did he recognize me. So I decided to go to a hotel. I knew the names of several. Taking a cab I asked to be driven to the Grand National Hotel. I saw the Manager and asked for a room. He eyed me for a moment, and politely saying, "I am very sorry, we are full up," bade me good-bye. So I asked the cabman to drive to Muhammad Kasam Kamruddin's shop. Here I found Abdul Gani Sheth expecting me, and he gave me a cordial greeting. He had a hearty laugh over the story of my experience at the hotel. "How ever did you expect to be admitted to a hotel?" he said.

"Why not?" I asked.

"You will come to know after you have stayed here a few days,"
said he. "Only we can live in a land like this, because, for making
money, we do not mind pocketing insults, and here we are." With
this he narrated to me the story of the hardships of Indians in
South Africa.

RELIGIOUS FERMENT
by M. K. Gandhi

*In Pretoria Gandhi attended to his legal work, but had
much time for other pursuits. He spent much of his free time
studying the condition of the Indian population in the Transvaal,
and himself constantly experienced discrimination. A Christian
legal associate, Mr. A. W. Baker, was also a lay preacher and
took Gandhi to noon-day prayer meetings. There he met Mr.
Coates, a Quaker, who discussed Christianity with him and introduced him to other Christian friends.*

MR. BAKER WAS getting anxious about my future. He took me to
the Wellington Convention. The Protestant Christians organize
such gatherings every few years for religious enlightenment or,
in other words, self-purification. One may call this religious restoration or revival. The Wellington Convention was of this type.
The chairman was the famous divine of the place, the Rev.
Andrew Murray. Mr. Baker had hoped that the atmosphere of
religious exaltation at the Convention, and the enthusiasm and
earnestness of the people attending it, would inevitably lead me
to embrace Christianity.

But his final hope was the efficacy of prayer. He had an abiding

* Reprinted with permission from *Gandhi's Autobiography* (Washington: Public Affairs Press, 1948), Part II, Chapter XV, pp. 169-72.

faith in prayer. It was his firm conviction that God could not but listen to prayer fervently offered. He would cite the instances of men like George Muller of Bristol, who depended entirely on prayer even for his temporal needs. I listened to his discourse on the efficacy of prayer with unbiased attention, and assured him that nothing could prevent me from embracing Christianity, should I feel the call. I had no hesitation in giving him this assurance, as I had long since taught myself to follow the inner voice. I delighted in submitting to it. To act against it would be difficult and painful to me.

So we went to Wellington. Mr. Baker was hard put to it in having "a colored man" like me for his companion. He had to suffer inconveniences on many occasions entirely on account of me. We had to break the journey on the way, as one of the days happened to be a Sunday, and Mr. Baker and his party would not travel on the sabbath. Though the manager of the station hotel agreed to take me in after much altercation, he absolutely refused to admit me to the dining room. Mr. Baker was not the man to give way easily. He stood by the rights of the guests of a hotel. But I could see his difficulty. At Wellington also I stayed with Mr. Baker. In spite of his best efforts to conceal the little inconveniences that he was put up to, I could see them all.

This Convention was an assemblage of devout Christians. I was delighted at their faith. I met the Rev. Murray. I saw that many were praying for me. I liked some of their hymns, they were very sweet.

The Convention lasted for three days. I could understand and appreciate the devoutness of those who attended it. But I saw no reason for changing my belief—my religion. It was impossible for me to believe that I could go to heaven or attain salvation only by becoming a Christian. When I frankly said so to some of the good Christian friends, they were shocked. But there was no help for it.

My difficulties lay deeper. It was more than I could believe that Jesus was the only incarnate son of God, and that only he who believed in him would have everlasting life. If God could have sons, all of us were His sons. If Jesus was like God, or God Himself, then all men were like God and could be God Himself. My reason was not ready to believe literally that Jesus by his death and by his blood redeemed the sins of the world. Metaphorically there might be some truth in it. Again, according to Christianity only human beings had souls, and not other living beings, for whom death meant complete extinction; while I held a contrary belief. I could accept Jesus as a martyr, an embodiment of sacrifice, and a divine teacher, but not as the most perfect man ever born. His death on the Cross was a great example to the world, but that there was anything like a mysterious or miraculous virtue in it my heart could not accept. The pious lives of Christians did not give me anything that the lives of men of other faiths had failed to give. I had seen in other lives just the same reformation that I had heard of among Christians. Philosophically there was nothing extraordinary in Christian principles. From the point of view of sacrifice, it seemed to me that the Hindus greatly surpassed the Christians. It was impossible for me to regard Christianity as a perfect religion or the greatest of all religions.

I shared this mental churning with my Christian friends whenever there was an opportunity, but their answers could not satisfy me.

Thus if I could not accept Christianity either as a perfect, or the greatest, religion, neither was I then convinced of Hinduism being such. Hindu defects were pressingly visible to me. If untouchability could be a part of Hinduism, it could but be a rotten part or an excrescence. I could not understand the raison d'être of a multitude of sects and castes. What was the meaning of saying that the Vedas were the inspired Word of God? If they were inspired, why not also the Bible and the Koran?

As Christians friends were endeavoring to convert me, even so were Musalman friends. Abdulla Sheth had kept on inducing me to study Islam, and of course he had always something to say regarding its beauty.

I expressed my difficulties in a letter to Raychandbhai.[1] I also corresponded with other religious authorities in India and received answers from them. Raychandbhai's letter somewhat pacified me. He asked me to be patient and to study Hinduism more deeply. One of his sentences was to this effect: "On a dispassionate view of the question I am convinced that no other religion has the subtle and profound thought of Hinduism, its vision of the soul, or its charity."

I purchased Sale's translation of the Koran and began reading it. I also obtained other books on Islam. I communicated with Christian friends in England. One of them introduced me to Edward Maitland,[2] with whom I opened correspondence. He sent me *The Perfect Way*, a book he had written in collaboration with Anna Kingsford. The book was a repudiation of the current Christian belief. He also sent me another book, *The New Interpretation of the Bible*. I liked both. They seemed to support Hinduism. Tolstoy's *The Kingdom of God Is Within You*[3] overwhelmed me. It left an abiding impression on me. Before the independent thinking, profound morality, and the truthfulness of this book, all the books given me by Mr. Coates seemed to pale into insignificance.

My studies thus carried me in a direction unthought of by the Christian friends. My correspondence with Edward Maitland was fairly prolonged, and that with Raychandbhai continued until his death. I read some of the books he sent me. These included *Panchikaran*, *Maniratnamala*, *Mumukshu Prakaran* of *Yogavasishtha*, Haribhadra Suri's *Shaddarshana Samuchchaya* and others.

Though I took a path my Christian friends had not intended for me, I have remained forever indebted to them for the religious quest that they awakened in me. I shall always cherish the memory of their contact. The years that followed had more, not less, of such sweet and sacred contacts in store for me.

A PARIAH

by C. F. Andrews

[GANDHI] had himself suffered terribly in South Africa, along with the whole Indian community, many of whom were High-Caste Hindus, owing to the treatment meted out to them by Christian people. . . . How can I ever forget, for instance, the shock of horror and dismay which I had on first landing in South Africa in 1913? The Archdeacon kindly met me on the wharf and asked me to preach in his church. It was the first Sunday after Christmas, and I preached a Christmas sermon of "peace and good will to all mankind." I had no idea whatever that anything had happened while I was preaching that sermon; but Mr. Gandhi had expressed to my friend and companion, Mr. W. W. Pearson, of Manchester, that he himself would like to hear me preach. Mr. Pearson had taken him to the church door, and he had been refused an entrance even after all the circumstances of the request had been courteously explained and it was known who was being refused. Mr. Gandhi was thus a pariah in South Africa to that European Christian congregation.

• Reprinted with permission from C. F. Andrews, *Mahatma Gandhi's Ideas* (London: Allen and Unwin, 1949), pp. 177-78.

MAN PROPOSES, GOD DISPOSES

by M. K. Gandhi

Although Gandhi was not the principal lawyer for his client in the lawsuit—for £40,000—he studied the bookkeeping involved in the case and did much translation. He concluded that his client had the stronger case, but that the interminable litigation would ruin both plaintiff and defendant. He successfully urged the appointment of an arbitrator and, in the end, his client won. Since the loser would be bankrupt if he had to pay the whole award, Gandhi induced his client to accept installment payments. Gandhi said, "My joy was boundless. I had learnt the true practice of law. I realized that the true function of a lawyer was to unite parties riven asunder."

THE CASE having been concluded, I had no reason for staying in Pretoria. So I went back to Durban and began to make preparations for my return home. But Abdulla Sheth was not the man to let me sail without a send-off. He gave a farewell party in my honor at Sydenham.

It was proposed to spend the whole day there. Whilst I was turning over the sheets of some of the newspapers I found there, I chanced to see a paragraph in a corner of one of them under the caption, "Indian Franchise." It was with reference to the Bill then before the House of Legislature, which sought to deprive the Indians of their right to elect members of the Natal Legislative Assembly. I was ignorant of the Bill, and so were the rest of the guests who had assembled there.

I inquired of Abdulla Sheth about it. He said: "What can we

• Reprinted with permission from *Gandhi's Autobiography* (Washington: Public Affairs Press, 1948), Part II, Chapter XVI, pp. 173-75.

understand in these matters? We can only understand things that affect our trade. As you know all our trade in the Orange Free State has been swept away. We agitated about it, but in vain. We are after all lame men, being unlettered. We generally take in newspapers simply to ascertain the daily market rates, etc. What can we know of legislation? Our eyes and ears are the European attorneys here."

"But," said I, "there are so many young Indians born and educated here. Do not they help you?"

"They!" exclaimed Abdulla Sheth in despair. "They never care to come to us, and to tell you the truth, we care less to recognize them. Being Christians, they are under the thumb of the white clergymen, who in their turn are subject to the Government."

This opened my eyes. I felt that this class should be claimed as our own. Was this the meaning of Christianity? Did they cease to be Indians because they had become Christians?

But I was on the point of returning home and hesitated to express what was passing through my mind in this matter. I simply said to Abdulla Sheth: "This Bill, if it passes into law, will make our lot extremely difficult. It is the first nail into our coffin. It strikes at the root of our self-respect."

"It may," echoed Sheth Abdulla. "I will tell you the genesis of the franchise question. We knew nothing about it. But Mr. Escombe, one of our best attorneys, whom you know, put the idea into our heads. It happened thus. He is a great fighter, and there being no love lost between him and the Wharf Engineer, he feared that the Engineer might deprive him of his votes and defeat him at the election. So he acquainted us with our position, and at his instance we all registered ourselves as voters, and voted for him. You will now see how the franchise has not for us the value that you attach to it. But we understand what you say. Well, then, what is your advice?"

The other guests were listening to this conversation with attention. One of them said: "Shall I tell you what should be done? You cancel your passage by this boat, stay here a month longer, and we will fight as you direct us."

All the others chimed in: "Indeed, indeed. Abdulla Sheth, you must detain Gandhibhai."

The Sheth was a shrewd man. He said: "I may not detain him now. Or rather, you have as much right as I to do so. But you are quite right. Let us *all* persuade him to stay on. But you should remember that he is a barrister. What about his fees?"

The mention of fees pained me, and I broke in: "Abdulla Sheth, fees are out of the question. There can be no fees for public work. I can stay, if at all, as a servant. And as you know, I am not acquainted with all these friends. But if you believe that they will cooperate, I am prepared to stay a month longer. There is one thing, however. Though you need not pay me anything, work of the nature we contemplate cannot be done without some funds to start with. Thus we may have to send telegrams. we may have to print some literature, some touring may have to be done, the local attorneys may have to be consulted, and as I am ignorant of your laws, I may need some law-books for reference. All this cannot be done without money. And it is clear that one man is not enough for this work. Many must come forward to help him."

And a chorus of voices was heard: "Allah is great and merciful. Money will come in. Men there are, as many as you may need. You please consent to stay, and all will be well."

The farewell party was thus turned into a working committee. I suggested finishing dinner etc. quickly and getting back home. I worked out in my own mind an outline of the campaign. I ascertained the names of those who were on the list of voters, and made up my mind to stay on for a month.

Thus God laid the foundations of my life in South Africa and sowed the seed of the fight for national self-respect.

MOBBED AT DURBAN

by M. K. Gandhi

In 1896, after Gandhi had been in South Africa three years, he asked permission to return to India for six months. He wanted to bring back his wife and children, who had remained in India, and he also hoped to arouse interest in the grievances of Indians in South Africa. To this end he wrote a popular brochure called The Green Pamphlet. He also traveled widely in India, until, in Calcutta, he received word to return at once to South Africa. He sailed with his wife and two sons from Bombay at the beginning of December 1896.

On reaching the port of Durban, his ship and another from India were put in quarantine, ostensibly because of the plague in Bombay, but really because of the presence of Gandhi. A garbled report of his pamphlet had reached South Africa and the white community was aroused against Gandhi, fearing that his returning with two ship-loads of Indians was a plot to invade the country. After riding at sea for twenty-three days outside Port Natal, the ships were allowed to discharge their passengers, who had in the meantime, together with Gandhi, received all kinds of threats.

A MESSAGE reached me from Mr. Escombe [4] advising me not to land with the others but to wait until evening when he would send the Superintendent of Water Police to escort me home, and adding that my family were free to land at any time. This was not an order according to law, but was by way of advice to the captain not to allow me to land and of warning to me of the danger that was hanging over my head. The captain had not the power forc-

• Reprinted with permission from M. K. Gandhi, Satyagraha in South Africa (Madras: Ganesan, 1928), pp. 91-103.

ibly to prevent me from landing. But I came to the conclusion that I should accept this suggestion. I sent my family to the residence of my old friend and client, Parsee Rustomji, instead of to my own place, and told them that I would meet them there. When the passengers had disembarked, Mr. Laughton, counsel for Dada Abdulla [5] and a personal friend of mine, came up and met me. He asked me why I had not yet landed. I told him about Mr. Escombe's letter. He said that he did not like the idea of my waiting till evening and then entering the city like a thief or offender, that if I was not afraid, I should accompany him there and then, and that we could walk to the town as if nothing had happened. I replied: "I do not think I am afraid. It is only a question of propriety whether or not I should accept Mr. Escombe's suggestion. And we should also consider whether the captain of the steamer is responsible in the matter." Mr. Laughton smiled and said: "What has Mr. Escombe done for you that you must needs heed his suggestion? And what reason have you to believe that he is actuated by kindliness and not by some ulterior motive? I know more than you what has happened in the town, and what hand Mr. Escombe had in the happenings there." I interrupted him with a shaking of the head. "We might assume," continued Mr. Laughton, "that he is actuated by the best of motives. But I am positively of opinion that if you comply with his suggestion, you will stand humiliated. I would, therefore, advise you, if you are ready, to accompany me just now. The captain is our man, and his responsibility is our responsibility. He is accountable only to Dada Abdulla. I know what they will think of the matter, as they have displayed great courage in the present struggle." I replied: "Let us then go. I have no preparations to make. All I have to do is to put on my turban. Let us inform the captain and start." We took the captain's leave.

Mr. Laughton was an old and well-known advocate of Durban. I had come in intimate contact with him before I returned to India. I used to consult him in difficult cases and often to engage him as my senior. He was a brave and powerfully built man.

Our road lay through the principal street of Durban. It was

about half past four in the evening when we started. The sky was slightly overcast and the sun was not to be seen. It would take a pedestrian at least one hour to reach Rustomji Sheth's place. The number of persons present about the wharf was not larger than what is to be usually seen there. As soon as we landed, some boys saw us. As I was the only Indian who put on a turban of a particular type, they at once recognized me, began to shout "Gandhi," "Gandhi," "thrash him," "surround him," and came up towards us. Some began to throw pebbles at us. A few elderly Europeans joined the boys. Gradually the party of rioters began to grow. Mr. Laughton thought that there was danger in our going on foot. He therefore hailed a rickshaw. I had never sat in a rickshaw before, as it was thoroughly disgusting to me to sit in a vehicle pulled by human beings. But I then felt that it was my duty to use that vehicle. I have experienced five or seven times in my life that one, whom God wishes to save, cannot fall even if he will. If I did not fall I cannot take any credit for it to myself. These rickshaws are pulled by Zulus. The elderly Europeans and the boys threatened the rickshaw puller that if he allowed me to sit in his rickshaw, they would beat him and smash his rickshaw to pieces. The rickshaw boy, therefore, said "Kha" (meaning "no") and went away. I was thus spared the shame of a rickshaw ride.

We had no alternative now but to proceed to our destination on foot. A mob followed us. With every step we advanced, it grew larger and larger. The gathering was enormous when we reached West Street. A man of powerful build took hold of Mr. Laughton and tore him away from me. He was not therefore in a position to come up with me. The crowd began to abuse me and shower upon me stones and whatever else they could lay their hands on. They threw down my turban. Meanwhile a burly fellow came up to me, slapped me in the face and then kicked me. I was about to fall down unconscious when I held on to the railings of a house near by. I took breath for a while and when the fainting was over, proceeded on my way. I had almost given up the hope of reaching home alive. But I remember well that even then my heart did not arraign my assailants.

While I was thus wending my way, the wife of the Superintendent of Police at Durban was coming from the opposite direction. We knew each other well. She was a brave lady. Although the sky was cloudy and the sun about to set, she opened her sunshade for my protection and began to walk at my side. The Europeans would not insult a lady, especially the wife of the old and popular Superintendent of Police, nor would they hurt her. They must avoid injuring her while aiming blows at me. The injuries, therefore, which I received after she joined me, were not serious. Meanwhile the Superintendent of Police came to know of the attack upon me and sent a party of constables for my protection. The police surrounded me. The Police Station was on our way. When we reached there I saw that the Superintendent of Police was waiting for us. He offered me asylum in the police station, but I declined the offer with thanks and said, "I must reach my destination. I have faith in the fair play of the citizens of Durban and in the righteousness of my own cause. I am thankful to you for sending the police party for my protection. Mrs. Alexander too has contributed to my safety."

I reached Rustomji's house without further trouble. It was nearly evening when I reached there. Dr. Dadibarjor, the medical officer of the *Courland*, who was with Rustomji Sheth, began to treat me. He examined my wounds. There were not many of them. One blind wound in particular was very painful. But I was not yet privileged to rest in peace. Thousands of Europeans gathered before Rustomji Sheth's house. After nightfall, hooligans also joined the crowd. The crowd sent word to Rustomji Sheth that if he did not hand me over to them, they would burn him and his house along with me. Rustomji Sheth was too good an Indian to be daunted. When Superintendent Alexander came to know how matters stood, he quietly joined the crowd with a number of detectives. He sent for a bench and stood upon it. Thus under the pretence of talking to the crowd, he took possession of the entrance to Rustomji's house so that none could break and enter it. He had already posted detectives at proper places. Immediately on arrival, he had instructed a subordinate to disguise himself as an Indian trader by putting on Indian dress and painting his face to see me and deliver to me the following message: "If you wish to save your friend, his guests and property, and your own family, I advise you to disguise yourself as an Indian constable, come out through Rustomji's go-down, steal through the crowd with my man and reach the Police Station. A carriage is awaiting you at the corner of the street. This is the only way in which I can save you and others. The crowd is so excited that I am not in a position to control it. If you are not prompt in following my directions, I am afraid the crowd will raze Rustomji's house to the ground and it is impossible for me to imagine how many lives will be lost and how much property destroyed."

I gauged the situation at once. I soon disguised myself as a constable and left Rustomji's house. The Police Officer and I reached the Police Station in safety. In the meantime Mr. Alexander was humoring the crowd by singing topical songs [6] and talking to them. When he knew that I had reached the Police Station, he became serious and asked:

"What do you want?"

"We want Gandhi."

"What will you do with him?"

"We will burn him."

"What harm has he done to you?"

"He has vilified us in India and wants to flood Natal with Indians."

"What if he does not come out?"

"We will then burn this house."

"His wife and children are also there. There are other men and women besides. Would you not be ashamed of burning women and children?"

"The responsibility for that will rest with you. What can we do when you make us helpless in the matter? We do not wish to hurt anyone else. It would be enough if you hand over Gandhi to us. If you do not surrender the culprit, and if others are injured in our endeavor to capture him, would it be fair on your part to blame us?"

The Superintendent gently smiled and informed the crowd that I had left Rustomji's house, passed through their midst, and reached another place already. The crowd laughed loudly and shouted, "It is a lie, it is a lie."

The Superintendent said: "If you will not believe your old Superintendent of Police, please appoint a committee of three or four men from amongst you. Let others promise that they will not enter the house, and that if the committee fail to find Gandhi in the house, you will peacefully return to your homes. You got excited today and did not obey the police. That reflects discredit on you, not on the police. The police therefore played a trick with you; it removed your prey from your midst and you have lost the game. You will certainly not blame the police for this. The police, whom you yourselves have appointed, have simply done their duty."

The Superintendent addressed the crowd with such suavity and determination, that they gave him the promise he had asked for. A committee was appointed. It searched Rustomji's house through and through, and reported to the crowd that the Superintendent was right and had beaten them in the game. The crowd was disappointed. But they kept their word and dispersed without committing any mischief. This happened on 13th January 1897.

The same morning after the quarantine on the steamers had been removed, the reporter of a Durban newspaper had seen me on the steamer. He had asked me everything. It was quite easy to dispose of the charges against me to his satisfaction. I showed to him in detail that I had not indulged in the least exaggeration. What I had done was only my duty. If I had failed to discharge it, I would be unworthy of the name of man. All this appeared in the newspapers the next day. Sensible people among the Europeans admitted their mistake. The newspapers expressed their sympathy with the standpoint of the Europeans in Natal, but at the same time fully defended my action. This enhanced my reputation as well as the prestige of the Indian community. It was proved that the Indians, poor as they were, were no cowards, and that the Indian traders were prepared to fight for their self-respect and for their country regardless of loss.

Thus though the Indian community had to suffer hardship and though Dada Abdulla incurred big losses, the ultimate result, I believe, was entirely beneficial. The community had an opportunity of measuring their own strength and their self-confidence increased in consequence. I had a most valuable experience, and whenever I think of that day, I feel that God was preparing me for the practice of Satyagraha.

The events in Natal had their repercussion in England. Mr. Chamberlain,[7] Secretary of State for the Colonies, cabled to the Government of Natal asking them to prosecute my assailants and to see that justice was done to me.

Mr. Escombe, who was Attorney-General with the Government of Natal, called me. He told me about Mr. Chamberlain's cable. He expressed his regret for the injuries I had sustained, and his pleasure that the consequences of the assault were not more serious. He added, "I can assure you that I did not at all intend that you or any other member of your community should be injured. As I feared that you might possibly be hurt, I sent you word to say that you should land at night. You did not like my suggestion. I do not wish to blame you in the least that you accepted Mr. Laughton's advice. You were perfectly entitled to do what you thought fit. The Government of Natal fully accepts Mr. Chamberlain's demand. We desire that the offenders should be brought to book. Can you identify any of your assailants?"

I replied: "I might perhaps be able to identify one or two of them. But I must say at once before this conversation proceeds that I have already made up my mind not to prosecute my assailants. I cannot see that they are at fault. What information they had, they had obtained from their leaders. It is too much to expect them to judge whether it was correct or otherwise. If all that they heard about me was true, it was natural for them to be excited and do something wrong in a fit of indignation. I would not blame them for it. Excited crowds have always tried to deal out justice in that manner. If any one is to blame it is the Committee of Europeans, you yourself and therefore, the Government of Natal. Reuter might have cabled any distorted account. But when you knew that I was coming to Natal, it was your duty and duty of the Committee to question me about the suspicions you entertained with regard to my activities in India, to hear what I had to say and then do what might appear proper in the circumstances. Now I cannot prosecute you or the Committee for the assault. And even if I could, I would not seek redress in a court of law. You took such steps as seemed advisable to you for safeguarding the interests of the Europeans of Natal. That is a political matter, and it remains for me to fight with you in the political field and to convince you and the other Europeans that the Indians who constitute a large proportion of the population of the British Empire wish to preserve their self-respect and safeguard their rights without injuring the Europeans in the least."

Mr. Escombe said, "I quite understand what you say, and I appreciate it. I was not prepared to hear that you were not willing to prosecute your assailants. I would not have been displeased in the least had you prosecuted them. But when you have signified your determination not to prosecute, I do not hesitate to say not only that you have come to a right decision in the matter, but you will render further service to your community by your self-restraint. I must at the same time admit that your refusal to prosecute your assailants will save the Government of Natal from a most awkward position. If you so desire, the Government will see that your assailants are arrested, but it is scarcely necessary to tell you that it would irritate the Europeans and give rise to all manner of criticism, which no Government would relish. But if you have finally made up your mind not to prosecute, you should write to me a note signifying your intention to that effect. I cannot defend my Government merely by sending Mr. Chamberlain a summary of our conversation. I should cable to him a summary of your note. I am not, however, asking you to let me have the note just now. You had better consult your friends. You consult Mr. Laughton also. And if after such consultations you still adhere to your resolution not to prosecute, you write to me. But your note should clearly state that you, on your own responsibility, refuse to prosecute your assailants. Then only can I make use of it."

I said: "I had no idea that you had sent for me in this connection. I have not consulted anyone on the subject, nor do I wish to consult anyone now. When I decided to land and proceed with Mr. Laughton, I had made up my mind that I should not feel aggrieved in case I was injured. Prosecuting my assailants is therefore out of the question. This is a religious question with me, and I believe with you that I shall serve my community as well as myself by this act of self-restraint. I propose, therefore, to take all the responsibility on my shoulders and to give you the note you ask for here and now." I then obtained blank paper from him, wrote out the desired note and handed it over to him.

FAMILY LIFE
by M. K. Gandhi

Gandhi was separated a great deal from his family in his early life. For this and other reasons, his family is only occasionally mentioned in his autobiography. Following are several separated narratives of family life between the time he brought his wife and children to South Africa in 1897 and his return to India in 1901-2.

WHEN I landed at Durban in January 1897, I had three children with me, my sister's son ten years old, and my own sons nine and five years of age. Where was I to educate them?

I could have sent them to the schools for European children, but only as a matter of favor and exception. No other Indian

• Reprinted with permission from *Gandhi's Autobiography* (Washington: Public Affairs Press, 1948), Part III, pp. 245-46, 250-51, 261-63, 338-40.

children were allowed to attend them. For these there were schools established by Christian missions, but I was not prepared to send my children there, as I did not like the education imparted in those schools. For one thing, the medium of instruction would be only English, or perhaps incorrect Tamil or Hindi; this too could only have been arranged with difficulty. I could not possibly put up with this and other disadvantages. In the meantime I was making my own attempt to teach them. But that was at best irregular, and I could not get hold of a suitable Gujarati teacher.

I was at my wits' end. I advertised for an English teacher who should teach the children under my direction. Some regular instruction was to be given them by this teacher, and for the rest they should be satisfied with what little I could give them irregularly. So I engaged an English governess on £7 a month. This went on for some time, but not to my satisfaction. The boys acquired some knowledge of Gujarati through my conversation and intercourse with them, which was strictly in the mother-tongue. I was loath to send them back to India, for I believed even then that young children should not be separated from their parents. The education that children naturally imbibe in a well-ordered household is impossible to obtain in hostels. I therefore kept my children with me. I did send my nephew and elder son to be educated at residential schools in India for a few months, but I soon had to recall them. Later, the eldest son, long after he had come of age, broke away from me, and went to India to join a High School in Ahmedabad. I have an impression that the nephew was satisfied with what I could give him. Unfortunately he died in the prime of youth after a brief illness. The other three of my sons have never been at a public school, though they did get some regular schooling in an improvised school which I started for the children of Satyagrahi parents in South Africa. . . .

The question of the rearing of children had been ever before me. I had two sons born in South Africa, and my service in the hospital was useful in solving the question of their upbringing.

My independent spirit was a constant source of trial. My wife and I had decided to have the best medical aid at the time of her delivery, but if the doctor and the nurse were to leave us in the lurch at the right moment, what was I to do? Then the nurse had to be an Indian. And the difficulty of getting a trained Indian nurse in South Africa can be easily imagined from the similar difficulty in India. So I studied the things necessary for safe labor. I read Dr. Tribhuvandas' book, Ma-ne Shikhaman—Advice to a Mother—and I nursed both my children according to the instructions given in the book, tempered here and there by such experience as I had gained elsewhere. The services of a nurse were utilized—not for more than two months each time—chiefly for helping my wife, and not for taking care of the babies, which I did myself.

The birth of the last child put me to the severest test. The travail came on suddenly. The doctor was not immediately available, and some time was lost in fetching the midwife. Even if she had been on the spot, she could not have helped delivery. I had to see through the safe delivery of the baby. My careful study of the subject in Dr. Tribhuvandas' work was of inestimable help. I was not nervous.

I am convinced that for the proper upbringing of children the parents ought to have a general knowledge of the care and nursing of babies. At every step I have seen the advantages of my careful study of the subject. My children would not have enjoyed the general health that they do today, had I not studied the subject and turned my knowledge to account. We labor under a sort of superstition that the child has nothing to learn during the first five years of its life. On the contrary the fact is that the child never learns in after life what it does in its first five years. The education of the child begins with conception. The physical and mental states of the parents at the moment of conception are reproduced in the baby. Then during the period of pregnancy it continues to be affected by the mother's moods, desires and temperament, as also by her ways of life. After birth the child imitates the parents, and for a considerable number of years entirely depends on them for its growth. . . .

I had started on a life of ease and comfort, but the experiment was short-lived. Although I had furnished the house with care, yet it failed to have any hold on me. So no sooner had I launched forth on that life, than I began to cut down expenses. The washerman's bill was heavy, and as he was besides by no means noted for his punctuality, even two to three dozen shirts and collars proved insufficient for me. Collars had to be changed daily and shirts, if not daily, at least every alternate day. This meant a double expense, which appeared to me unnecessary. So I equipped myself with a washing outfit to save it. I bought a book on washing, studied the art and taught it also to my wife. This no doubt added to my work, but its novelty made it a pleasure.

I shall never forget the first collar that I washed myself. I had used more starch than necessary, the iron had not been made hot enough, and for fear of burning the collar I had not pressed it sufficiently. The result was that, though the collar was fairly stiff, the superfluous starch continually dropped off it. I went to court with the collar on, thus inviting the ridicule of brother barristers, but even in those days I could be impervious to ridicule. . . .

In the same way, as I freed myself from slavery to the washerman, I threw off dependence on the barber. All people who go to England learn there at least the art of shaving, but none, to my knowledge, learn to cut their own hair. I had to learn that too. I once went to an English hair-cutter in Pretoria. He contemptuously refused to cut my hair. I certainly felt hurt, but immediately purchased a pair of clippers and cut my hair before the mirror. I succeeded more or less in cutting the front hair, but I spoiled the back. The friends in the court shook with laughter.

"What's wrong with your hair, Gandhi? Rats have been at it?"

"No. The white barber would not condescend to touch my black hair," said I, "so I preferred to cut it myself, no matter how badly." . . .

When I was practicing in Durban, my office clerks often stayed with me, and there were among them Hindus and Christians, or to describe them by their provinces, Gujaratis and Tamilians. I do not recollect having ever regarded them as anything but my kith and kin. I treated them as members of my family, and had unpleasantness with my wife if ever she stood in the way of my treating them as such. One of the clerks was a Christian, born of Panchama [8] parents.

The house was built after the Western model and the rooms rightly had no outlets for dirty water. Each room had therefore chamber-pots. Rather than have these cleaned by a servant or a sweeper, my wife or I attended to them. The clerks who made themselves completely at home would naturally clean their own pots, but the Christian clerk was a newcomer, and it was our duty to attend to his bedroom. My wife managed the pots of the others, but to clean those used by one who had been a Panchama seemed to her to be the limit, and we fell out. She could not bear the pots being cleaned by me, neither did she like doing it herself. Even today I can recall the picture of her chiding me, her eyes red with anger, and pearl drops streaming down her cheeks, as she descended the ladder, pot in hand. But I was a cruelly kind husband. I regarded myself as her teacher, and so harassed her out of my blind love for her.

I was far from being satisfied by her merely carrying the pot. I would have her do it cheerfully. So I said, raising my voice: "I will not stand this nonsense in my house."

The words pierced her like an arrow.

She shouted back: "Keep your house to yourself and let me go." I forgot myself, and the spring of compassion dried up in me. I caught her by the hand, dragged the helpless woman to the gate, which was just opposite the ladder, and proceeded to open it with the intention of pushing her out. The tears were running down her cheeks in torrents, and she cried: "Have you no sense of shame? Must you so far forget yourself? Where am I to go? I have no parents or relatives here to harbor me. Being your wife, you think I must put up with your cuffs and kicks? For Heaven's sake behave yourself, and shut the gate. Let us not be found making scenes like this!"

I put on a brave face, but was really ashamed and shut the gate. If my wife could not leave me, neither could I leave her. We have had numerous bickerings, but the end has always been peace between us. The wife, with her matchless powers of endurance, has always been the victor.

Today I am in a position to narrate the incident with some detachment, as it belongs to a period out of which I have fortunately emerged. I am no longer a blind, infatuated husband, I am no more my wife's teacher. Kasturba can, if she will, be as unpleasant to me today, as I used to be to her before. We are tried friends, the one no longer regarding the other as the object of lust. She has been a faithful nurse throughout my illnesses, serving without any thought of reward. . . .

THE MAGIC SPELL OF A BOOK
• by M. K. Gandhi

In 1904 the journal, Indian Opinion, was launched in South Africa. Gandhi paid most of the deficits and wrote for it as well. "Week after week," he says, "I poured out my soul in its columns." At this time, in a vegetarian restaurant, Gandhi made the acquaintance of Mr. Henry S. L. Polak, of whom he later wrote, "We seemed to hold closely similar views on the essential things of life."

MR. POLAK . . . came to see me off at the station, and left with me a book to read during the journey, which he said I was sure to like. It was Ruskin's *Unto This Last.*

• Reprinted with permission from *Gandhi's Autobiography* (Washington: Public Affairs Press, 1948), Part IV, Chapters XVIII and XIX, pp. 364-68.

The book was impossible to lay aside, once I had begun it. It gripped me. Johannesburg to Durban was a twenty-four hours' journey. The train reached there in the evening. I could not get any sleep that night. I determined to change my life in accordance with the ideals of the book.

This was the first book of Ruskin I had ever read. During the days of my education I had read practically nothing outside textbooks, and after I launched into active life I had very little time for reading. I cannot therefore claim much book knowledge. However, I believe I have not lost much because of this enforced restraint. On the contrary, the limited reading may be said to have enabled me thoroughly to digest what I did read. Of these books, the one that brought about an instantaneous and practical transformation in my life was *Unto This Last*. I translated it later into Gujarati, entitling it *Sarvodaya* (the welfare of all).

I believe that I discovered some of my deepest convictions reflected in this great book of Ruskin, and that is why it so captured me and made me transform my life. A poet is one who can call forth the good latent in the human breast. Poets do not influence all alike, for everyone is not evolved in an equal measure.

The teaching of *Unto This Last* I understood to be:

1. That the good of the individual is contained in the good of all.
2. That a lawyer's work has the same value as the barber's, inasmuch as all have the same right of earning their livelihood from their work.
3. That a life of labor, i.e., the life of the tiller of the soil and the handicraftsman, is the life worth living.

The first of these I knew. The second I had dimly realized. The third had never occurred to me. *Unto This Last* made it as clear as daylight for me that the second and third were contained in the first. I arose with the dawn, ready to reduce these principles to practice.

I talked over the whole thing with Mr. West,[9] described to him the effect *Unto This Last* had produced on my mind, and proposed that *Indian Opinion* should be removed to a farm, on which everyone should labor, drawing the same living wage, and attending to the press work in spare time. Mr. West approved of the proposal, and £3 was laid down as the monthly allowance per head, irrespective of color or nationality.

But it was a question whether all the ten or more workers in the press would agree to go and settle on an out-of-the-way farm, and be satisfied with bare maintenance. We therefore proposed that those who could not fit in with the scheme should continue to draw their salaries and gradually try to reach the ideal of becoming members of the settlement.

I talked to the workers in the terms of this proposal. It did not appeal to Sjt. Madanjit,[10] who considered my proposal to be foolish and held that it would ruin a venture on which he had staked his all, that the workers would bolt, *Indian Opinion* would come to a stop, and the press would have to be closed down.

Among the men working in the press was Chhaganlal Gandhi, one of my cousins. I had put the proposal to him at the same time as to West. He had a wife and children, but he had from childhood chosen to be trained and to work under me. He had full faith in me. So without any argument he agreed to the scheme and has been with me ever since. The machinist Govindaswami also fell in with the proposal. The rest did not join the scheme, but agreed to go wherever I removed the press.

I do not think I took more than two days to fix up these matters with the men. Thereafter I at once advertised for a piece of land situated near a railway station in the vicinity of Durban. An offer came in respect of Phoenix. Mr. West and I went to inspect the estate. Within a week we purchased twenty acres of land. It had a nice little spring and a few orange and mango trees. Adjoining it was a piece of 80 acres which had many more fruit trees and a dilapidated cottage. We purchased this too, the total cost being a thousand pounds.

The late Mr. Rustomji always supported me in such enterprises. He liked the project. He placed at my disposal secondhand corrugated iron sheets of a big godown and other building material, with which we started work. Some Indian carpenters

and masons, who had worked with me in the Boer War, helped
me in erecting a shed for the press. This structure, which was 75
feet long and 50 feet broad, was ready in less than a month. Mr.
West and others, at great personal risk, stayed with the carpenters and masons. The place, uninhabited and thickly overgrown
with grass, was infested with snakes and obviously dangerous to
live in. At first all lived under canvas. We carted most of our
things to Phoenix in about a week. It was fourteen miles from
Durban, and two and a half miles from Phoenix station.

Only one issue of *Indian Opinion* had to be printed outside, in
the Mercury press.

I now endeavored to draw to Phoenix those relations and
friends who had come with me from India to try their fortune,
and who were engaged in business of various kinds. They had
come in search of wealth, and it was therefore difficult to persuade
them; but some agreed. Of these I can single out here only
Maganlal Gandhi's name. The others went back to business.
Maganlal Gandhi left his business for good to cast in his lot
with me, and by ability, sacrifice and devotion stands foremost
among my original coworkers in my ethical experiments. As a
self-taught handicraftsman his place among them is unique.

Thus the Phoenix Settlement was started in 1904, and there
in spite of numerous odds *Indian Opinion* continues to be published.

3 BEGINNINGS OF *SATYAGRAHA* (1906-1908)

THE ADVENT OF *SATYAGRAHA*
• by M. K. Gandhi

In August 1906 the Transvaal government Gazette printed a proposed ordinance which would require all Indians to register with the authorities and to carry a certificate at all times, on penalty of imprisonment or deportation from the Transvaal. This ordinance was named "the Black Act" and Gandhi, on first reading it, felt that if it were adopted it would mean "absolute ruin for the Indians of South Africa." The leading Indians held a small meeting and after Gandhi explained the meaning of the ordinance to them, it was agreed to hold a public meeting at which a number of resolutions about the Black Act would be proposed.

THE MEETING was duly held on the 11th September 1906. It was attended by delegates from various places in the Transvaal. But I must confess that even I myself had not then understood all the implications of the resolutions I had helped to frame; nor had I gauged all the possible conclusions to which they might lead. The old Empire Theatre was packed from floor to ceiling. I could read in every face the expectation of something strange to be done or to happen. Mr. Abdul Gani, Chairman of the Transvaal British Indian Association, presided. He was one of the oldest Indian

• Reprinted with permission from M. K. Gandhi, *Satyagraha in South Africa* (Madras: Ganesan, 1928), Chapter XII, pp. 161-73.

59

residents of the Transvaal, and partner and manager of the Johannesburg branch of the well-known firm of Mamad Kasam Kamrudin. The most important among the resolutions passed by the meeting was the famous Fourth Resolution, by which the Indians solemnly determined not to submit to the Ordinance in the event of its becoming law in the teeth of their opposition and to suffer all the penalties attaching to such non-submission.

I fully explained this resolution to the meeting and received a patient hearing. The business of the meeting was conducted in Hindi or Gujarati; it was impossible therefore that anyone present should not follow the proceedings. For the Tamils and Telugus who did not know Hindi there were Tamil and Telugu speakers who fully explained everything in their respective languages. The resolution was duly proposed, seconded and supported by several speakers one of whom was Sheth Haji Habib. He too was a very old and experienced resident of South Africa and made an impassioned speech. He was deeply moved and went so far as to say that we must pass this resolution with God as witness and must never yield a cowardly submission to such degrading legislation. He then went on solemnly to declare in the name of God that he would never submit to that law, and advised all present to do likewise. Others also delivered powerful and angry speeches in supporting the resolution.

When in the course of his speech Sheth Haji Habib came to the solemn declaration, I was at once startled and put on my guard. Only then did I fully realize my own responsibility and the responsibility of the community. The community had passed many a resolution before and amended such resolutions in the light of further reflection or fresh experience. There were cases in which resolutions passed had not been observed by all concerned. Amendments in resolutions and failure to observe resolutions on the part of persons agreeing thereto are ordinary experiences of public life all the world over. But no one ever imports the name of God into such resolutions. In the abstract there should not be any distinction between a resolution and an oath taken in the name of God. When an intelligent man makes a resolution deliberately he never swerves from it by a hair's breadth. With him his resolution carries as much weight as a declaration made with God as witness does. But the world takes no note of abstract principles and imagines an ordinary resolution and an oath in the name of God to be as poles asunder. A man who makes an ordinary resolution is not ashamed of himself when he deviates from it, but a man who violates an oath administered to him is not only ashamed of himself, but is also looked upon by society as a sinner. This imaginary distinction has struck such a deep root in the human mind that a person making a statement on oath before a judge is held to have committed an offence in law if the statement is proved to be false and receives drastic punishment.

Full of these thoughts as I was, possessing as I did much experience of solemn pledges, having profited by them, I was simply taken aback by Sheth Haji Habib's suggestion of an oath. I thought out the possible consequences of it in a single moment. My perplexity gave place to enthusiasm. And although I had no intention of taking an oath or inviting others to do so when I went to the meeting, I warmly approved of the Sheth's suggestion. But at the same time it seemed to me that the people should be apprised of all the consequences and should have explained to them clearly the meaning of a pledge. And if even then they were prepared to pledge themselves, they should be encouraged to do so; otherwise I must understand that they were not still ready to stand the final test. I therefore asked the President for permission to explain to the meeting the implications of Sheth Haji Habib's suggestion. The President readily granted it and I rose to address the meeting. I give below a summary of my remarks just as I can recall them now:

"I wish to explain to this meeting that there is a vast difference between this resolution and every other resolution we have passed up to date and that there is a wide divergence also in the manner of making it. It is a very grave resolution we are making, as our existence in South Africa depends upon our fully observing it. The manner of making the resolution suggested by our friend is as much of a novelty as of a solemnity. I did not come to the meeting with a view to getting the resolution passed in that manner, which redounds to the credit of Sheth Haji Habib as well as it lays a burden of responsibility upon him. I tender my congratulations to him. I deeply appreciate his suggestion, but if you adopt it you too will share his responsibility. You must understand what is this responsibility, and as an adviser and servant of the community, it is my duty fully to explain it to you.

"We all believe in one and the same God, the differences of nomenclature in Hinduism and Islam notwithstanding. To pledge ourselves or to take an oath in the name of that God or with Him as witness is not something to be trifled with. If having taken such an oath we violate our pledge we are guilty before God and man. Personally I hold that a man, who deliberately and intelligently takes a pledge and then breaks it, forfeits his manhood. And just as a copper coin treated with mercury not only becomes valueless when found out but also makes its owner liable to punishment, in the same way a man who lightly pledges his word and then breaks it becomes a man of straw and fits himself for punishment here as well as hereafter. Sheth Haji Habib is proposing to administer an oath of such a serious character. There is no one in this meeting who can be classed as an infant or as wanting in understanding. You are all well advanced in age and have seen the world; many of you are delegates and have discharged responsibilities in a greater or lesser measure. No one present, therefore, can ever hope to excuse himself by saying that he did not know what he was about when he took the oath.

"I know that pledges and vows are, and should be, taken on rare occasions. A man who takes a vow every now and then is sure to stumble. But if I can imagine a crisis in the history of the Indian community of South Africa when it would be in the fitness of things to take pledges that crisis is surely now. There is wisdom in taking serious steps with great caution and hesitation. But caution and hesitation have their limits, which we have now passed. The Government have taken leave of all sense of decency. We would only be betraying our unworthiness and cowardice, if we cannot stake our all in the face of the conflagration which envelopes us and sit watching it with folded hands. There is no doubt, therefore, that the present is a proper occasion for taking pledges. But every one of us must think out for himself if he has the will and the ability to pledge himself. Resolutions of this nature cannot be passed by a majority vote. Only those who take a pledge can be bound by it. This pledge must not be taken with a view to produce an effect on outsiders. No one should trouble to consider what impression it might have upon the Local Government, the Imperial Government, or the Government of India. Every one must only search his own heart, and if the inner voice assures him that he has the requisite strength to carry him through, then only should he pledge himself and then only would his pledge bear fruit.

"A few words now as to the consequences. Hoping for the best, we may say that if a majority of the Indians pledge themselves to resistance and if all who take the pledge prove true to themselves, the Ordinance may not even be passed and, if passed, may be soon repealed. It may be that we may not be called upon to suffer at all. But if on the one hand who takes a pledge must be a robust optimist, on the other hand he must be prepared for the worst. It is therefore that I would give you an idea of the worst that might happen to us in the present struggle. Imagine that all of us present here numbering 3,000 at the most pledge ourselves. Imagine again that the remaining 10,000 Indians take no such pledge. We will only provoke ridicule in the beginning. Again, it is quite possible that in spite of the present warning some or many of those who pledge themselves might weaken at the very first trial. We might have to go to jail, where we might be insulted. We might have to go hungry and suffer extreme heat or cold. Hard labor might be imposed upon us. We might be flogged by rude warders. We might be fined heavily and our property might be attached and held up to auction if there are only a few resisters left. Opulent today we might be reduced to abject poverty tomorrow. We might be deported. Suffering from starvation and similar hardships in jail, some of us might fall ill and even die. In short, therefore, it is not at all impossible that we might have to endure every hardship that we can imagine, and wisdom lies in pledging ourselves on the understanding that we shall have to suffer all that and worse. If some one asks me when and how the struggle may end, I may say that if the entire community manfully stands the test, the end will be near. If many of us fall back under storm and stress, the struggle will be prolonged. But I can boldly declare, and with certainty, that so long as there is even a handful of men true to their pledge, there can only be one end to the struggle, and that is victory.

"A word about my personal responsibility. If I am warning you of the risks attendant upon the pledge, I am at the same time inviting you to pledge yourselves, and I am fully conscious of my responsibility in the matter. It is possible that a majority of those present here might take the pledge in a fit of enthusiasm or indignation but might weaken under the ordeal, and only a handful might be left to face the final test. Even then there is only one course open to the like of me, to die but not to submit to the law. It is quite unlikely but even if everyone else flinched leaving me alone to face the music, I am confident that I would never violate my pledge. Please do not misunderstand me. I am not saying this out of vanity, but I wish to put you, especially the leaders upon the platform, on your guard. I wish respectfully to suggest it to you that if you have not the will or the ability to stand firm even when you are perfectly isolated, you must not only not take the pledge yourselves but you must declare your opposition before the resolution is put to the meeting and before its members begin to take pledges and you must not make yourselves parties to the resolution. Although we are going to take the pledge in a body, no one should imagine that default on the part of one or many can absolve the rest from their obligation. Everyone should fully realize his responsibility, then only pledge himself independently of others and understand that he himself must be true to his pledge even unto death, no matter what others do."

I spoke to this effect and resumed my seat. The meeting heard me word by word in perfect quiet. Other leaders too spoke. All dwelt upon their own responsibility and the responsibility of the audience. The President rose. He too made the situation clear, and at last all present, standing with upraised hands, took an oath with God as witness not to submit to the Ordinance if it became law. I can never forget the scene, which is present before my mind's eye as I write. The community's enthusiasm knew no bounds. The very next day there was some accident in the theatre in consequence of which it was wholly destroyed by fire. On the third day friends brought me the news of the fire and congratulated the community upon this good omen, which signified to them that the Ordinance would meet the same fate as the theatre. I have never been influenced by such so-called signs and therefore did not attach any weight to the coincidence. I have taken note of it here only as a demonstration of the community's courage and faith. The reader will find in the subsequent chapters many proofs of these two high qualities of the people. . . .

None of us knew what name to give to our movement. I then used the term "passive resistance" in describing it. I did not quite understand the implications of "passive resistance" as I called it. I only knew that some new principle had come into being. As the struggle advanced, the phrase "passive resistance" gave rise to confusion and it appeared shameful to permit this great struggle to be known only by an English name. Again, that foreign phrase could hardly pass as current coin among the community. A small prize was therefore announced in *Indian Opinion* to be awarded to the reader who invented the best designation for our struggle. We thus received a number of suggestions. The meaning of the struggle had been then fully discussed in *Indian Opinion* and the competitors for the prize had fairly sufficient material to serve as a basis for their exploration. Sr. Maganlal Gandhi was one of the competitors and he suggested the word "Sadagraha," meaning "firmness in a good cause." I liked the word, but it did not fully represent the whole idea I wished it to connote. I therefore corrected it to "Satyagraha." Truth (Satya) implies love and firmness (Agraha) engenders and therefore serves as a synonym for force. I thus began to call the Indian movement "Satyagraha," that is to say, the Force which is born of Truth and Love or non-violence, and gave up the use of the phrase "passive resist-ance," in connection with it, so much so that even in English writing we often avoided it and used instead the word "Saty-agraha" itself or some other equivalent English phrase. This then was the genesis of the movement which came to be known as Satyagraha, and of the word used as a designation for it. . . .

FIRST IMPRISONMENT
by M. K. Gandhi

The Black Act was put into effect in July 1907, and called for the registration of all Asians in South Africa. When only a few Indians registered, the government decided to make arrests to enforce the Act. During Christmas week, 1907, some of the leaders of the Indian community, including Gandhi, were served with a notice to appear before the magistrate to show cause why, having failed to apply for registration as required by the new law, they should not be ordered to leave the Transvaal.

THE MAGISTRATE conducted each case separately, and ordered all the accused to leave the Transvaal within forty-eight hours in some cases and seven or fourteen days in others.

The time limit expired on 10th January, 1908 and the same day we were called upon to attend court for sentence.

None of us had to offer any defence. All were to plead guilty to the charge of disobeying the order to leave the Transvaal within the stated period, issued by the Magistrate, on failure to satisfy him that they were lawful holders of certificates of registration.

I asked leave to make a short statement, and on its being

• Reprinted with permission from M. K. Gandhi, *Satyagraha in South Africa* (Madras: Ganesan, 1928), pp. 230-38.

granted, I said I thought there should be a distinction made between my case and those that were to follow. I had just heard from Pretoria that my compatriots there had been sentenced to three months' imprisonment with hard labor, and had been fined a heavy amount, in lieu of payment of which they would receive a further period of three months' hard labor. If these men had committed an offence, I had committed a greater offence and I therefore asked the Magistrate to impose upon me the heaviest penalty. The Magistrate, however, did not accede to my request and sentenced me to two months' simple imprisonment. I had some slight feeling of awkwardness due to the fact that I was standing as an accused in the very Court where I had often appeared as counsel. But I well remember that I considered the former role as far more honorable than the latter, and did not feel the slightest hesitation in entering the prisoner's box.

In the Court there were hundreds of Indians as well as brother members of the Bar in front of me. On the sentence being pronounced I was at once removed in custody and was then quite alone. The policeman asked me to sit on a bench kept there for prisoners, shut the door on me and went away. I was somewhat agitated and fell into deep thought. Home, the Courts where I practiced, the public meeting—all these passed away like a dream, and I was now a prisoner. What will happen in two months? Will I have to serve the full term? If the people courted imprisonment in large numbers, as they had promised, there would be no question of serving the full sentence. But if they failed to fill the prisons, two months would be as tedious as an age. These thoughts passed through my mind in less than one hundredth of the time that it has taken me to dictate them. And they filled me with shame. How vain I was! I, who had asked the people to consider the prisons as His Majesty's hotels, the suffering consequent upon disobeying the Black Act as perfect bliss, and the sacrifice of one's all and of life itself in resisting it as supreme enjoyment! Where had all this knowledge vanished today? This second train of thought acted upon me as a bracing tonic, and I began to laugh at my own folly. I began to think what kind of imprisonment would be awarded to the others and whether they would be kept with me in the prison. But I was disturbed by the police officer who opened the gate and asked me to follow him, which I did. He then made me go before him, following me himself, took me to the prisoner's closed van and asked me to take my seat in it. I was driven to Johannesburg jail.

In jail I was asked to put off my own private clothing. I knew that convicts were made naked in jails. We had all decided as Satyagrahis voluntarily to obey all jail regulations so long as they were not inconsistent with one's self-respect or with one's religious convictions. The clothes which were given to me to wear were very dirty. I did not like to put them on at all. It was not without pain that I reconciled myself to them from an idea that I must put up with some dirt. After the officers had recorded my name and address, I was taken to a large cell, and in a short time was joined by my compatriots who came laughing and told me how they received the same sentence as myself, and what took place after I had been removed. I understood from them that when my case was over, the Indians, some of whom were excited, took out a procession with black flags in their hands. The police disturbed the procession and flogged some of its members. We were all happy at the thought that we were kept in the same jail and in the same cell.

The cell door was locked at 6 o'clock. The door was not made up of bars but was quite solid, there being high up in the wall a small aperture for ventilation, so that we felt as if we had been locked up in a safe.

No wonder the jail authorities did not accord us the good treatment which they had meted out to Rama Sundara. As Rama Sundara was the first Satyagrahi prisoner, the authorities had no idea even as to how he was to be treated. Our batch was fairly large and further arrests were in contemplation. We were therefore kept in the Negro ward. In South Africa only two classes of convicts are recognized, namely Whites and Blacks, i.e. the Negroes, and the Indians were classed with Negroes.

The next morning we found that prisoners without hard labor

had the right to keep on their own private clothing, and if they would not exercise this right, they were given special jail clothing assigned to that class of prisoners. We decided that it was not right to put on our own clothing and that it was appropriate to take the jail uniform, and we informed the authorities accordingly. We were therefore given the clothes assigned to Negro convicts not punished with hard labor. But Negro prisoners sentenced to simple imprisonment are never numerous, and hence there was a shortage of simple imprisonment prisoners' clothing as soon as other Indians sentenced to simple imprisonment began to arrive. As the Indians did not wish to stand upon ceremony in this matter, they readily accepted clothing assigned to hard labor prisoners. Some of those who came in later preferred to keep on their own clothing rather than put on the uniform of the hard labor convicts. I thought this improper, but did not care to insist upon their following the correct procedure in the matter.

From the second or third day Satyagrahi prisoners began to arrive in large numbers. They had all courted arrest and were most of them hawkers. In South Africa, every hawker, Black or White, has to take out a license, always to carry it with him and show it to the police when asked to do so. Nearly every day some policeman would ask to see the licenses and arrest those who had none to show. The community had resolved to fill up the jail after our arrests. In this the hawkers took the lead. It was easy for them to be arrested. They must refuse to show their licenses and that was enough to ensure their arrest. In this way the number of Satyagrahi prisoners swelled to more than a hundred in one week. And as some few were sure to arrive every day, we received the daily budget of news without a newspaper. When Satyagrahis began to be arrested in large numbers, they were sentenced to imprisonment with hard labor, either because the magistrates lost patience, or because, as we thought, they received some such instructions from the Government. Even today, I think we were right in our conjecture, as, if we leave out the first few cases in which simple imprisonment was awarded, never afterwards throughout the long drawn out struggle was there pronounced a sentence of simple imprisonment, even ladies having been punished with hard labor. If all the magistrates had not received the same orders or instructions, and if yet by mere coincidence they sentenced all men and women at all times to hard labor, that must be held to be almost a miracle.

In Johannesburg jail prisoners not condemned to hard labor got "mealie pap" in the morning. There was no salt in it, but each prisoner was given some salt separately. At noon the prisoners were given four ounces of rice, four ounces of bread, one ounce of *ghi* and a little salt, and in the evening "mealie pap" and some vegetable, chiefly potatoes of which two were given if they were small and only one if they were big in size. None of us were satisfied with this diet. The rice was cooked soft. We asked the prison medical officer for some condiments, and told him that condiments were allowed in the jails in India. "This is not India," was the stern answer. "There is no question of taste about prison diet and condiments therefore cannot be allowed." We asked for pulse on the ground that the regulation diet was lacking in muscle-building properties. "Prisoners must not indulge in arguments on medical grounds," replied the doctor. "You do get muscle-building food, as twice a week you are served boiled beans instead of maize." The doctor's argument was sound if the human stomach was capable of extracting the various elements out of various foods taken at various times in a week or fortnight. As a matter of fact he had no intention whatever of looking to our convenience. The Superintendent permitted us to cook our food ourselves. We elected Thambi Naidoo [1] as our chef, and as such he had to fight many a battle on our behalf. If the vegetable ration issued was short in weight, he would insist on getting full weight. On vegetable days which were two in a week we cooked twice and on other days only once, as we were allowed to cook other things for ourselves only for the noonday meal. We were somewhat better off after we began to cook our own food.

But whether or not we succeeded in obtaining these conveniences, everyone of us was firm in his resolution of passing his term in jail in perfect happiness and peace. The number of Satyagrahi prisoners gradually rose to over 150. As we were all simple imprisonment convicts, we had no work to do except keeping the cells etc. clean. We asked the Superintendent for work, and he replied: "I am sorry I cannot give you work, as, if I did, I should be held to have committed an offense. But you can devote as much time as you please to keeping the place clean." We asked for some such exercise as drill, as we had observed even the Negro prisoners with hard labor being drilled in addition to their usual work. The Superintendent replied, "If your warder has time and if he gives you drill, I will not object to it; nor will I require him to do it, as he is hard worked as it is, and your arrival in unexpectedly large numbers has made his work harder still." The warder was a good man and this qualified permission was quite enough for him. He began to drill us every morning with great interest. This drill must be performed in the small yard before our cells and was therefore in the nature of a merry-go-round. When the warder finished the drill and went away, it was continued by a Pathan compatriot of ours named Nawabkhan, who made us all laugh with his quaint pronunciation of English words of command. He rendered "Stand at ease" as "sundlies." We could not for the life of us understand what Hindustani word it was, but afterwards it dawned upon us that it was not Hindustani but only Nawabkhani English.

FIRST ATTACK ON HIS LIFE
by M. K. Gandhi

Gandhi was in prison less than three weeks when he was summoned to Pretoria to confer with General Jan Christiaan

• Reprinted with permission from M. K. Gandhi, *Satyagraha in South Africa* (Madras: Ganesan, 1928), pp. 257-63, 288-89.

Smuts. A compromise was reached whereby if the Asians in South Africa would register voluntarily, Smuts promised to repeal the Black Act. Gandhi was immediately released from prison, but encountered much opposition in trying to convince his fellow Indians that this was a reasonable compromise. Gandhi, however, announced that he would be the first to register and give his fingerprints under the new agreement.

ON THE MORNING of 10th February 1908 some of us got ready to go and take out certificates of registration.[2] The supreme necessity of getting through the registration business with all possible expedition had been fully impressed on the community, and it had been agreed, that the leaders should be the first to take out certificates on the first day, with a view to break down shyness, to see if the officers concerned discharged their duties with courtesy and generally to have an eye over all the arrangements.

When I reached my office, which was also the office of the Satyagraha Association, I found Mir Alam and his companions standing outside the premises. Mir Alam was an old client of mine, and used to seek my advice in all his affairs. Many Pathans in the Transvaal employed laborers to manufacture straw or coir[3] mattresses, which they sold at a good profit, and Mir Alam did the same. He was fully six feet in height and of a large and powerful build. Today for the first time I saw Mir Alam outside my office instead of inside it, and although his eyes met mine, he for the first time refrained from saluting me. I saluted him and he saluted me in return. As usual I asked him, "How do you do?", and my impression is that he said he was all right. But he did not today wear his usual smile on the face. I noticed his angry eyes and took a mental note of the fact. I thought that something was going to happen. I entered the office. The Chairman Mr. Essop Mian and other friends arrived, and we set out for the Asiatic Office. Mir Alam and his companions followed us.

The Registration Office was at Von Brandis Square, less than a mile away from my office. On our way to it we had to pass through high roads. As we were going along Von Brandis Street, outside the premises of Messrs. Arnot and Gibson, not more than three minutes' walk from the Registration Office, Mir Alam accosted me and asked me, "Where are you going?"

"I propose to take out a certificate of registration, giving the ten finger-prints," I replied. "If you will go with me, I will first get you a certificate, with an impression only of the two thumbs, and then I will take one for myself, giving the finger-prints."

I had scarcely finished the last sentence when a heavy cudgel blow descended on my head from behind. I at once fainted with the words *He Rama* (Oh God!) on my lips, lay prostrate on the ground and had no notion of what followed. But Mir Alam and his companions gave me more blows and kicks, some of which were warded off by Essop Mian and Thambi Naidoo with the result that they too became a target for attack in their turn. The noise attracted some European passers-by to the scene. Mir Alam and his companions fled but were caught by the Europeans. The police arrived in the meanwhile and took them in custody. I was picked up and carried into Mr. J. C. Gibson's private office. When I regained consciousness, I saw Mr. Doke[4] bending over me. "How do you feel?" he asked me.

"I am all right," I replied, "but there is pain in the teeth and the ribs. Where is Mir Alam?"

"He has been arrested along with the rest."

"They should be released."

"That is all very well. But here you are in a stranger's office with your lip and cheek badly lacerated. The police are ready to take you to the hospital, but if you will go to my place, Mrs. Doke and I will minister to your comforts as best we can."

"Yes, please take me to your place. Thank the police for their offer but tell them that I prefer to go with you."

Mr. Chamney the Registrar of Asiatics too now arrived on the scene. I was taken in a carriage to this good clergyman's residence in Smit Street and a doctor was called in. Meanwhile I said to Mr. Chamney: "I wished to come to your office, give ten finger-prints and take out the first certificate of registration, but God willed it otherwise. However, I have now to request you to bring

the papers and allow me to register at once. I hope that you will
not let anyone else register before me."

"Where is the hurry about it?" asked Mr. Chamney. "The doctor will be here soon. You please rest yourself and all will be well.
I will issue certificates to others but keep your name at the head
of the list."

"Not so," I replied. "I am pledged to take out the first certificate if I am alive and if it is acceptable to God. It is therefore
that I insist upon the papers being brought here and now."

Upon this Mr. Chamney went away to bring the papers.

The second thing for me to do was to wire to the Attorney-
General that I did not hold Mir Alam and others guilty for the
assault committed upon me, that in any case I did not wish them
to be prosecuted and that I hoped they would be discharged for
my sake. But the Europeans of Johannesburg addressed a strong
letter to the Attorney-General saying that whatever views Gandhi
might hold as regards the punishment of criminals, they could not
be given effect to in South Africa. Gandhi himself might not take
any steps, but the assault was committed not in a private place
but on the high roads and was therefore a public offense. Several
Englishmen too were in a position to tender evidence and the
offenders must be prosecuted. Upon this the Attorney-General re-
arrested Mir Alam and one of his companions who were sentenced to three months' hard labor. Only I was not summoned
as a witness.

But let us return to the sick room. Dr. Thwaites came in while
Mr. Chamney was still away. He examined me and stitched up
the wounds in the cheek and on the upper lip. He prescribed
some medicine to be applied to the ribs and enjoined silence upon
me so long as the stitches were not removed. He restricted my diet
to liquids only. He said that none of the injuries was serious, that
I should be able to leave my bed and take up my ordinary activities in a week, but that I should be careful not to undertake much
physical strain for two months more. So saying he left.

Thus speech was forbidden me, but I was still master of my

hands. I addressed a short note as follows to the community through the Chairman and sent it for publication:

"I am well in the brotherly and sisterly hands of Mr. and Mrs. Doke. I hope to take up my duty shortly.

"Those who have committed the act did not know what they were doing. They thought that I was doing what was wrong. They have had their redress in the only manner they know. I therefore request that no steps be taken against them.

"Seeing that the assault was committed by a Mussalman or Mussalmans, the Hindus might probably feel hurt. If so, they would put themselves in the wrong before the world and their Maker. Rather let the blood spilt today cement the two communities indissolubly—such is my heartfelt prayer. May God grant it.

"Assault or no assault, my advice remains the same. The large majority of Asiatics ought to give finger-prints. Those who have real conscientious scruples will be exempted by the Government. To ask for more would be to show ourselves as children.

"The spirit of Satyagraha rightly understood should make the people fear none and nothing but God. No cowardly fear therefore should deter the vast majority of sober-minded Indians from doing their duty. The promise of repeal of the Act against voluntary registration having been given, it is the sacred duty of every good Indian to help the Government and the Colony to the uttermost."

Mr. Chamney returned with the papers and I gave my finger-prints but not without pain. I then saw that tears stood in Mr. Chamney's eyes. I had often to write bitterly against him, but this showed me how man's heart may be softened by events.

The reader will easily imagine that all this did not take more than a few minutes. Mr. Doke and his good wife were anxious that I should be perfectly at rest and peaceful, and were therefore pained to witness my mental activity after the assault. They were afraid that it might react in a manner prejudicial to my health. They, therefore, by making signs and similar devices, removed all persons from near my bed, and asked me not to write or do anything. I made a request in writing, that before and in order that I might lie down quietly, their daughter Olive, who was then only a little girl, should sing for me my favorite English hymn, "Lead, kindly light." Mr. Doke liked this very much and acceded to my request with a sweet smile. He called Olive by signs and asked her to stand at the door and sing the hymn in a low tone. The whole scene passes before my eyes as I dictate this, and the melodious voice of little Olive reverberates in my ears. . . .

Just suppose that Mir Alam and his friends, instead of only wounding, had actually destroyed my body. And suppose also that the community had deliberately remained calm and unperturbed, and forgiven the offenders perceiving that according to their lights they could not behave otherwise than they did. Far from injuring the community, such a noble attitude would have greatly benefited them. All misunderstanding would have disappeared, and Mir Alam and party would have had their eyes opened to the error of their ways. As for me, nothing better can happen to a Satyagrahi than meeting death all unsought in the very act of Satyagraha, i.e., pursuing Truth. All these propositions are true only of a struggle like the Satyagraha movement, where there is no room for hatred, where self-reliance is the order of the day, where no one has to look expectantly at another, where there are no leaders and hence no followers, or where all are leaders and all are followers, so that the death of a fighter, however eminent, makes not for slackness but on the other hand intensifies the struggle.

A BONFIRE OF CERTIFICATES
by M. K. Gandhi

General Smuts did not carry out his part of the compromise; he refused to take steps for the repeal of the Black Act. The dissatisfaction of the Asian community grew and the Indians

• Reprinted with permission from M. K. Gandhi, *Satyagraha in South Africa* (Madras: Ganesan, 1928), pp. 310-14.

were ready to resume the struggle and, if necessary, go to jail again. They finally sent a so-called ultimatum to General Smuts indicating that, if the decision to repeal the Act were not communicated to the Indian community by a specific date—August 16, 1908—the voluntary certificates would be collected and burned.

THE ULTIMATUM was to expire on the same day that the new Asiatic bill was to be carried through the Legislature. A meeting had been called some two hours after the expiry of the time limit to perform the public ceremony of burning the certificates. The Satyagraha Committee thought that the meeting would not be fruitless even if quite unexpectedly perhaps a favorable reply was received from the Government, as in that case the meeting could be utilized for announcing the Government's favorable decision to the community.

The Committee however believed that the Government would not reply to the ultimatum at all. We had all reached the place of meeting early, and arranged for the Government's reply by wire, if any, to be brought promptly to the meeting, which was held at four o'clock on the grounds of the Hamidia Mosque at Johannesburg (16th August 1908). Every inch of space available was taken up by Indians of all classes. The Negroes of South Africa take their meals in iron cauldrons resting on four legs. One such cauldron of the largest size available in the market had been requisitioned from an Indian trader's shop and set up on a platform in a corner of the grounds in order to burn the certificates.

As the business of the meeting was about to commence, a volunteer arrived on a cycle with a telegram from the Government in which they regretted the determination of the Indian community and announced their inability to change their line of action. The telegram was read to the audience which received it with cheers, as if they were glad that the auspicious opportunity of burning the certificates did not after all slip out of their hands as it would have if the Government had complied with the demands formulated in the ultimatum. It is difficult to pronounce any categorical opinion on the propriety or the reverse of such a feeling of gladness without a knowledge of the motives which prompted each of the audience who greeted the Government reply with applause. This much however can be said, that these cheers were a happy sign of the enthusiasm of the meeting. The Indians had now some consciousness of their strength.

The meeting began. The chairman put the meeting on their guard and explained the whole situation to them. Appropriate resolutions were adopted. I clearly detailed the various stages of the protracted negotiations and said, "If there is any Indian who has handed his certificate to be burnt but wants it to be returned to him, let him step forward and have it. Merely burning the certificates is no crime, and will not enable those who court imprisonment to win it. By burning the certificates we only declare our solemn resolution never to submit to the Black Act and divest ourselves of the power of even showing the certificates. But it is open to anyone to take a copy tomorrow of the certificate that may be burned to ashes today, and if there are any persons here who contemplate such a cowardly act or doubt their own ability to stand the ordeal, there is still time for them to have their certificates back, and these can be given back to them. No one need be ashamed of getting his certificate back just now, as in doing so he will be exhibiting a certain kind of courage. But it would be not only shameful but also detrimental to the best interests of the community to get a copy of the certificate afterwards. Again let us take note that this is going to be a protracted struggle. We know that some of us have fallen out of the marching army, and the burden of those who remain has been made heavier to that extent. I would advise you to ponder over all these considerations and only then to take the plunge proposed today." ,

Even during my speech there were voices saying, "We do not want the certificates back, burn them." Finally I suggested that if anyone wanted to oppose the resolution, he should come forward, but no one stood up. Mir Alam too was present at this meeting. He announced that he had done wrong to assault me as he did, and to the great joy of the audience, handed his original certificate to be burnt, as he had not taken a voluntary certificate. I took hold of his hand, pressed it with joy, and assured him once more that I had never harbored in my mind any resentment against him.

The Committee had already received upwards of 2,000 certificates to be burnt. These were all thrown into the cauldron, saturated with paraffin and set ablaze by Mr. Essop Mian. The whole assembly rose to their feet and made the place resound with the echoes of their continuous cheers during the burning process. Some of those who had still withheld their certificates brought them in numbers to the platform, and these too were consigned to the flames. When asked why he handed his certificate only at the last moment, one of these friends said that he did so as it was more appropriate and would create a greater impression on the onlookers. Another frankly admitted his want of courage and a feeling that the certificates might not be burnt after all. But he could not possibly withhold the certificate after he had seen the bonfire and gave it up, from an idea that the fate of all might well be his own fate too. Such frankness was a matter of frequent experience during this struggle.

The reporters of English newspapers present at the meeting were profoundly impressed with the whole scene and gave graphic descriptions of the meeting in their papers. A description of the meeting was sent to *The Daily Mail* (London) by its Johannesburg correspondent, in course of which he compared the act of the Indians in burning their certificates with that of the Boston Tea Party. I do not think this comparison did more than justice to the Indians, seeing that if the whole might of the British Empire was ranged against the hundreds of thousands of able Europeans in America, here in South Africa a helpless body of 13,000 Indians had challenged the powerful Government of the Transvaal. The Indians' only weapon was a faith in the righteousness of their own cause and in God. There is no doubt that this weapon is all-sufficient and all-powerful for the devout, but so long as that is not the view of the man in the street, 13,000 unarmed Indians might appear insignificant before the well-armed Europeans of America. As God is the strength of the weak, it is as well that the world despises them.

THE MAN HIMSELF
by Joseph J. Doke

Reverend Joseph J. Doke was a Baptist minister in Johannesburg who was a friend and co-worker of Gandhi. He was his first biographer. This biography of Gandhi, entitled An Indian Patriot in South Africa, was published in London in 1909. The following excerpts tell of Doke's first encounter with Gandhi in 1907 and of his efforts to induce Gandhi to give him material for the biography.

It was late in December, 1907, when I saw Mr. Gandhi for the first time. Rumor had been very busy with his name. The Passive Resistance movement had come into prominence. Some small stir had been made in the newspapers by the imprisonment of a Pundit, and in one way or another, Mr. Gandhi's name had been bandied from lip to lip. One evening, a friend raised the Asiatic Question at the supper-table, and as we were comparatively new to Johannesburg, although not new to the country, he told us what he thought of the Indians. His account was so strange and so completely opposed to all our previous experience, that it made us curious, and more than anything else decided me to interview the leader.

The office, at the corner of Rissik and Anderson Streets, I found to be like other offices. It was intended for work and not for show. The windows and door were adorned with the name of the occupant with the denomination of Attorney attached to it. The first room was given up to a lady-typist; the second, into which I was ushered, was the SANCTUM SANCTORUM. It was meagerly furnished

• Reprinted from Joseph J. Doke, *An Indian Patriot in South Africa* (London: London Indian Chronicle, 1909), pp. 5-10.

and dusty. A few pictures were scattered along the walls. They were chiefly photographs of no great merit. The Indian Stretcher-bearer Corps was in evidence—photographs of Mrs. Besant, Sir William Wilson Hunter, and Justice Ranade—several separate Indian portraits—and a beautiful picture of Jesus Christ. Some indifferent chairs, and shelves filled with law books completed the inventory.

All this I confess to have noted afterwards. Just then, my whole attention was centered in the man who greeted me, and in an effort to readjust my ideas to unexpected experiences. Having travelled in India, I had almost unconsciously selected some typical face and form as likely to confront me, probably a tall and stately figure, and a bold, masterful face, in harmony with the influence which he seemed to exert in Johannesburg. Perhaps a bearing haughty and aggressive. Instead of this, to my surprise, a small, lithe, spare figure stood before me, and a refined, earnest face looked into mine. The skin was dark, the eyes dark, but the smile which lighted up the face, and that direct fearless glance, simply took one's heart by storm. I judged him to be of some thirty-eight years of age, which proved correct. But the strain of his work showed its traces in the sprinkling of silver hairs on his head. He spoke English perfectly, and was evidently a man of great culture.

Asking me to be seated, he listened to an explanation of my visit, noting the points raised with a nod of the head, and a quick "Yes," until I had done. Then he went straight to the mark. Using his fingers to emphasize his thoughts, he gave the most luminous statement of the Asiatic position, in a few crisp sentences, that I have ever heard. I was anxious to know what the religious elements in the struggle were, and he gave them with convincing clearness, explaining patiently every little involved issue, and satisfying himself that I understood each before dealing with the next. Once, when he paused longer than usual, to see whether I had grasped the thought or had only assented for the sake of courtesy, I closed my note-book, thinking he had finished. "Don't close it," he said, "the chief point is yet to come."

There was a quiet assured strength about him, a greatness of heart, a transparent honesty, that attracted me at once to the Indian leader. We parted friends.

When I think of him now, one or two scenes stand out more vividly than others.

There is the trial in the "B" Criminal Court, a great mass of excited Asiatics crushed in at the door, and spreading to a great crowd outside. The cynical Magistrate, with his face flushed, presiding at the Bench; the horseshoe of legal offices below.

Then I can see again that spare, lithe form responding to the call, "Mohandas Karamchand Gandhi," and taking the prisoner's place with alacrity to receive a sentence of "two months' imprisonment" for the sake of his suffering people. Just prior to this, he had addressed these words to the hundreds of Asiatics who had gathered at the Mosque: "No matter what may be said, I will always repeat that it is a struggle for religious liberty. By religion, I do not mean formal religion, or customary religion, but that religion which underlies all religions, which brings us face to face with our Maker. If you cease to be men, if, on taking a deliberate vow, you break that vow, in order that you remain in the Transvaal without physical inconvenience, you undoubtedly forsake God. To repeat again the words of the Jew of Nazareth, those who would follow God have to leave the world, and I call upon my countrymen, in this particular instance, to leave the world and cling to God, as a child clings to its mother's breast." Notable and brave words.

Another scene recurs to my mind with equal vividness. The Pathans had attacked him, striking him down and beating him with savage brutality. When he recovered consciousness, he was lying in an office near by to which he had been carried. I saw him a moment later. He was helpless and bleeding, the doctor was cleansing his wounds, the police officers watching and listening beside him, while he was using what little strength he had to insist that no action should be taken to punish his would-be murderers. "They thought they were doing right," he said, "and I have no desire to prosecute them." They were punished, but Mr. Gandhi took no part in it.

These are scenes one can never forget; they serve to reveal the man. Our Indian friend lives on a higher plane than most men do. His actions, like the actions of Mary of Bethany, are often counted eccentric, and not infrequently misunderstood. Those who do not know him think there is some unworthy motive behind, some Oriental "slimness," to account for such profound unworldliness. But those who know him well are ashamed of themselves in his presence.

Money, I think, has no charm for him. His compatriots are angry; they say, "He will take nothing. The money we gave him when he went as our deputy to England he brought back to us again. The presents we made him in Natal, he handed over to our public funds. He is poor because he will be poor."

They wonder at him, grow angry at his strange unselfishness, and love him with the love of pride and trust. He is one of those outstanding characters, with whom to walk is a liberal education, whom to know is to love.

This morning, as usual, the sanctum was full of Indians when I entered, discussing earnestly the latest phase of the Asiatic difficulty. When, however, it became clear that Mr. Gandhi and I wished for a quiet chat, with the well-bred instinct of Orientals they silently left the room. Mr. Gandhi swung round on his office-chair and faced me, his dark eyes alert and watchful, his hair a little more silvered, I thought, than yesterday, his whole attitude alert and expectant.

"My friend," I began, "I want to ask you a strange question—how far are you prepared to make a martyr of yourself for the good of the cause?" He looked a little surprised, but said quietly, "I think you should know that by this time." "No," I said, "candidly I do not." "Well," said he, his face kindling, "it is a matter with me of complete surrender. I am nothing, I am willing to die at any time, or to do anything for the cause." "Take care," I rejoined, "perhaps I shall ask something too great." "You cannot do that," he replied, calmly. Then I saw my opportunity, and drew the toils about him. "Listen," I said. "It appears to me that what

we are doing now is merely tinkering at the Asiatic settlement—
our fight with this Government is only part of a much greater
fight, to be fought out on a larger battlefield. The question of the
status of British Indians throughout the whole Empire will have
to be solved, and in the settlement of that vast problem, you
should have much to say. The question is—how can we best prepare for that future?" He nodded in his own quick, incisive way.
I proceeded: "You know very well that, with us Europeans, character and personality are of the first importance. It is so here, and
it must be so at home. You yourself are the chief asset of the Indian cause. It is a great thing to know and trust the leader of such
a movement." He was about to speak, but I stopped him. "Let me
continue," I said. "Your position as leader makes your personality
of great importance to the cause. It has occurred to me that if I
could write a short book—bright, graphic, and reliable—making
your personality real to the people of England, it might do something to help the cause in the great struggle that is to come." The
emphatic nods became appreciably weaker, but they did not altogether cease, so I went on; "You will see, however, that my
power to do this depends altogether upon yourself. You must tell
me about your childhood and youth, allow me to picture your
personality, and depict your character, and if I know anything of
you, to submit to this will be the severest kind of martyrdom that
you can suffer." "Ah," he said, as my purpose dawned upon him,
"you have caught me completely." "But," said I, "would this help
your people?" He thought a moment, and then replied. "Yes, in
England." "Well, can you go so far?" "For the cause, I can," he
said. And then, "What do you want me to do? You don't want
me to write anything, do you?" "No," I replied, "not a word; just
let me question you about that Indian city where you were born,
that beautiful home of yours far away in the East, the very
thoughts of your heart, your struggles and sacrifices and victories.
What you cannot tell me, others will help me to discover." So,
silently, with a grip of the hand, we confirmed the bond, and this
is how this story was born.

4 SOUTH AFRICAN CLIMAX
(1913–1914)

PREPARING FOR THE MARCH
by M. K. Gandhi

By early 1913 the Indians in South Africa had three main grievances: a ban on Asian immigrants, a three-pound annual tax to be paid by each indentured laborer who remained in South Africa as a free man, and a court decision holding that only Christian marriages were legal. Indian women, especially, protested this last issue, and groups of them marched across the borders of the Transvaal and Natal to court arrest. Those entering the Transvaal were arrested, but those entering Natal were not detained and went to Newcastle, where they urged the indentured miners to strike. When the government arrested these women, the strike of the miners spread. Gandhi arrived in Newcastle and advised the miners to leave the compounds and begin a march to Charlestown, on the Natal-Transvaal border, and thence into the Transvaal in order to court arrest. While preparations for the march were being made, Gandhi was invited by the mine-owners to confer with them in Durban, but no settlement was reached.

I RETURNED TO NEWCASTLE. Laborers were still pouring in from all directions. I clearly explained the whole situation to the "army."

• Reprinted with permission from M. K. Gandhi, *Satyagraha in South Africa* (Madras: Ganesan, 1928), pp. 444-46, 452-53, 455-56.

85

I said they were still free to return to work if they wished. I told them about the threats held out by the coalowners, and pictured before them the risks of the future. I pointed out that no one could tell when the struggle would end. I described to the men the hardships of jail, and yet they would not flinch. They fearlessly replied that they would never be down-hearted so long as I was fighting by their side, and they asked me not to be anxious about them as they were inured to hardships.

It was now only left for us to march. The laborers were informed one evening that they were to commence the march early next morning (28th October 1913), and the rules to be observed on the march were read to them. It was no joke to control a multitude of five or six thousand men. I had no idea of the exact number, nor did I know their names or places of residence. I was merely content with as many of them as chose to remain. I could not afford to give them anything on the road beyond a daily ration of one pound and a half of bread and an ounce of sugar per each "soldier." If possible I would try to get something more from the Indian traders on the way. But if I failed they must rest content with bread and sugar. My experience of the Boer war and the Zulu "rebellion" [1] stood me in good stead on the present occasion. None of the "invaders" was to keep with him any more clothes than necessary. None was to touch any one's property on the way. They were to bear it patiently if any official or non-official European met them and abused or even flogged them. They were to allow themselves to be arrested if the police offered to arrest them. The march must continue even if I was arrested. All these points were explained to the men and I also announced the names of those who should successively lead the "army" in place of me.

The men understood the instructions issued to them, and our caravan safely reached Charlestown where the traders rendered us great help. They gave us the use of their houses, and permitted us to make our cooking arrangements on the grounds of the mosque. The ration supplied on the march would be exhausted when camp was reached and therefore we were in need of cooking pots, which were cheerfully supplied by the traders. We had with us a plentiful store of rice etc. to which also the traders contributed their share. . . .

I wrote to the Government, that we did not propose to enter the Transvaal with a view to domicile, but as an effective protest against the minister's breach of pledge and as a pure demonstration of our distress at the loss of our self-respect. Government would be relieving us of all anxiety if they were good enough to arrest us where we then were, that is in Charlestown. But if they did not arrest us, and if any of us surreptitiously entered the Transvaal, the responsibility would not be ours. There was no secrecy about our movement. None of us had a personal axe to grind. We would not like it if any of us secretly entered the Transvaal. But we could not hold ourselves responsible for the acts of any as we had to deal with thousands of unknown men and as we could not command any other sanction but that of love. Finally I assured the Government that if they repealed the £3 tax, the strike would be called off and the indentured laborers would return to work, as we would not ask them to join the general struggle directed against the rest of our grievances.

The position therefore was quite uncertain, and there was no knowing when the Government would arrest us. But at a crisis like this we could not await the reply of the Government for a number of days, but only for one or two returns of the post. We therefore decided to leave Charlestown and enter the Transvaal at once if the Government did not put us under arrest. If we were not arrested on the way, the "army of peace" was to march twenty to twenty-four miles a day for eight days together, with a view to reach Tolstoy Farm, and to stop there till the struggle was over and in the meanwhile to maintain themselves by working the Farm. . . .

When all the preparations for the march were completed, I made one more effort to achieve a settlement. I had already sent letters and telegrams. I now decided to 'phone even at the risk of my overtures being answered by an insult. From Charlestown I 'phoned to General Smuts in Pretoria. I called his secretary and said: "Tell General Smuts that I am fully prepared for the march.

The Europeans in Volksrust are excited and perhaps likely to violate even the safety of our lives. They have certainly held out such a threat. I am sure that even the General would not wish any such untoward event to happen. If he promises to abolish the £3 tax, I will stop the march, as I will not break the law merely for the sake of breaking it but I am driven to it by inexorable necessity. Will not the General accede to such a small request?" I received this reply within half a minute: "General Smuts will have nothing to do with you. You may do just as you please." With this the message closed.

I had fully expected this result, though I was not prepared for the curtness of the reply. I hoped for a civil answer, as my political relations with the General since the organization of Satyagraha had now subsisted for six years. But as I would not be elated by his courtesy, I did not weaken in the face of his incivility. The strait and narrow path I had to tread was clear before me. The next day (6th November 1913) at the appointed stroke of the hour (6:30) we offered prayers and commenced the march in the name of God. The pilgrim band was composed of 2,037 men, 127 women and 57 children.

THE GREAT MARCH

by M. K. Gandhi

THE CARAVAN of pilgrims thus started punctually at the appointed hour. There is a small spruit [2] one mile from Charlestown, and as soon as one crosses it, one has entered Volksrust or the Transvaal. A small patrol of mounted policemen was on duty at the border gate. I went up to them, leaving instructions with the

• Reprinted with permission from M. K. Gandhi, Satyagraha in South Africa (Madras: Ganesan, 1928), pp. 457-63, 466-71, 472-73.

"army" to cross over when I signaled to them. But while I was still talking with the police, the pilgrims made a sudden rush and crossed the border. The police surrounded them, but the surging multitude was not easy of control. The police had no intention of arresting us. I pacified the pilgrims and got them to arrange themselves in regular rows. Everything was in order in a few minutes and the march into the Transvaal began.

Two days before this the Europeans of Volksrust held a meeting where they offered all manner of threats to the Indians. Some said that they would shoot the Indians if they entered the Transvaal. Mr. Kallenbach [3] attended this meeting to reason with the Europeans who were however not prepared to listen to him. Indeed some of them even stood up to assault him. Mr. Kallenbach is an athlete, having received physical training at the hands of Sandow,[4] and it was not easy to frighten him. One European challenged him to a duel. Mr. Kallenbach replied, "As I have accepted the religion of peace, I may not accept the challenge. Let him who will come and do his worst with me. But I will continue to claim a hearing at this meeting. You have publicly invited all Europeans to attend, and I am here to inform you that not all Europeans are ready as you are to lay violent hands upon innocent men. There is one European who would like to inform you that the charges you level at the Indians are false. The Indians do not want what you imagine them to do. The Indians are not out to challenge your position as rulers. They do not wish to fight with you or to fill the country. They only seek justice pure and simple. They propose to enter the Transvaal not with a view to settle there, but only as an effective demonstration against the unjust tax which is levied upon them. They are brave men. They will not injure you in person or in property, they will not fight with you, but enter the Transvaal they will, even in the face of your gunfire. They are not the men to beat a retreat from the fear of your bullets or your spears. They propose to melt, and I know they will melt, your hearts by self-suffering. This is all I have to say. I have had my say and, I believe, thus rendered you a service. Beware and save yourselves from perpetrating a wrong." With these words Mr. Kallenbach resumed his seat. The audience was rather abashed. The pugilist who had invited Mr. Kallenbach to a single combat became his friend.

We had heard about this meeting and were prepared for any mischief by the Europeans in Volksrust. It was possible that the large number of policemen massed at the border was intended as a check upon them. However that may be, our procession passed through the place in peace. I do not remember that any European attempted even a jest. All were out to witness this novel sight, while there was even a friendly twinkle in the eyes of some of them.

On the first day we were to stop for the night at Palmford about eight miles from Volksrust, and we reached the place at about five o'clock in the evening. The pilgrims took their ration of bread and sugar, and spread themselves in the open air. Some were talking while others were singing *bhajans*. Some of the women were thoroughly exhausted by the march. They had dared to carry their children in their arms, but it was impossible for them to proceed further. I therefore, according to my previous warning, kept them as lodgers with a good Indian shopkeeper who promised to send them to Tolstoy Farm if we were permitted to go there, and to their homes if we were arrested.

As the night advanced, all noises ceased and I too was preparing to retire when I heard a tread. I saw a European coming lantern in hand. I understood what it meant, but had no preparations to make. The police officer said,

"I have a warrant of arrest for you. I want to arrest you."

"When?" I asked.

"Just now."

"Where will you take me?"

"To the adjoining railway station now, and to Volksrust when we get a train for it."

"I will go with you without informing anyone, but I will leave some instructions with one co-worker."

"You may do so."

I roused P. K. Naidoo who was sleeping near me. I informed

him about my arrest and asked him not to awake the pilgrims before morning. At daybreak they must regularly resume the march. The march would commence before sunrise, and when it was time for them to halt and get their rations, he must break to them the news of my arrest. He might inform anyone who inquired about me in the interval. If the pilgrims were arrested, they must allow themselves to be arrested. Otherwise they must continue the march according to the program. Naidoo had no fears at all. I also told him what was to be done in case he was arrested. Mr. Kallenbach too was in Volksrust at the time.

I went with the police officer, and we took the train for Volksrust the next morning. I appeared before the Court in Volksrust, but the prosecutor himself asked for a remand until the 14th as he was not still ready with the evidence. The case was postponed accordingly. I applied for bail as I had over 2,000 men, 122 women and 50 children in my charge whom I should like to take on to their destination within the period of postponement. The Public Prosecutor opposed my application. But the Magistrate was helpless in the matter, as every prisoner not charged with a capital offense is in law entitled to be allowed to give bail for his appearance, and I could not be deprived of that right. He therefore released me on bail of £50. Mr. Kallenbach had already kept a car ready for me, and he took me at once to rejoin the "invaders." The special reporter of *The Transvaal Leader* wanted to go with us. We took him in the car, and he published at the time a vivid description of the case, the journey, and the meeting with the pilgrims, who received me with enthusiasm and were transported with joy. Mr. Kallenbach at once returned to Volksrust, as he had to look after the Indians stopping at Charlestown as well as fresh arrivals there.

We continued the march, but it could not suit the Government to leave me in a state of freedom. I was therefore re-arrested at Standerton on the 8th. Standerton is comparatively a bigger place. There was something rather strange about the manner of my arrest here. I was distributing bread to the pilgrims. The Indian storekeepers at Standerton presented us with some tins of marmalade, and the distribution therefore took more time than usual. Meanwhile the Magistrate came and stood by my side. He waited till the distribution of rations was over, and then called me aside. I knew the gentleman, who, I thought, perhaps wanted to talk with me. He laughed and said,

"You are my prisoner."

"It would seem I have received promotion in rank," I said, "as magistrates take the trouble to arrest me instead of mere police officials. But you will try me just now."

"Go with me," replied the Magistrate, "the courts are still in session."

I asked the pilgrims to continue their march, and then left with the Magistrate. As soon as I reached the court room, I found that some of my co-workers had also been arrested. There were five of them there, P. K. Naidoo, Biharilal Maharaj, Ramnarayan Sinha, Raghu Narasu and Rahimkhan.

I was at once brought before the court and applied for remand and bail on the same grounds as in Volksrust. Here too the application was strongly opposed by the Public Prosecutor and here too I was released on my own recognizance of £50 and the case was remanded till the 21st. The Indian traders had kept a carriage ready for me and I rejoined the pilgrims again when they had hardly proceeded three miles further. The pilgrims thought, and I thought too, that we might now perhaps reach Tolstoy Farm. But that was not to be. It was no small thing however that the invaders got accustomed to my being arrested. The five co-workers remained in jail. . . .

Mr. Polak [5] joined us on the 9th at Teakworth between Standerton and Greylingstad. We were in the midst of our consultation and had nearly done with it. It was about 3 o'clock in the afternoon. Polak and I were walking at the head of the whole body of pilgrims. Some of the co-workers were listening to our conversation. Polak was to take the evening train for Durban. But God does not always permit man to carry out his plans. Rama had to retire to the forest on the very day that was fixed for his coronation. While we were thus engaged in talking, a Cape cart came and stopped before us and from it alighted Mr. Chamney, the Principal Immigration Officer of the Transvaal and a police officer. They took me somewhat aside and one of them said, "I arrest you."

I was thus arrested thrice in four days.

"What about the marchers?" I asked.

"We shall see to that," was the answer.

I said nothing further. I asked Polak to assume charge of and go with the pilgrims. The police officer permitted me only to inform the marchers of my arrest. As I proceeded to ask them to keep the peace etc., the officer interrupted me and said,

"You are now a prisoner and cannot make any speeches."

I understood my position, but it was needless. As soon as he stopped me speaking, the officer ordered the driver to drive the cart away at full speed. In a moment the pilgrims passed out of my sight.

The officer knew that for the time being I was master of the situation, for trusting to our non-violence, he was alone in this desolate veld [6] confronted by two thousand Indians. He also knew that I would have surrendered to him even if he had sent me a summons in writing. Such being the case, it was hardly necessary to remind me that I was a prisoner. And the advice which I would have given the pilgrims would have served the Government's purpose no less than our own. But how could an officer forego an opportunity of exercising his brief authority? I must say, however, that many officers understood us better than this gentleman. They knew that not only had arrest no terrors for us but on the other hand we hailed it as the gateway of liberty. They therefore allowed us all legitimate freedom and thankfully sought our aid in conveniently and expeditiously effecting arrests. The reader will come across apposite cases of both kinds in these pages.

I was taken to Greylingstad, and from Greylingstad via Balfour to Heidelberg where I passed the night.

The pilgrims with Polak as leader resumed their march and halted for the night at Greylingstad where they were met by Sheth Amad Mamad Kachhalia and Sheth Amad Bhayat who had come to know that arrangements were complete for arresting the whole body of marchers. Polak therefore thought that when his responsibility ceased in respect of the pilgrims upon their arrest, he could reach Durban even if a day later and take the steamer for India after all. But God had willed otherwise. At about 9 o'clock in the morning on the 10th the pilgrims reached Balfour where three special trains were drawn up at the station to take them and deport them to Natal. The pilgrims were there rather obstinate. They asked for me to be called and promised to be arrested and to board the trains if I advised them to that effect. This was a wrong attitude. And the whole game must be spoiled and the movement must receive a setback unless it was given up. Why should the pilgrims want me for going to jail? It would ill become soldiers to claim to elect their commanders or to insist upon their obeying only one of them. Mr. Chamney approached Mr. Polak and Kachhalia Sheth to help him in arresting them. These friends encountered difficulty in explaining the situation to the marchers. They told them that jail was the pilgrims' goal and they should therefore appreciate the Government's action when they were ready to arrest them. Only thus could the Satyagrahis show their quality and bring their struggle to a triumphant end. They must realize that no other procedure could have my approval. The pilgrims were brought round and all entrained peacefully.

I, on my part, was again hauled up before the Magistrate. I knew nothing of what transpired after I was separated from the pilgrims. I asked for a remand once again. I said that a remand had been granted by two courts, and that we had not now much to go to reach our destination. I therefore requested that either the Government should arrest the pilgrims or else I should be permitted to see them safe in Tolstoy Farm. The Magistrate did not comply with my request, but promised to forward it at once to the Government. This time I was arrested on a warrant from Dundee where I was to be prosecuted on the principal charge of inducing indentured laborers to leave the province of Natal. I was therefore taken to Dundee by rail the same day.

Mr. Polak was not only not arrested at Balfour but he was even thanked for the assistance he had rendered to the authorities. Mr. Chamney even said, that the Government had no intention of arresting him. But these were Mr. Chamney's own views or the views of the Government in so far as they were known to that officer. Government in fact would be changing their mind every now and then. And finally they reached the decision that Mr. Polak should not be allowed to sail for India and should be arrested along with Mr. Kallenbach who was working most energetically on behalf of the Indians. Mr. Polak therefore was arrested in Charlestown whilst waiting for the corridor train. Mr. Kallenbach was also arrested and both these friends were confined in Volksrust jail.

I was tried in Dundee on the 11th and sentenced to nine months' imprisonment with hard labor. I had still to take my second trial at Volksrust on the charge of aiding and abetting prohibited persons to enter the Transvaal. From Dundee I was therefore taken on the 13th to Volksrust where I was glad to meet Kallenbach and Polak in the jail.

I appeared before the Volksrust court on the 14th. The beauty of it was that the charge was proved against me only by witnesses furnished by myself at Kromdraai. The police could have secured witnesses but with difficulty. They had therefore sought my aid in the matter. The courts here would not convict a prisoner merely upon his pleading guilty.

This was arranged as regards me, but who would testify against Mr. Kallenbach and Mr. Polak? It was impossible to convict them in the absence of evidence, and it was also difficult at once to secure witnesses against them. Mr. Kallenbach intended to plead guilty as he wished to be with the pilgrims. But Mr. Polak was bound for India, and was not deliberately courting jail at this moment. After a joint consultation therefore we three resolved that we should say neither yes nor no in case we were asked whether Mr. Polak was guilty of the offense with which he was charged.

I provided the evidence for the crown against Mr. Kallenbach and I appeared as witness against Mr. Polak. We did not wish that the cases should be protracted, and we therefore did our best to see that each case was disposed of within a day. The proceedings against me were completed on the 14th, against Kallenbach on the 15th and against Polak on the 17th, and the Magistrate passed sentence of three months' imprisonment on all three of us. We now thought we could live together in Volksrust jail for these three months. But the Government could not afford to allow it. . . .

Government would not like that men should thus be attracted to jail, nor did they appreciate the fact that prisoners upon their release should carry my messages outside. They therefore decided to separate Kallenbach, Polak and me, send us away from Volksrust, and take me in particular to a place where no Indian could go and see me. I was sent accordingly to the jail in Bloemfontein, the capital of Orangia, where there were not more than 50 Indians, all of them serving as waiters in hotels. I was the only Indian prisoner there, the rest being Europeans and Negroes. I was not troubled at this isolation but hailed it as a blessing. There was no need now for me to keep my eyes or ears open, and I was glad that a novel experience was in store for me. Again, I never had had time for study for years together, particularly since 1893, and the prospect of uninterrupted study for a year filled me with joy.

FAREWELL SPEECH
by M. K. Gandhi

Although Gandhi was confined to prison after the Great March, several of his associates avoided arrest in order to com-

• Reprinted with permission from *Souvenir of the Passive Resistance Movement in South Africa (1906–14)* (Golden Number, *Indian Opinion*, Natal: Phoenix Farm, 1914), pp. 10-12.

municate with India and England. Increasing pressure was put on the government of South Africa to come to terms with the Indians. Suddenly, on December 18, 1913, Gandhi, Kallenbach, and Polak were released from prison, and a commission was appointed to investigate the grievances of the Indian community. After prolonged negotiations between Smuts and Gandhi, an agreement was reached on June 30, 1914. This agreement became, with the support of Smuts, the basis of the Indian Relief Act, which went into effect in July 1914. The Act made non-Christian marriages valid, abolished the three-pound tax on indentured laborers who remained in Natal, banned the importation of indentured laborers from India after 1920, and allowed Indians born in South Africa to enter the Cape Colony, although otherwise Indians could not move freely from one South African province to another.

Having achieved this partial victory, Gandhi resolved to leave South Africa forever. Accompanied by his wife and Kallenbach, he sailed for England on July 18, 1914. Before he left, he was everywhere feted by the Indian community. One of the biggest demonstrations was in Johannesburg, where he made a farewell speech which, unfortunately for posterity, is recorded only in the third person.

MR. GANDHI said that they or circumstances had placed him that evening in a most embarrassing position. Hitherto those who had known him in Johannesburg had known him in the capacity of one of many hosts at gatherings of that kind, but that evening they had placed him in the unfortunate position of being a guest, and he did not know how he would be able to discharge that duty. For the other he thought long experience had fitted him, if he might say so with due humility, most admirably; but the present position was entirely new to him and Mrs. Gandhi, and he was exceedingly diffident as to how he was going to discharge the new duty that had been imposed upon him. So much had been said about Mrs. Gandhi and himself, their so-called devotion, their so-called self-sacrifice, and many other things. There was one injunction of his religion, and he thought it was true of all religions, and that was that when one's praises were sung one should fly from those praises, and, if one could not do that, one should stop one's ears, and if one could not do either of these things, one should dedicate everything that was said in connection with one to the Almighty, the Divine Essence, which pervaded everyone and everything in the Universe, and he hoped that Mrs. Gandhi and he would have the strength to dedicate all that had been said that evening to the Divine Essence. . . .

Johannesburg was not a new place to him. . . . It was in Johannesburg that he had found his most precious friends. It was in Johannesburg that the foundation for the great struggle of Passive Resistance was laid in the September of 1906. . . . It was last, but not least, Johannesburg that had given Valiamma,[7] that young girl, whose picture rose before him even as he spoke, who had died in the cause of truth. Simple-minded in faith—she had not the knowledge that he had, she did not know what Passive Resistance was, she did not know what it was the community would gain, but she was simply taken up with unbounded enthusiasm for her people—went to jail, came out of it a wreck, and within a few days died. It was in Johannesburg again that produced a Nagappan [8] and Naryansamy, two lovely youths hardly out of their teens, who also died. But both Mrs. Gandhi and he stood living before them. He and Mrs. Gandhi had worked in the limelight; those others had worked behind the scenes, not knowing where they were going, except this, that what they were doing was right and proper, and, if any praise was due anywhere at all, it was due to those three who died. . . .

No wonder if Passive Resistance had fired and quickened the conscience of South Africa! And, therefore, whenever he had spoken, he had said that, if the Indian community had gained anything through this settlement, it was certainly due to Passive Resistance; but it was certainly not due to Passive Resistance alone. He thought that the cablegram that had been read that evening showed that they had to thank that noble Viceroy, Lord Hardinge, for his great effort. He thought, too, that they had to thank the Imperial Government, who, during the past few years, in season and out of season, had been sending dispatches to General Botha,[9] and asking him to consider their standpoint—the Imperial standpoint. They had to thank also the Union Government for the spirit of justice they had adopted that time. They had, too, to thank the noble members of both Houses of the Legislature who had made those historic speeches and brought about the settlement; and, lastly, they had to thank the Opposition also for their cooperation with the Government in bringing about the passage of the Bill, in spite of the jarring note produced by the Natal members.

When one considered all those things, the service that he and Mrs. Gandhi might have rendered could be only very little. They were but two out of many instruments that had gone to make this settlement. And what was that settlement? In his humble opinion, the value of the settlement, if they were to examine it, would consist not in the intrinsic things they had received, but in the sufferings and the sorrows long drawn out that were necessary in order to achieve those things. . . . What was there to gloat over in having an intolerable burden removed which might have been removed years ago? What was there in a lawful wife's being recognized in a place like South Africa? . . . Behind that struggle for concrete rights lay the great spirit which asked for an abstract principle, and the fight which was undertaken in 1906, although it was a fight against a particular law, was a fight undertaken in order to combat the spirit that was seen about to overshadow the whole of South Africa, and to undermine the glorious British Constitution, of which the Chairman had spoken so loftily that evening, and about which he [the speaker] shared his views.

It was his knowledge, right or wrong, of the British Constitution, which bound him to the Empire. Tear that Constitution to shreds and his loyalty also would be torn to shreds. Keep that Constitution intact, and they held him bound a slave to that Constitution. He had felt that the choice lay for himself and his fellow-countrymen between two courses, when his spirit was brooding over South Africa, either to sunder themselves from the

British Constitution, or to fight in order that the ideals of that Constitution might be preserved—but only the ideals. Lord Ampthill [10] had said, in a preface to Mr. Doke's book, that the theory of the British Constitution must be preserved at any cost if the British Empire was to be saved from the mistakes that all the previous Empires had made. Practice might bend to the temporary aberration through which local circumstances might compel them to pass, it might bend before unreasoning or unreasonable prejudice, but theory once recognized could never be departed from, and this principle must be maintained at any cost. And it was that spirit which had been acknowledged now by the Union Government, and acknowledged now nobly and loftily.

The words that General Smuts so often emphasized still rang in his ears. He had said, "Gandhi, this time we want no misunderstanding, we want no mental or other reservations, let all the cards be on the table, and I want you to tell me wherever you think that a particular passage or word does not read in accordance with your own reading," and it was so.

That was the spirit in which he approached the negotiations. When he remembered General Smuts of a few years ago, when he told Lord Crewe [11] that South Africa would not depart from its policy of racial distinction, that it was bound to retain that distinction, and that, therefore, the sting that lay in this Immigration Law would not be removed, many a friend, including Lord Ampthill, asked whether they could not for the time being suspend their activity. He had said, "No." If they did that it would undermine his loyalty, and even though he might be the only person he would still fight on. Lord Ampthill had congratulated him, and that great nobleman had never deserted the cause even when it was at its lowest ebb, and they saw the result that day. They had not by any means to congratulate themselves on a victory gained. There was no question of a victory gained, but the question of the establishment of the principle that, so far as the Union of South Africa at least was concerned, its legislation would never contain the racial taint, would never contain the color disability. The practice would certainly be different.

There was the Immigration Law—it recognized no racial distinctions, but in practice they had arranged, they had given a promise, that there should be no undue influx from India as to immigration. That was a concession to present prejudice. Whether it was right or wrong was not for him to discuss then. But it was the establishment of that principle which had made the struggle so important to the British Empire, and the establishment of that principle which had made those sufferings perfectly justifiable and perfectly honorable, and he thought that, when they considered the struggle from that standpoint, it was a perfectly dignified thing for any gathering to congratulate itself upon such a vindication of the principles of the British Constitution.

One word of caution he wished to utter regarding the settlement. The settlement was honorable to both parties. He did not think there was any room left for misunderstanding, but whilst it was final in the sense that it closed the great struggle, it was not final in the sense that it gave to Indians all that they were entitled to. There was still the Gold Law[12] which had many a sting in it. There was still the Licensing Laws throughout the Union, which also contained many a sting. There was still a matter which the Colonial-born Indians especially could not understand or appreciate, namely, the water-tight compartments in which they had to live; whilst there was absolutely free intercommunication and inter-migration between the Provinces for Europeans, Indians had to be cooped up in their respective Provinces. Then there was undue restraint on their trading activity. There was the prohibition as to holding landed property in the Transvaal, which was degrading, and all these things took Indians into all kinds of undesirable channels. These restrictions would have to be removed. But for that, he thought, sufficient patience would have to be exercised. Time was now at their disposal, and how wonderfully the tone had been changed! And here he had been told in Capetown, and he believed it implicitly, the spirit of Mr. Andrews had pervaded all those statesmen and leading men whom he saw. He came and went away after a brief

period, but he certainly fired those whom he saw with a sense
of their duty to the Empire of which they were members. . . .

To his countrymen he would say that they should wait and
nurse the settlement, which he considered was all that they could
possibly and reasonably have expected, and that they would now
live to see, with the cooperation of their European friends, that
what was promised was fulfilled, that the administration of the
existing laws was just, and that vested rights were respected in
the administration; that after they had nursed these things, if
they cultivated European public opinion, making it possible for
the Government of the day to grant a restoration of the other
rights of which they had been deprived, he did not think that
there need be any fear about the future. He thought that, with
mutual cooperation, with mutual goodwill, with due response on
the part of either party, the Indian community need never
be a source of weakness to that Government or to any Government. On the contrary, he had full faith in his countrymen
that, if they were well treated, they would always rise to the
occasion and help the Government of the day. If they had insisted on their rights on many an occasion, he hoped that the
European friends who were there would remember that they had
also discharged the responsibilities which had faced them.

And now it was time for him to close his remarks and say a
few words of farewell only. He did not know how he could express those words. The best years of his life had been passed in
South Africa. India, as his distinguished countryman, Mr. Gokhale, had reminded him, had become a strange land to him. South
Africa he knew, but not India. He did not know what impelled
him to go to India, but he did know that the parting from them
all, the parting from the European friends who had helped him
through thick and thin, was a heavy blow, and one he was least
able to bear; yet he knew he had to part with them. He could
only say farewell and ask them to give him their blessing, to
pray for them that their heads might not be turned by the praise
they had received, that they might still know how to do their

duty to the best of their ability, that they might still learn that first, second, and last should be the approbation of their own conscience, and that then whatever might be due to them would follow in its own time.

5 "INDIAN HOME RULE" (1909)

• ## "INDIAN HOME RULE" (1909)
by M. K. Gandhi

The first important work written by Gandhi was a pamphlet entitled Hind Swaraj, or Indian Home Rule, composed in 1909, which has been frequently reprinted. Its genesis and evolution are best described in "A Word of Explanation" written by Gandhi himself in 1921: [1]

"It is certainly my good fortune that this booklet of mine is receiving wide attention. The original is in Gujarati. It has a checkered career. It was first published in the columns of the Indian Opinion of South Africa. It was written in 1908 [2] during my return voyage from London to South Africa in answer to the Indian school of violence and its prototype in South Africa. I came in contact with every known Indian anarchist in London. Their bravery impressed me, but I felt that their zeal was misguided. I felt that violence was no remedy for India's ills, and that her civilization required the use of a different and higher weapon for self-protection. The Satyagraha of South Africa was still an infant hardly two years old. But it had developed sufficiently to permit me to write of it with some degree of confidence. What I

• Reprinted with permission from M. K. Gandhi, Hind Swaraj, or Indian Home Rule (Ahmedabad: Navajivan, 1946), pp. 24-27, 43-46, 56-63, 71-76.

wrote was so much appreciated that it was published as a booklet. It attracted some attention in India. The Bombay Government prohibited its circulation. I replied by publishing its translation. I thought that it was due to my English friends that they should know its contents. In my opinion it is a book which can be put into the hands of a child. It teaches the gospel of love in place of that of hate. It replaces violence with self-sacrifice. It pits soul force against brute force. It has gone through several editions and I commend it to those who would care to read it. I withdraw nothing except one word of it, and that in deference to a lady friend. The booklet is a severe condemnation of 'modern civilization.' It was written in 1908. My conviction is deeper today than ever. I feel that if India will discard 'modern civilization' she can only gain by doing so."

Of the twenty chapters in this pamphlet, only portions of four can be given here.

CIVILIZATION (Chapter VI)

READER: . . . Now will you tell me something of what you have read and thought of this civilization?

EDITOR: Let us first consider what state of things is described by the word "civilization." Its true test lies in the fact that people living in it make bodily welfare the object of life. We will take some examples. The people of Europe today live in better-built houses than they did a hundred years ago. This is considered an emblem of civilization, and this is also a matter to promote bodily happiness. Formerly, they wore skins, and used spears as their weapons. Now, they wear long trousers, and, for embellishing their bodies, they wear a variety of clothing, and, instead of spears, they carry with them revolvers containing five or more chambers. If people of a certain country, who have hitherto not been in the habit of wearing much clothing, boots, etc., adopt European clothing, they are supposed to have become civilized out of savagery. Formerly, in Europe, people ploughed their lands mainly by manual labor. Now, one man can plough a vast tract by means of steam engines and can thus amass great wealth. This is called a sign of civilization. Formerly, only a few men wrote valuable books. Now, anybody writes and prints anything he likes and poisons people's minds. Formerly, men traveled in wagons. Now, they fly through the air in trains at the rate of four hundred and more miles per day. This is considered the height of civilization. It has been stated that, as men progress, they shall be able to travel in airships and reach any part of the world in a few hours. Men will not need the use of their hands and feet. They will press a button, and they will have their clothing by their side. They will press another button, and they will have their newspaper. A third, and a motor-car will be in waiting for them. They will have a variety of delicately dished up food. Everything will be done by machinery. Formerly, when people wanted to fight with one another, they measured between them their bodily strength; now it is possible to take away thousands of lives by one man working behind a gun from a hill. This is civilization. Formerly, men worked in the open air only as much as they liked. Now thousands of workmen meet together and for the sake of maintenance work in factories or mines. Their condition is worse than that of beasts. They are obliged to work, at the risk of their lives, at most dangerous occupations, for the sake of millionaires. Formerly, men were made slaves under physical compulsion. Now they are enslaved by temptation of money and of the luxuries that money can buy. There are now diseases of which people never dreamt before, and an army of doctors is engaged in finding out their cures, and so hospitals have increased. This is a test of civilization. Formerly, special messengers were required and much expense was incurred in order to send letters; today, anyone can abuse his fellow by means of a letter for one penny. True, at the same cost, one can send one's thanks also. Formerly, people had two or three meals consisting of home-made bread and vegetables; now, they require something to eat every two hours so that they have hardly leisure for anything else. What more need I say? All this you can ascertain from several authoritative books. These are all true tests of civilization. And if anyone speaks to the contrary, know that he is ignorant. This civilization takes note neither of morality nor of religion. Its votaries calmly state that their business is not to teach religion. Some even consider it to be a superstitious growth. Others put on the cloak of religion, and prate about morality. Even a child can understand that in all I have described above there can be no inducement to morality. Civilization seeks to increase bodily comforts, and it fails miserably even in doing so.

This civilization is irreligion, and it has taken such a hold on the people in Europe that those who are in it appear to be half mad. They lack real physical strength or courage. They keep up their energy by intoxication. They can hardly be happy in solitude. Women, who should be the queens of households, wander in the streets or they slave away in factories. For the sake of a pittance, half a million women in England alone are laboring under trying circumstances in factories or similar institutions. This awful fact is one of the causes of the daily growing suffragette movement.

This civilization is such that one has only to be patient and it will be self-destroyed. According to the teaching of Mahomed this would be considered a Satanic Civilization. Hinduism calls it the Black Age. I cannot give you an adequate conception of it. It is eating into the vitals of the English nation. It must be shunned. Parliaments are really emblems of slavery. If you will sufficiently think over this, you will entertain the same opinion and cease to blame the English. They rather deserve our sympathy. They are a shrewd nation and I therefore believe that they will cast off the evil. They are enterprising and industrious, and their mode of thought is not inherently immoral. Neither are they bad at heart. I therefore respect them. Civilization is not an incurable disease, but it should never be forgotten that the English people are at present afflicted by it.

WHAT IS TRUE CIVILIZATION? (Chapter XIII)

READER: You have denounced railways, lawyers and doctors. I can see that you will discard all machinery. What, then, is civilization?
EDITOR: The answer to that question is not difficult. I believe that

the civilization India has evolved is not to be beaten in the world. Nothing can equal the seeds sown by our ancestors. Rome went, Greece shared the same fate; the might of the Pharaohs was broken; Japan has become westernized; of China nothing can be said; but India is still, somehow or other, sound at the foundation. The people of Europe learn their lessons from the writings of the men of Greece or Rome, which exist no longer in their former glory. In trying to learn from them, the Europeans imagine that they will avoid the mistakes of Greece and Rome. Such is their pitiable condition. In the midst of all this India remains immovable and that is her glory. It is a charge against India that her people are so uncivilized, ignorant and stolid, that it is not possible to induce them to adopt any changes. It is a charge really against our merit. What we have tested and found true on the anvil of experience, we dare not change. Many thrust their advice upon India, and she remains steady. This is her beauty: it is the sheet-anchor of our hope.

Civilization is that mode of conduct which points out to man the path of duty. Performance of duty and observance of morality are convertible terms. To observe morality is to attain mastery over our mind and our passions. So doing, we know ourselves. The Gujarati equivalent for civilization means "good conduct."

If this definition be correct, then India, as so many writers have shown, has nothing to learn from anybody else, and this is as it should be. We notice that the mind is a restless bird; the more it gets the more it wants, and still remains unsatisfied. The more we indulge our passions the more unbridled they become. Our ancestors, therefore, set a limit to our indulgences. They saw that happiness was largely a mental condition. A man is not necessarily happy because he is rich, or unhappy because he is poor. The rich are often seen to be unhappy, the poor to be happy. Millions will always remain poor. Observing all this, our ancestors dissuaded us from luxuries and pleasures. We have managed with the same kind of plough as existed thousands of years ago. We have retained the same kind of cottages that we had in former times and our indigenous education remains the same as before. We have had no system of life-corroding competition. Each followed his own occupation or trade and charged a regulation wage. It was not that we did not know how to invent machinery, but our fore-fathers knew that, if we set our hearts after such things, we would become slaves and lose our moral fibre. They, therefore, after due deliberation decided that we should only do what we could with our hands and feet. They saw that our real happiness and health consisted in a proper use of our hands and feet. They further reasoned that large cities were a snare and a useless en-cumbrance and that people would not be happy in them, that there would be gangs of thieves and robbers, prostitution and vice flourishing in them and that poor men would be robbed by rich men. They were, therefore, satisfied with small villages. They saw that kings and their swords were inferior to the sword of ethics, and they, therefore, held the sovereigns of the earth to be inferior to the Rishis [3] and the Fakirs.[4] A nation with a constitution like this is fitter to teach others than to learn from others. This nation had courts, lawyers and doctors, but they were all within bounds. Everybody knew that these professions were not particularly superior; moreover, these vakils and vaids [5] did not rob people; they were considered people's dependents, not their masters. Justice was tolerably fair. The ordinary rule was to avoid courts. There were no touts to lure people into them. This evil, too, was notice-able only in and around capitals. The common people lived independently and followed their agricultural occupation. They enjoyed true Home Rule. . . .

Now you see what I consider to be real civilization. Those who want to change conditions such as I have described are enemies of the country and are sinners.

READER: It would be all right if India were exactly as you have described it, but it is also India where there are hundreds of child widows, where two year old babies are married, where twelve year old girls are mothers and house wives, where women practice polyandry, where the practice of Niyoga [6] obtains, where, in the name of religion, girls dedicate themselves to prostitution, and in the name of religion, sheep and goats are killed. Do you consider these also symbols of the civilization that you have described? EDITOR: You make a mistake. The defects that you have shown are defects. Nobody mistakes them for ancient civilization. They remain in spite of it. Attempts have always been made and will be made to remove them. We may utilize the new spirit that is born in us for purging ourselves of these evils. But what I have described to you as emblems of modern civilization are accepted as such by its votaries. The Indian civilization, as described by me, has been so described by its votaries. In no part of the world, and under no civilization, have all men attained perfection. The tendency of the Indian civilization is to elevate the moral being, that of the Western civilization is to propagate immorality. The latter is godless, the former is based on a belief in God. So understanding and so believing, it behooves every lover of India to cling to the old Indian civilization even as a child clings to the mother's breast.

PASSIVE RESISTANCE (Chapter XVII)

READER: Is there any historical evidence as to the success of what you have called soul-force or truth-force? No instance seems to have happened of any nation having risen through soul-force. I still think that the evil-doers will not cease doing evil without physical punishment.

EDITOR: The poet Tulsidas has said: "Of religion, pity, or love, is the root, as egotism of the body. Therefore, we should not abandon pity so long as we are alive." This appears to me to be a scientific truth. I believe in it as much as I believe in two and two being four. The force of love is the same as the force of the soul or truth. We have evidence of its working at every step. The universe would disappear without the existence of that force. But you ask for historical evidence. It is, therefore, necessary to know what history means. The Gujarati equivalent means; "It so happened." If that is the meaning of history, it is possible to give copious evidence. But, if it means the doings of kings and emperors, there can be no evidence of soul-force or passive resistance in such history. You cannot expect silver ore in a tin mine. History, as we know it, is a record of the wars of the world, and so there is a proverb among Englishmen that a nation which has no history, that is, no wars, is a happy nation. How kings played, how they became enemies of one another, how they murdered one another, is found accurately recorded in history, and if this were all that had happened in the world, it would have been ended long ago. If the story of the universe had commenced with wars, not a man would have been found alive today. Those people who have been warred against have disappeared as, for instance, the natives of Australia of whom hardly a man was left alive by the intruders. Mark, please, that these natives did not use soul-force in self-defense, and it does not require much foresight to know that the Australians will share the same fate as their victims. "Those that take the sword shall perish by the sword." With us the proverb is that professional swimmers will find a watery grave.

The fact that there are so many men still alive in the world shows that it is based not on the force of arms but on the force of truth or love. Therefore, the greatest and most unimpeachable evidence of the success of this force is to be found in the fact that, in spite of the wars of the world, it still lives on.

Thousands, indeed tens of thousands, depend for their existence on a very active working of this force. Little quarrels of millions of families in their daily lives disappear before the exercise of this force. Hundreds of nations live in peace. History does not and cannot take note of this fact. History is really a record of every interruption of the even working of the force of love or of the soul. Two brothers quarrel; one of them repents and re-awakens the love that was lying dormant in him; the two again begin to live in peace; nobody takes note of this. But if the two brothers, through the intervention of solicitors or some other reason, take up arms or go to law—which is another form of the exhibition of brute force—their doings would be immediately noticed in the press, they would be the talk of their neighbors and would probably go down to history. And what is true of families and communities is true of nations. There is no reason to believe that there is one law for families and another for nations. History, then, is a record of an interruption of the course of nature. Soul-force, being natural, is not noted in history.

READER: According to what you say, it is plain that instances of this kind of passive resistance are not to be found in history. It is necessary to understand this passive resistance more fully. It will be better, therefore, if you enlarge upon it.

EDITOR: Passive resistance is a method of securing rights by personal suffering; it is the reverse of resistance by arms. When I refuse to do a thing that is repugnant to my conscience, I use soul-force. For instance, the Government of the day has passed a law which is applicable to me. I do not like it. If by using violence I force the Government to repeal the law, I am employing what may be termed body-force. If I do not obey the law and accept the penalty for its breach, I use soul-force. It involves sacrifice of self.

Everybody admits that sacrifice of self is infinitely superior to sacrifice of others. Moreover, if this kind of force is used in a cause that is unjust, only the person using it suffers. He does not make others suffer for his mistakes. Men have before now done many things which were subsequently found to have been wrong. No man can claim that he is absolutely in the right or that a particular thing is wrong because he thinks so, but it is wrong for him so long as that is his deliberate judgment. It is therefore meet that he should not do that which he knows to be wrong, and suffer the consequence whatever it may be. This is the key to the use of soul-force.

READER: You would then disregard laws—this is rank disloyalty. We have always been considered a law-abiding nation. You seem to be going even beyond the extremists. They say that we must obey the laws that have been passed, but that if the laws be bad, we must drive out the law-givers even by force.

EDITOR: Whether I go beyond them or whether I do not is a matter of no consequence to either of us. We simply want to find out what is right and to act accordingly. The real meaning of the statement that we are a law-abiding nation is that we are passive resisters. When we do not like certain laws, we do not break the heads of law-givers but we suffer and do not submit to the laws. That we should obey laws whether good or bad is a new-fangled notion. There was no such thing in former days. The people disregarded those laws they did not like and suffered the penalties for their breach. It is contrary to our manhood if we obey laws repugnant to our conscience. Such teaching is opposed to religion and means slavery. If the Government were to ask us to go about without any clothing, should we do so? If I were a passive resister, I would say to them that I would have nothing to do with their law. But we have so forgotten ourselves and become so compliant that we do not mind any degrading law.

A man who has realized his manhood, who fears only God, will fear no one else. Man-made laws are not necessarily binding on him. Even the Government does not expect any such thing from us. They do not say: "You must do such and such a thing," but they say: "If you do not do it, we will punish you." We are sunk so low that we fancy that it is our duty and our religion to do what the law lays down. If man will only realize that it is unmanly to obey laws that are unjust, no man's tyranny will enslave him. This is the key to self-rule or home-rule.

It is a superstition and ungodly thing to believe that an act of a majority binds a minority. Many examples can be given in which acts of majorities will be found to have been wrong and those of minorities to have been right. All reforms owe their origin to the initiation of minorities in opposition to majorities. If among a band of robbers a knowledge of robbing is obligatory, is a pious man to accept the obligation? So long as the superstition that men should obey unjust laws exists, so long will their slavery exist. And a passive resister alone can remove such a superstition.

To use brute-force, to use gunpowder, is contrary to passive resistance, for it means that we want our opponent to do by force that which we desire but he does not. And if such a use of force is justifiable, surely he is entitled to do likewise by us. And so we should never come to an agreement. We may simply fancy, like the blind horse moving in a circle round a mill, that we are making progress. Those who believe that they are not bound to obey laws which are repugnant to their conscience have only the remedy of passive resistance open to them. Any other must lead to disaster.

READER: From what you say I deduce that passive resistance is a splendid weapon of the weak, but that when they are strong they may take up arms.

EDITOR: This is a gross ignorance. Passive resistance, that is, soul-force, is matchless. It is superior to the force of arms. How, then, can it be considered only a weapon of the weak? Physical-force men are strangers to the courage that is requisite in a passive resister. Do you believe that a coward can ever disobey a law that he dislikes? Extremists are considered to be advocates of brute force. Why do they, then, talk about obeying laws? I do not blame them. They can say nothing else. When they succeed in driving out the English and they themselves become governors, they will want you and me to obey their laws. And that is a fitting thing for their constitution. But a passive resister will say he will not obey a law that is against his conscience, even though he may be blown to pieces at the mouth of a cannon.

What do you think? Wherein is courage required—in blowing others to pieces from behind a cannon, or with a smiling face to approach a cannon and be blown to pieces? Who is the true warrior—he who keeps death always as a bosom-friend, or he who controls the death of others? Believe me that a man devoid of courage and manhood can never be a passive resister.

This, however, I will admit: that even a man weak in body is capable of offering this resistance. One man can offer it just as well as millions. Both men and women can indulge in it. It does not require the training of an army; it needs no jiu-jitsu. Control over the mind is alone necessary, and when that is attained, man is free like the king of the forest and his very glance withers the enemy.

Passive resistance is an all-sided sword, it can be used anyhow; it blesses him who uses it and him against whom it is used. Without drawing a drop of blood it produces far-reaching results.

It never rusts and cannot be stolen. Competition between passive resisters does not exhaust. The sword of passive resistance does not require a scabbard. It is strange indeed that you should consider such a weapon to be a weapon merely of the weak. . . .

READER: From what you say, then, it would appear that it is not a small thing to become a passive resister, and, if that is so, I should like you to explain how a man may become one.

EDITOR: To become a passive resister is easy enough but it is also equally difficult. I have known a lad of fourteen years become a passive resister; I have known also sick people do likewise; and I have also known physically strong and otherwise happy people unable to take up passive resistance. After a great deal of experience it seems to me that those who want to become passive resisters for the service of the country have to observe perfect chastity, adopt poverty, follow truth, and cultivate fearlessness.

Chastity is one of the greatest disciplines without which the mind cannot attain requisite firmness. A man who is unchaste loses stamina, becomes emasculated and cowardly. He whose mind is given over to animal passions is not capable of any great effort. . . .

Just as there is necessity for chastity, so is there for poverty. Pecuniary ambition and passive resistance cannot go well together. Those who have money are not expected to throw it away, but they are expected to be indifferent about it. They must be prepared to lose every penny rather than give up passive resistance.

Passive resistance has been described in the course of our discussion as truth-force. Truth, therefore, has necessarily to be followed and that at any cost. In this connection, academic questions such as whether a man may not lie in order to save a life, etc., arise, but these questions occur only to those who wish to justify lying. Those who want to follow truth every time are not placed in such a quandary; and if they are, they are still saved from a false position.

Passive resistance cannot proceed a step without fearlessness. Those alone can follow the path of passive resistance who are free from fear, whether as to their possessions, false honor, their relatives, the government, bodily injuries or death.

These observances are not to be abandoned in the belief that they are difficult. Nature has implanted in the human breast ability to cope with any difficulty or suffering that may come to man unprovoked. These qualities are worth having, even for those who do not wish to serve the country. Let there be no mistake, as those who want to train themselves in the use of arms are also obliged to have these qualities more or less. Everybody does not become a warrior for the wish. A would-be warrior will have to observe chastity and to be satisfied with poverty as his lot. A warrior without fearlessness cannot be conceived of. It may be thought that he would not need to be exactly truthful, but that quality follows real fearlessness. When a man abandons truth, he does so owing to fear in some shape or form. The above four attributes, then, need not frighten anyone. It may be as well here to note that a physical-force man has to have many other useless qualities which a passive resister never needs. And you will find that whatever extra effort a swordsman needs is due to lack of fearlessness. If he is an embodiment of the latter, the sword will drop from his hand that very moment. He does not need its support. One who is free from hatred requires no sword. A man with a stick suddenly came face to face with a lion and instinctively raised his weapon in self-defense. The man saw that he had only prated about fearlessness when there was none in him. That moment he dropped the stick and found himself free from all fear.

CONCLUSION (Chapter XX)

READER: From your views I gather that you would form a third party. You are neither an extremist nor a moderate.

EDITOR: That is a mistake. I do not think of a third party at all. We do not all think alike. We cannot say that all the moderates hold identical views. And how can those who want only to serve have a party? I would serve both the moderates and the extremists.

Where I differ from them, I would respectfully place my position before them and continue my service.

READER: What, then, would you say to both the parties?

EDITOR: I would say to the extremists: "I know that you want Home Rule for India; it is not to be had for your asking. Everyone will have to take it for himself. What others get for me is not Home Rule but foreign rule; therefore, it would not be proper for you to say that you have obtained Home Rule if you have merely expelled the English. I have already described the true nature of Home Rule. This you would never obtain by force of arms. Brute-force is not natural to Indian soil. You will have, therefore, to rely wholly on soul-force. You must not consider that violence is necessary at any stage for reaching our goal."

I would say to the moderates: "Mere petitioning is derogatory; we thereby confess inferiority. To say that British rule is indispensable, is almost a denial of the Godhead. We cannot say that anybody or anything is indispensable except God. Moreover, common sense should tell us that to state that, for the time being, the presence of the English in India is a necessity, is to make them conceited.

"If the English vacated India, bag and baggage, it must not be supposed that she would be widowed. It is possible that those who are forced to observe peace under their pressure would fight after their withdrawal. There can be no advantage in suppressing an eruption; it must have its vent. If, therefore, before we can remain at peace, we must fight amongst ourselves, it is better that we do so. There is no occasion for a third party to protect the weak. It is this so-called protection which has unnerved us. Such protection can only make the weak weaker. Unless we realize this, we cannot have Home Rule. I would paraphrase the thought of an English divine and say that anarchy under Home Rule were better than orderly foreign rule. Only, the meaning that the learned divine attached to Home Rule is different from Indian Home Rule according to my conception. We have to learn, and to teach others, that we do not want the tyranny of either English rule or Indian rule."

If this idea were carried out, both the extremists and the moderates could join hands. There is no occasion to fear or distrust one another.

READER: What then, would you say to the English?

EDITOR: To them I would respectfully say: "I admit you are my rulers. It is not necessary to debate the question whether you hold India by the sword or by my consent. I have no objection to your remaining in my country, but although you are the rulers, you will have to remain as servants of the people. It is not we who have to do as you wish, but it is you who have to do as we wish. You may keep the riches that you have drained away from this land, but you may not drain riches henceforth. Your function will be, if you so wish, to police India; you must abandon the idea of deriving any commercial benefit from us. We hold the civilization that you support to be the reverse of civilization. We consider our civilization to be far superior to yours. If you realize this truth, it will be to your advantage and, if you do not, according to your own proverb, you should only live in our country in the same manner as we do. You must not do anything that is contrary to our religions. It is your duty as rulers that for the sake of the Hindus you should eschew beef, and for the sake of Mahomedans you should avoid bacon and ham. We have hitherto said nothing because we have been cowed down, but you need not consider that you have not hurt our feelings by your conduct. We are not expressing our sentiments either through base selfishness or fear, but because it is our duty now to speak out boldly. We consider your schools and law courts to be useless. We want our own ancient schools and courts to be restored. The common language of India is not English but Hindi. You should, therefore, learn it. We can hold communication with you only in our national language.

"We cannot tolerate the idea of your spending money on railways and the military. We see no occasion for either. You may fear Russia; we do not. When she comes we shall look after her. If you are with us, we may then receive her jointly. We do not need any European cloth. We shall manage with articles produced and manufactured at home. You may not keep one eye on Manchester and the other on India. We can work together only if our interests are identical.

"This has not been said to you in arrogance. You have great military resources. Your naval power is matchless. If we wanted to fight with you on your own ground, we should be unable to do so, but if the above submissions be not acceptable to you, we cease to play the part of the ruled. You may, if you like, cut us to pieces. You may shatter us at the cannon's mouth. If you act contrary to our will, we shall not help you; and without our help, we know that you cannot move one step forward.

"It is likely that you will laugh at all this in the intoxication of your power. We may not be able to disillusion you at once; but if there be any manliness in us, you will see shortly that your intoxication is suicidal and that your laugh at our expense is an aberration of intellect. We believe that at heart you belong to a religious nation. We are living in a land which is the source of religions. How we came together need not be considered, but we can make mutual good use of our relations.

"You, English, who have come to India are not good specimens of the English nation, nor can we, almost half-Anglicized Indians, be considered good specimens of the real Indian nation. If the English nation were to know all you have done, it would oppose many of your actions. The mass of the Indians have had few dealings with you. If you will abandon your so-called civilization and search into your own scriptures, you will find that our demands are just. Only on condition of our demands being fully satisfied may you remain in India; and if you remain under those conditions, we shall learn several things from you and you will learn many from us. So doing we shall benefit each other and the world. But that will happen only when the root of our relationship is sunk in a religious soil."

READER: What will you say to . . . those of us who are affected by European civilization, and who are eager to have Home Rule[?]
EDITOR: To these I would say, "It is only those Indians who are imbued with real love who will be able to speak to the English

in the above strain without being frightened, and only those can be said to be so imbued who conscientiously believe that Indian civilization is the best and that the European is a nine days' wonder. Such ephemeral civilizations have often come and gone and will continue to do so. Those only can be considered to be so imbued who, having experienced the force of the soul within themselves, will not cower before brute-force, and will not, on any account, desire to use brute-force. Those only can be considered to have been so imbued who are intensely dissatisfied with the present pitiable condition, having already drunk the cup of poison.

"If there be only one such Indian, he will speak as above to the English and the English will have to listen to him.

"These are not demands, but they show our mental state. We shall get nothing by asking; we shall have to take what we want, and we need the requisite strength for the effort. . . ."

READER: This is a large order. When will all carry it out?

EDITOR: You make a mistake. You and I have nothing to do with the others. Let each do his duty. If I do my duty, that is, serve myself, I shall be able to serve others. Before I leave you, I will take the liberty of repeating:

1. Real home-rule is self-rule or self-control.

2. The way to it is passive resistance; that is soul-force or love-force.

3. In order to exert this force, Swadeshi [7] in every sense is necessary.

4. What we want to do should be done, not because we object to the English or because we want to retaliate but because it is our duty to do so. Thus, supposing that the English remove the salt-tax, restore our money, give the highest posts to Indians, withdraw the English troops, we shall certainly not use their machine-made goods, nor use the English language, nor many of their industries. It is worth noting that these things are, in their nature, harmful; hence we do not want them. I bear no enmity towards the English but I do towards their civilization.

In my opinion, we have used the term "Swaraj" [8] without understanding its real significance. I have endeavored to explain it as I understand it, and my conscience testifies that my life henceforth is dedicated to its attainment.

PART TWO 1915–1931

6

A NEW START IN INDIA
(1915–1918)

ADMITTING AN UNTOUCHABLE

by M. K. Gandhi

Gandhi arrived in England, from South Africa, just at the beginning of the first World War. He organized an Indian Ambulance Corps in England, but was obliged to leave the British Isles and sail for India because of pleurisy. By May 1915 he was settled enough in India to establish his first religious community— the Satyagraha Ashram—at Kochrab, near Ahmedabad, in his native district of Gujarat.

THE ASHRAM had been in existence only a few months when we were put to a test such as I had scarcely expected. I received a letter from Amritlal Thakkar to this effect: "A humble and honest untouchable family is desirous of joining your Ashram. Will you accept them?"

I was perturbed. I had never expected that an untouchable family with an introduction from no less a man than Thakkar Bapa would so soon be seeking admission to the Ashram. I shared the letter with my companions. They welcomed it.

I wrote to Amritlal Thakkar expressing our willingness to ac-

• Reprinted with permission from *Gandhi's Autobiography* (Washington: Public Affairs Press, 1948), Part V, Chapter X, pp. 485-87.

cept the family, provided all the members were ready to abide
by the rules of the Ashram.

The family consisted of Dudabhai, his wife Danibehn and
their daughter Lakshmi,[1] then a mere toddling babe. Dudabhai
had been a teacher in Bombay. They all agreed to abide by the
rules and were accepted.

But their admission created a flutter amongst the friends who
had been helping the Ashram. The very first difficulty was found
with regard to the use of the well, which was partly controlled
by the owner of the bungalow. The man in charge of the water-
lift objected that drops of water from our bucket would pollute
him. So he took to swearing at us and molesting Dudabhai. I
told everyone to put up with the abuse and continue drawing
water at any cost. When he saw that we did not return his abuse,
the man became ashamed and ceased to bother us.

All monetary help, however, was stopped. The friend who had
asked that question about an untouchable being able to follow
the rules of the Ashram had never expected that any such would
be forthcoming.

With the stopping of monetary help came rumors of proposed
social boycott. We were prepared for all this. I had told my companions that, if we were boycotted and denied the usual facilities,
we would not leave Ahmedabad. We would rather go and stay
in the untouchables' quarter and live on whatever we could get
by manual labor.

Matters came to such a pass that Maganlal Gandhi one day
gave me this notice: "We are out of funds and there is nothing
for the next month."

I quietly replied: "Then we shall go to the untouchables'
quarter."

This was not the first time I had been faced with such a trial.
On all such occasions God has sent help at the last moment.
One morning, shortly after Maganlal had given me warning of
our monetary plight, one of the children came and said that a
Sheth [2] who was waiting in a car outside wanted to see me. I

went out to him. "I want to give the Ashram some help. Will you accept it?" he asked.

"Most certainly," said I. "And I confess I am at the present moment at the end of my resources."

"I shall come tomorrow at this time," he said. "Will you be here?"

"Yes," said I, and he left.

Next day, exactly at the appointed hour, the car drew up near our quarters, and the horn was blown. The children came with the news. The Sheth did not come in. I went out to see him. He placed in my hands currency notes of the value of Rs. 13,000 and drove away.

I had never expected this help, and what a novel way of rendering it! The gentleman had never before visited the Ashram. So far as I can remember, I had met him only once. No visit, no enquiries, simply rendering help and going away! This was a unique experience for me. The help deferred the exodus to the untouchables' quarter. We now felt quite safe for a year.

Just as there was a storm outside, so was there a storm in the Ashram itself. Though in South Africa untouchable friends used to come to my place and live and feed with me, my wife and other women did not seem quite to relish the admission into the Ashram of the untouchable friends. My eyes and ears easily detected their indifference, if not their dislike, towards Danibehn. The monetary difficulty had caused me no anxiety; but this internal storm was more than I could bear. Danibehn was an ordinary woman. Dudabhai was a man with slight education but of good understanding. I liked his patience. Sometimes he did flare up, but on the whole I was well impressed with his forbearance. I pleaded with him to swallow minor insults. He not only agreed, but prevailed upon his wife to do likewise.

The admission of this family proved a valuable lesson to the Ashram. In the very beginning we proclaimed to the world that the Ashram would not countenance untouchability. Those who wanted to help the Ashram were thus put on their guard, and the work of the Ashram in this direction was considerably simplified. The fact that it is mostly the real orthodox Hindus who have met the daily growing expenses of the Ashram is perhaps a clear indication that untouchability is shaken to its foundation. There are indeed many other proofs of this, but the fact that good Hindus do not scruple to help an Ashram where we go the length of dining with the untouchables is no small proof.

BENARES UNIVERSITY SPEECH
by M. K. Gandhi

During World War I, although most Indians remained loyal to the government, the demand for home rule was growing and seditious activity was suppressed by the authorities. Indian nationalists were divided between moderate reformists and extremists who advocated direct action. Professor G. K. Gokhale, Gandhi's political mentor, advised him to spend his first year with "his ears open but his mouth shut." Gandhi traveled a great deal and kept his ears open, but did not always heed Gokhale's advice. He was moving toward the conviction that the British had no right to rule India, but that many evils in Indian society would have to be corrected before India would be fit to govern herself. Some of these ideas found expression in a speech delivered on February 4, 1916 at the dedication of the Hindu Central University College at Benares, a great ceremony attended by the Viceroy, Lord Hardinge, and other notables. Mrs. Annie Besant, the famous Englishwoman who became a religious and political leader in India (and who had founded the college in 1892), presided at the meeting. Gandhi's frankness in criticizing both British and Indian shortcomings led to such an uproar in the audience that he was unable to finish his speech.

· Reprinted with permission from M. K. Gandhi, *To the Students* (Ahmedabad: Navajivan, 1949), pp. 14-22.

FRIENDS. I WISH to tender my humble apology for the long delay that took place before I am able to reach this place. And you will readily accept the apology when I tell you that I am not responsible for the delay, nor is any human agency responsible for it. [Laughter] The fact is that I am like an animal on show and my keepers in their over-kindness always manage to neglect a necessary chapter in this life and that is pure accident. In this case, they did not provide for the series of accidents that happened to us—to me, my keepers, and my carriers. Hence, this delay.

Friends, under the influence of the matchless eloquence of the lady [Mrs. Besant] who has just sat down, pray, do not believe that our University has become a finished product and that all the young men who are to come to the University that has yet to rise and come into existence, have also come and returned from it finished citizens of a great Empire. Do not go away with any such impression, and, if you, the student world, to which my remarks are supposed to be addressed this evening, consider for one moment that the spiritual life, for which this country is noted and for which this country has no rival, can be transmitted through the lip, pray, believe me, you are wrong. You will never be able merely through the lip to give the message that India, I hope, will one day deliver to the world. I myself have been "fed up" with speeches and lectures. I except the lectures that have been delivered here during the last two days from this category, because they were necessary. But I do venture to suggest to you that we have now reached almost the end of our resources in speech-making, and it is not enough that our ears are feasted, that our eyes are feasted, but it is necessary that our hearts have got to be touched and that our hands and feet have got to be moved. We have been told during the last two days how necessary it is, if we are to retain our hold upon the simplicity of Indian character, that our hands and feet should move in unison with our hearts. But this is only by way of preface.

I wanted to say it is a matter of deep humiliation and shame for us that I am compelled this evening, under the shadow of this great college in this sacred city, to address my countrymen in a language that is foreign to me. I know that if I was appointed an examiner to examine all those who have been attending during these two days this series of lectures, most of those who might be examined upon these lectures would fail. And why? Because they have not been touched. I was present at the sessions of the great Congress [3] in the month of December. There was a much vaster audience, and will you believe me when I tell you that the only speeches that touched that huge audience in Bombay were the speeches that were delivered in Hindustani? In Bombay, mind you, not in Benares where everybody speaks Hindi. But between the vernaculars of the Bombay Presidency on the one hand, and Hindi on the other, no such great dividing line exists as there does between English and the sister languages of India; and the Congress audience was better able to follow the speakers in Hindi. I am hoping that this University will see to it that the youths who come to it will receive their instruction through the medium of their vernaculars. Our language is the reflection of ourselves, and if you tell me that our languages are too poor to express the best thought, then I say that the sooner we are wiped out of existence the better for us. Is there a man who dreams that English can ever become the national language of India? [Cries of "Never"] Why this handicap on the nation? Just consider for one moment what an unequal race our lads have to run with every English lad. I had the privilege of a close conversation with some Poona professors. They assured me that every Indian youth, because he reached his knowledge through the English language, lost at least six precious years of life. Multiply that by the number of students turned out by our schools and colleges and find out for yourselves how many thousand years have been lost to the nation. The charge against us is that we have no initiative. How can we have any if we are to devote the precious years of our life to the mastery of a foreign tongue? We fail in this attempt also. Was it possible for any speaker yesterday and today to impress his audience as was possible for Mr. Higginbotham? It was not the fault of the previous speakers that they could not engage the audience. They had more than substance enough for us in their addresses. But their addresses could not go home to us. I have heard it said that after all it is English-educated India which is leading and which is doing all the things for the nation. It would be monstrous if it were otherwise. The only education we receive is English education. Surely, we must show something for it. But suppose that we had been receiving, during the past fifty years, education through our vernaculars, what should we have today? We should have today a free India, we should have our educated men, not as if they were foreigners in their own land but speaking to the heart of the nation; they would be working among the poorest of the poor, and whatever they would have gained during the past fifty years would be a heritage for the nation. [Applause] Today even our wives are not the sharers in our best thought. Look at Professor Bose and Professor Ray [4] and their brilliant researches. Is it not a shame that their researches are not the common property of the masses? Let us now turn to another subject.

The Congress has passed a resolution about self-government, and I have no doubt that the All-India Congress Committee and the Moslem League will do their duty and come forward with some tangible suggestions. But I, for one, must frankly confess that I am not so much interested in what they will be able to produce, as I am interested in anything that the student world is going to produce or the masses are going to produce. No paper contribution will ever give us self-government. No amount of speeches will ever make us fit for self-government. It is only our conduct that will fit us for it. [Applause] And, how are we trying to govern ourselves? I want to think audibly this evening. I do not want to make a speech, and if you find me this evening speaking without reserve, pray, consider that you are only sharing the thoughts of a man who allows himself to think audibly, and if you think that I seem to transgress the limits that courtesy imposes upon me, pardon me for the liberty I may be taking. I visited the Viswanath Temple last evening and as I was walking through those lanes, these were the thoughts that touched me. If a stranger dropped from above on to this great Temple and he had to consider what we as Hindus were, would he not be justified in condemning us? Is not this great Temple a reflection of our own character? I speak feelingly as a Hindu. Is it right that the lanes of our sacred Temple should be as dirty as they are? The houses round about are built anyhow. The lanes are tortuous and narrow. If even our temples are not models of roominess and cleanliness, what can our self-government be? Shall our temples be abodes of holiness, cleanliness and peace as soon as the English have retired from India, either of their own pleasure or by compulsion, bag and baggage?

I entirely agree with the President of the Congress that before we think of self-government, we shall have to do the necessary plodding. In every city there are two divisions, the cantonment and the city proper. The city mostly is a stinking den. But we are a people unused to city life. But if we want city life, we cannot reproduce the easy-going hamlet life. It is not comforting to think that people walk about the streets of Indian Bombay under the perpetual fear of dwellers in the storied buildings spitting upon them. I do a great deal of railway travelling. I observe the difficulty of third class passengers. But the Railway Administration is by no means to blame for all their hard lot. We do not know the elementary laws of cleanliness. We spit anywhere on the carriage floor, irrespective of the thought that it is often used as sleeping space. We do not trouble ourselves as to how we use it; the result is indescribable filth in the compartment. The so-called better class passengers over-awe their less fortunate brethren. Among them I have seen the student world also. Sometimes they behave no better. They can speak English and they have worn Norfolk jackets and, therefore, claim the right to force their way in and command seating accommodation. I have turned the searchlight all over, and as you have given me the privilege of speaking to you, I am laying my heart bare. Surely, we must set these things right in our progress towards self-government.

I now introduce you to another scene. His Highness the Maharajah, who presided yesterday over our deliberations, spoke about the poverty of India. Other speakers laid great stress upon it. But what did we witness in the great *pandal* [5] in which the foundation ceremony was performed by the Viceroy? Certainly a most gorgeous show, an exhibition of jewellery which made a splendid feast for the eyes of the greatest jeweller who chose to come from Paris. I compare with the richly bedecked noblemen the millions of the poor. And I feel like saying to those noblemen: "There is no salvation for India unless you strip yourselves of this jewellery and hold it in trust for your countrymen in India." [Hear, hear and applause] I am sure it is not the desire of the King-Emperor or Lord Hardinge that, in order to show the truest loyalty to our King-Emperor, it is necessary for us to ransack our jewellery-boxes and to appear bedecked from top to toe. I would undertake, at the peril of my life, to bring to you a message from King George himself that he expects nothing of the kind. Sir, whenever I hear of a great palace rising in any great city of India, be it in British India or be it in India which is ruled by our great chiefs, I become jealous at once and I say: "Oh, it is the money that has come from the agriculturists." Over 75 per cent of the population are agriculturists, and Mr. Higginbotham told us last night in his own felicitous language that they are the men who grow two blades of grass in the place of one. But there cannot be much spirit of self-government about us if we take away or allow others to take away from them almost the whole of the results of their labor. Our salvation can only come through the farmer. Neither the lawyers, nor the doctors, nor the rich landlords are going to secure it.

Now, last but not the least, it is my bounden duty to refer to what agitated our minds during these two or three days. All of us have had many anxious moments while the Viceroy was going through the streets of Benares. There were detectives stationed in many places. We were horrified. We asked ourselves: "Why this distrust. Is it not better that even Lord Hardinge should die than live a living death?" But a representative of a mighty Sovereign may not. He might find it necessary even to live a living death. But why was it necessary to impose these detectives on us? We may foam, we may fret, we may resent, but let us not forget that India of today in her impatience has produced an army of anarchists. I myself am an anarchist, but of another type. But there is a class of anarchists amongst us, and if I was able to reach this class, I would say to them that their anarchism has no room in India, if India is to conquer the conqueror. It is a sign of fear. If we trust and fear God, we shall have to fear no one, not Maharajahs, not Viceroys, not the detectives, not even King George. I honor the anarchist for his love of the country. I honor him for his bravery in being willing to die for his country; but I ask him: "Is killing honorable? Is the dagger of an assassin a fit precursor of an honorable death?" I deny it. There is no warrant for such methods in any scriptures. If I found it necessary for the salvation of India that the English should retire, that they should be driven out, I would not hesitate to declare that they would have to go, and I hope, I would be prepared to die in defense of that belief. That would, in my opinion, be an honorable death. The bomb-thrower creates secret plots, is afraid to come out into the open, and when caught pays the penalty of misdirected zeal. I have been told: "Had we not done this, had some people not thrown bombs, we should never have gained what we have got with reference to the Partition Movement." [Mrs. Besant: "Please stop it"] This was what I said in Bengal when Mr. Lyon presided at the meeting. I think what I am saying is necessary. If I am told to stop I shall obey. [Turning to the Chairman] I await your orders. If you consider that by my speaking as I am, I am not serving the country and the Empire, I shall certainly stop. [Cries of "Go on"] [The chairman: "Please explain your object"] I am explaining my object. I am simply—[another interruption]. My friends, please do not resent this interruption. If Mrs. Besant this evening suggests that I should stop, she does so because she loves India so well, and she considers that I am erring in thinking audibly before you, young men. But even so, I simply say this, that I want to purge

India of the atmosphere of suspicion on either side; if we are to reach our goal, we should have an empire which is to be based upon mutual love and mutual trust. Is it not better that we talk under the shadow of this college than that we should be talking irresponsibly in our homes? I consider that it is much better that we talk these things openly. I have done so with excellent results before now. I know that there is nothing that the students are not discussing. There is nothing that the students do not know. I am, therefore, turning the searchlight towards ourselves. I hold the name of my country so dear to me that I exchange these thoughts with you, and submit to you that there is no reason for anarchism in India. Let us frankly and openly say whatever we want to say to our rulers and face the consequences, if what we have to say does not please them. But let us not abuse. I was talking the other day to a member of the much-abused Civil Service. I have not very much in common with the members of that Service; but I could not help admiring the manner in which he was speaking to me. He said: "Mr. Gandhi, do you for one moment suppose that all we, Civil Servants, are a bad lot, that we want to oppress the people whom we have come to govern?" "No," I said. "Then, if you get an opportunity put in a word for the much-abused Civil Service." And I am here to put in that word. Yes, many members of the Indian Civil Service are most decidedly over-bearing; they are tyrannical, at times thoughtless. Many other adjectives may be used. I grant all these things and I grant also that, after having lived in India for a certain number of years, some of them become somewhat degraded. But what does that signify? They were gentlemen before they came here, and if they have lost some of the moral fibre, it is a reflection upon ourselves. [Cries of "No"] Just think out for yourselves, if a man who was good yesterday has become bad after having come in contact with me, is he responsible that he has deteriorated or am I? The atmosphere of sycophancy and falsity that surrounds them on their coming to India demoralizes them, as it would many of us. It is well to take the blame sometimes. If we are to receive self-government we shall have to take it. We shall never be granted self-government. Look at the history of the British Empire and the British nation; freedom-loving as it is, it will not be a party to give freedom to a people who will not take it themselves. Learn your lessons, if you wish to, from the Boer War. Those who were enemies of that empire only a few years ago, have now become friends. [At this point there was an interruption and there was a movement on the platform to leave; the speech, therefore, ended here abruptly.]

THE SATYAGRAHA ASHRAM
by M. K. Gandhi

An ashram is a religious community or retreat. In India, many spiritual leaders have established their own ashrams as a living embodiment of their spiritual ideas. In South Africa Gandhi organized two communities which were, in effect, ashrams: Phoenix Farm in 1904 near Durban and Tolstoy Farm in 1910 near Johannesburg. Returning to India in 1914, Gandhi transferred many of his entourage to Shantiniketan, Rabindranath Tagore's ashram near Calcutta.

In May 1915 Gandhi established his own Satyagraha Ashram with twenty-five inmates in a rented bungalow at Kochrab, a small village near Ahmedabad, in his native Gujarati-speaking section of India. Because of an outbreak of plague, this ashram in 1917 was removed to Sabarmati, across the river of that name from Ahmedabad. This ashram was under his direction until 1933, when it was disbanded and given for a center for the removal of untouchability. Gandhi then established his headquarters at

• Reprinted with permission from C. F. Andrews, *Mahatma Gandhi's Ideas* (London: Allen and Unwin, 1929), pp. 101-11.

Wardha, a small town in the Central Provinces. In 1936 he visited Segaon, a village near Wardha and decided to settle there. This was renamed Sevagram in 1940 and eventually became an ashram.

Early in the establishment of the Satyagraha Ashram Gandhi devised certain rules and regulations for inhabitants of this retreat.

No WORK done by any man, however great, will really prosper unless it has a distinct religious backing. But what is Religion? I for one would answer: "Not the Religion you will get after reading all the scriptures of the world. Religion is not really what is grasped by the brain, but a heart grasp."

Religion is a thing not alien to us. It has to be evolved out of us. It is always within us: with some, consciously so; with others, quite unconsciously. But it is always there. And whether we wake up this religious instinct in us through outside assistance or by inward growth, no matter how it is done, it has got to be done, if we want to do anything in the right manner, or to achieve anything that is going to persist.

Our scriptures have laid down certain rules as maxims of human life. They tell us that without living according to these maxims we are incapable of having a reasonable perception of Religion. Believing in these implicitly, I have deemed it necessary to seek the association of those who think with me in founding this Institution [the Satyagraha Ashram]. The following are the rules that have been drawn up and have to be observed by everyone who seeks to be a member.

The first and foremost is

THE VOW OF TRUTH

Not simply as we ordinarily understand it, not truth which merely answers the saying, "Honesty is the best policy," implying that if it is not the best policy we may depart from it. Here Truth as it is conceived means that we may have to rule our life by this law of Truth at any cost; and in order to satisfy the definition I have drawn upon the celebrated illustration of the life of Prahlad.[6] For the sake of Truth he dared to oppose his own father; and he defended himself, not by paying his father back in his own coin. Rather, in defense of Truth as he knew it, he was prepared to die without caring to return the blows that he had received from his father, or from those who were charged with his father's instructions. Not only that, he would not in any way even parry the blows; on the contrary, with a smile on his lips, he underwent the innumerable tortures to which he was subjected, with the result that at last Truth rose triumphant. Not that he suffered the tortures because he knew that some day or other in his very lifetime he would be able to demonstrate the infallibility of the Law of Truth. That fact was there; but if he had died in the midst of tortures he would still have adhered to Truth. That is the Truth which I would like to follow. In our Ashram we make it a rule that we must say "No" when we mean No, regardless of consequences.

Then we come to

THE DOCTRINE OF AHIMSA

Literally speaking, Ahimsa means "non-killing." But to me it has a world of meaning, and takes me into realms much higher, infinitely higher. It really means that you may not offend anybody; you may not harbor an uncharitable thought, even in connection with one who may consider himself to be your enemy. To one who follows this doctrine there is no room for an enemy. But there may be people who consider themselves to be his enemies. So it is held that we may not harbor an evil thought even in connection with such persons. If we return blow for blow we depart from the doctrine of Ahimsa. But I go farther. If we resent a friend's action, or the so-called enemy's action, we still fall short of this doctrine. But when I say we should not resent, I do not say that we should acquiesce: by the word "resenting" I mean wishing that some harm should be done to the enemy; or that he should be put out of the way, not even by any action of ours, but by the action of somebody else, or, say, by divine agency. If we harbor even this thought we depart from this doctrine of Non-Violence. Those who join the Ashram have literally to accept that meaning.

This does not mean that we practice that doctrine in its entirety. Far from it. It is an ideal which we have to reach, and it is an ideal to be reached even at this very moment, if we are capable of doing so. But it is not a proposition in Geometry; it is not even like solving difficult problems in higher mathematics—it is infinitely more difficult. Many of us have burnt the midnight oil in solving those problems. But if you want to follow out this doctrine you will have to do much more than burn the midnight oil. You will have to pass many a sleepless night, and go through many a mental torture, before you can even be within measurable distance of this goal. It is the goal, and nothing less than that, which you and I have to reach, if we want to understand what a religious life means.

A man who believes in the efficacy of this doctrine finds in the ultimate stage, when he is about to reach the goal, the whole world at his feet. If you express your love—Ahimsa—in such a manner that it impresses itself indelibly upon your so-called enemy, he must return that love. Under this rule there is no room for organized assassinations, or for murders openly committed, or for any violence for the sake of your country, and even for guarding the honor of precious ones that may be under your charge. After all, that would be a poor defense of their honor. This doctrine tells us that we may guard the honor of those under our charge by delivering our own lives into the hands of the man who would commit the sacrilege. And that requires far greater courage than delivering of blows. If you do not retaliate, but stand your ground between your charge and the opponent, simply receiving the blows without retaliating, what happens? I give you my promise that the whole of his violence will be expended on you, and your friend will be left unscathed. Under this plan of life there is no conception of patriotism which justifies such wars as you witness today in Europe.

Then again there is

THE VOW OF CELIBACY

Those who want to perform national service, or to have a gleam of the real religious life, must lead a celibate life, whether married or unmarried. Marriage only brings a woman closer to man, and they become friends in a special sense, never to be parted either in this life or in the lives to come. But I do not think that, in our conception of marriage, our lusts should enter. Be that as it may, that is what is placed before those who come to the Ashram. I do not deal with it at any length.

Then we have, further,

THE VOW OF THE CONTROL OF THE PALATE

A man who wants to control his animal passions easily does so if he controls his palate. I fear this is one of the most difficult vows to follow. Unless we are prepared to rid ourselves of stimulating, heating, and exciting condiments we shall certainly not be able to control the over-abundant, unnecessary, and exciting stimulation of the animal passions. If we do not do that we are likely to abuse the sacred trust of our bodies that has been given us, and to become less than animals and brutes, eating, drinking, and indulging in passions which we share with animals. But have you ever seen a horse or cow indulging in the abuse of the palate as we do? Do you suppose that it is a sign of civilization, a sign of real life, that we should multiply our eatables so far that we do not even know where we are; and seek dishes until at last we have become absolutely mad and run after the newspaper sheets which give us advertisements about these dishes?

Then we have once more

THE VOW OF NON-THIEVING

I suggest that we are thieves in a way. If I take anything that I do not need for my own immediate use and keep it, I thieve it from somebody else. It is the fundamental law of Nature, without exception, that Nature produces enough for our wants from day to day; and if only everybody took enough for himself and nothing more there would be no pauperism in this world, there would be no man dying of starvation. I am no Socialist, and I do not want to dispossess those who have got possessions; but I do say that personally those of us who want to see light out of darkness have to follow this rule. I do not want to dispossess anybody; I should then be departing from the rule of Non-Violence. If somebody else possesses more than I do, let him. But so far as my own life has to be regulated I dare not possess anything which I do not want. In India we have got many millions of people who have to be satisfied with one meal a day, and that meal consisting of a *chapatti*[7] containing no fat in it and a pinch of salt. You and I have no right to anything that we really have until these many millions are clothed and fed. You and I, who ought to know better, must adjust our wants, and even undergo voluntary privation, in order that they may be nursed, fed, and clothed.

Then there is the "Vow of Non-Possession," which follows as a matter of course, and needs no further explanation at this point, where only a brief summary of various difficulties and their answer is being given.

Then I go to

THE VOW OF SWADESHI

The vow of Swadeshi is a necessary vow. We are departing from one of the sacred laws of our being when we leave our neighborhood and go somewhere else to satisfy our wants. If a man comes from Bombay and offers you wares, you are not justified in supporting the Bombay merchant so long as you have got a merchant at your very door, born and bred in Madras.

That is my view on Swadeshi. In your village you are bound to support your village barber to the exclusion of the finished barber who may come to you from Madras. If you find it necessary that your village barber should reach the attainments of the barber from Madras you may train him to that. Send him to Madras by all means, if you wish, in order that he may learn his calling. Until you do that you are not justified in going to another barber. That is Swadeshi. So when we find that there are many things that we cannot get in India we must try to do without them. We may have to do without many things; but, believe me, when you have that frame of mind you will find a great burden taken off your shoulders, even as the Pilgrim did in that inimitable book _Pilgrim's Progress_. There came a time when the mighty burden that the Pilgrim was carrying unconsciously dropped from him, and he felt a freer man than he was when he started on the journey. So will you feel freer men than you are now, if immediately you adopt this Swadeshi life.

We have also

THE VOW OF FEARLESSNESS

I found, through my wanderings in India, that my country is seized with a paralyzing fear. We may not open our lips in public; we may only talk about our opinions secretly. We may do anything we like within the four walls of our house; but those things are not for public consumption.

If we had taken a vow of silence I would have nothing to say. I suggest to you that there is only One whom we have to fear; that is God. When we fear God, then we shall fear no man, however high-placed he may be; and if you want to follow the vow of Truth, then fearlessness is absolutely necessary. Before we can aspire to guide the destinies of India we shall have to adopt this habit of fearlessness.

And then we have also

THE VOW REGARDING THE "UNTOUCHABLES"

There is an ineffaceable blot that Hinduism today carries with it. I have declined to believe that it has been handed down to us from immemorial times. I think that this miserable, wretched, enslaving spirit of "untouchableness" must have come to us when we were at our lowest ebb. This evil has stuck to us and still remains with us. It is, to my mind, a curse that has come to us;

and as long as that curse remains with us, so long I think we are bound to consider that every affliction in this sacred land is a proper punishment for the indelible crime that we are committing. That any person should be considered untouchable because of his calling passes my comprehension; and you, the student world, who receive all this modern education, if you become a party to this crime, it were better that you received no education whatsoever.

EDUCATION THROUGH THE VERNACULARS

In Europe every cultured man learns, not only his own language, but also other languages. In order to solve the problem of language in India, we in this Ashram must make it a point to learn as many Indian vernaculars as possible. The trouble of learning these languages is nothing compared to that of mastering English. How dare we rub off from our memory all the years of our infancy? But that is precisely what we do when we commence our higher life through the medium of a foreign tongue. This creates a breach for which we shall have to pay dearly. And you will see now the connection between this education and untouchability—this persistence of the latter in spite of the spread of knowledge and education. Education has enabled us to see the horrible crime, but we are seized with fear, and therefore we cannot take this doctrine to our homes.

THE VOW OF KHADDAR [8]

You may ask, "Why should we use our hands?" You may say, "Manual work has got to be done by those who are illiterate. I can only occupy myself with reading literature and political essays." We have to realize the dignity of labor. If a barber or shoemaker attends a college he ought not to abandon his profession. I consider that such professions are just as good as the profession of medicine.

Last of all, when you have conformed to these rules you may come to

THE RELIGIOUS USE OF POLITICS

Politics, divorced from religion, has absolutely no meaning. If the student world crowd the political platforms of this country, that is not necessarily a healthy sign of national growth; but this does not mean that you, in your student life, ought not to study politics. Politics are a part of our being; we ought to understand our national institutions. We may do this from our infancy. So in our Ashram every child is taught to understand the political institutions of our country and to know how the country is vibrating with new emotions, with new aspirations, with new life. But we want also the steady light, the infallible light of religious faith; not a faith which merely appeals to the intelligence, but a faith which is indelibly inscribed on the heart. First we want to realize our religious consciousness, and immediately we have done that the whole department of life is open to us; and it should then be a sacred privilege of all, so that when young men grow to manhood they may do so properly equipped to battle with life. Today what happens is this: much of the political life is confined to the students, but immediately they cease to be students they sink into oblivion, seeking miserable employments, knowing nothing about God, nothing of fresh air or bright light, or of real vigorous independence, such as comes out of obedience to those laws that I have placed before you on this occasion.

FACE TO FACE WITH *AHIMSA*
by M. K. Gandhi

While Gandhi was attending the annual meetings of the Indian National Congress at Lucknow in December 1916, he was approached by a peasant. He later recalled the incident as follows: ". . . a peasant came up to me looking like any other peasant in India, poor and emaciated, and said, 'I am Rajkumar Shulka. I am from Champaran, and I want you to come to my district." This was in Bihar, in the Himalayan foothills, near Nepal. Gandhi had other immediate plans, but Shulka followed him around India so persistently that finally Gandhi yielded and in 1917 took a train for Bihar.

There Gandhi found that the Indian peasants, who were in effect sharecroppers, were very poor and complained of unjust treatment by the English landlords. They had to plant 15 per cent of their land in indigo, which was turned over to the landlords as rent. With aniline dyes lessening the value of natural indigo, some of the peasants were released from this obligation, but only on condition of paying a lump sum in cash. Gandhi's arrival aroused new hopes in the peasants and they flocked to tell him their story.

[ONE] DAY we heard that about five miles from Motihari a tenant had been ill-treated. It was decided that, in company with Babu Dharanidhar Prasad, I should go and see him the next morning, and we accordingly set off for the place on elephant's back. An elephant, by the way, is about as common in Champaran as a bullock-cart in Gujarat. We had scarcely gone half way when

· Reprinted with permission from *Gandhi's Autobiography* (Washington: Public Affairs Press, 1948), pp. 502-503, 505-507.

a messenger from the Police Superintendent overtook us and said that the latter had sent his compliments. I saw what he meant. Having left Dharanidharbabu to proceed to the original destination, I got into the hired carriage which the messenger had brought. He then served on me a notice to leave Champaran, and drove me to my place. On his asking me to acknowledge the service of the notice, I wrote to the effect that I did not propose to comply with it and leave Champaran till my inquiry was finished. Thereupon I received a summons to take my trial the next day for disobeying the order to leave Champaran.

I kept awake that whole night writing letters and giving necessary instructions to Babu [9] Brajkishore Prasad.

The news of the notice and the summons spread like wildfire, and I was told that Motihari that day witnessed unprecedented scenes. Gorakhbabu's house and the court house overflowed with men. Fortunately I had finished all my work during the night and so was able to cope with the crowds. My companions proved the greatest help. They occupied themselves with regulating the crowds, for the latter followed me wherever I went.

A sort of friendliness sprang up between the officials—Collector, Magistrate, Police Superintendent—and myself. I might have legally resisted the notices served on me. Instead I accepted them all, and my conduct towards the officials was correct. They thus saw that I did not want to offend them personally, but that I wanted to offer civil resistance to their orders. In this way they were put at ease, and instead of harassing me they gladly availed themselves of my and my co-worker's cooperation in regulating the crowds. But it was an ocular demonstration to them of the fact that their authority was shaken. The people had for the moment lost all fear of punishment and yielded obedience to the power of love which their new friend exercised. . . .

The trial began. The Government pleader, the Magistrate and other officials were on tenterhooks. They were at a loss to know what to do. The Government pleader was pressing the Magistrate to postpone the case. But I interfered and requested the Magistrate not to postpone the case, as I wanted to plead guilty to having disobeyed the order to leave Champaran, and read a brief statement as follows:

"With the permission of the Court I would like to make a brief statement showing why I have taken the very serious step of seemingly disobeying the order passed under Sec. 144 of Cr. P. C. In my humble opinion it is a question of difference of opinion between the Local Administration and myself. I have entered the country with motives of rendering humanitarian and national service. I have done so in response to a pressing invitation to come and help the ryots,[10] who urge they are not being fairly treated by the indigo planters. I could not render any help without studying the problem. I have, therefore, come to study it with the assistance, if possible, of the Administration and the planters. I have no other motive, and cannot believe that my coming can in any way disturb public peace and cause loss of life. I claim to have considerable experience in such matters. The Administration, however, have thought differently. I fully appreciate their difficulty, and I admit too that they can only proceed upon information they received. As a law-abiding citizen my first instinct would be, as it was, to obey the order served upon me. But I could not do so without doing violence to my sense of duty to those for whom I have come. I feel that I could just now serve them only by remaining in their midst. I could not, therefore, voluntarily retire. Amid this conflict of duties I could only throw the responsibility for removing me from them on the Administration. I am fully conscious of the fact that a person holding, in the public life of India, a position such as I do, has to be most careful in setting an example. It is my firm belief that in the complex constitution under which we are living, the only safe and honorable course for a self-respecting man is, in the circumstances such as face me, to do what I have decided to do, that is, to submit without protest to the penalty of disobedience.

"I venture to make this statement not in any way in extenuation of the penalty to be awarded against me, but to show that I have disregarded the order served upon me not for want of respect for lawful authority, but in obedience to the higher law of our being, the voice of conscience."

There was now no occasion to postpone the hearing, but as both Magistrate and the Government pleader had been taken by surprise, the Magistrate postponed judgment. Meanwhile I had wired full details to the Viceroy, to Patna friends, as also to Pandit Madan Mohan Malaviya and others.

Before I could appear before the Court to receive the sentence, the Magistrate sent a written message that the Lieutenant Governor had ordered the case against me to be withdrawn, and the Collector wrote to me saying that I was at liberty to conduct the proposed inquiry, and that I might count on whatever help I needed from the officials. None of us was prepared for this prompt and happy issue. . . .

The country thus had its first direct object-lesson in Civil Disobedience.

GANDHI IN BIHAR

by Rajendra Prasad

After continuing to hear many witnesses about the injustices in Champaran, Gandhi asked the Governor either to redress the peasant grievances or appoint an official commission of inquiry. The Governor appointed a commission, with Gandhi as a member representing the peasants. In the end, the Commission recommended that the planters should repay part of the money they had previously exacted from the peasants and that the compulsory growing of indigo should be abolished. Thus Gandhi won his first major struggle on Indian soil. Later he commented: "What

• Reprinted with permission from Rajendra Prasad, *Mahatma Gandhi and Bihar* (Bombay: Hind Kitabs, 1949), pp. 24-29.

I did was a very ordinary thing. I declared that the British could not order me around in my own country."

Gandhi also worked among the peasants and gathered a number of helpers around him. Among these was Rajendra Prasad, a Bihar lawyer, who was to become his lifelong associate and later President of the Indian National Congress and first President of the Republic of India. At Bihar also Gandhi was joined by Mahadev Desai, who was to be his personal secretary for more than two decades.

[THE] PURELY SOCIAL WORK [which Gandhi did in Champaran] was remarkable though it did not attract much attention at the time. Bihar was a province in which orthodoxy reigned supreme among the Hindus. We also have our mode of living which, we found, was not helpful in the kind of work we were engaged in. As soon as Mahatmaji [Gandhi] discovered that a large number of workers would be required to assist him who would have to make a prolonged stay with him, he made up his mind that we should have a separate house and establishment where we could stay and work instead of billeting ourselves on friends as we did on our arrival at Motihari. He said a house must be found and, if necessary, taken on rent, and he fixed the day on which we should shift. A house was found and everything was ready for removal, but according to our habits of procrastination, and busy as we had been the whole day, we felt it would be better if we shifted the next day. But Mahatmaji had fixed the day for removal and that day had passed and it was about 9 o'clock at night. He felt that if we did not move that night the first decision of moving that day would remain unfulfilled on account of our laziness. The next day we would have again a large number of ryots anxious to get their statements recorded who would have to be kept waiting while we were busy shifting to another house. So at about 10 o'clock at night the order went forth that we must move the same night and when he found us hesitating and discussing how to get a carriage or laborers to carry our things, he rose, packed his bedding and started, carrying the load. We had no option but to run after him with whatever we could carry. Fortunately, the new house was at a short distance. On reaching there we found that it was not as clean as it should be. He immediately took a broom and started sweeping. We were shamed into taking away the broom from him and sweeping the house clean. This was the first of the many lessons which we had to learn from him.

It is an inveterate habit with Biharees [11] to depend upon servants for personal service even in small matters. We had several of us our own servants and so the number of inmates of the camp or Ashram, as you might call it, was practically double that of workers. We had besides a cook who came a few days later. Our orthodoxy was such that none of us had taken kachi [12] food from the hands of anyone except a Brahmin or a fellow caste-man. And this we had carried and preserved in spite of the fact that some of us had been educated in Calcutta and spent years in that big metropolis, and in spite of the fact that some of us had taken part in the agitation for the readmission of English-returned gentlemen to caste. The question was—were we going to keep our caste intact? Mahatmaji was of course living on groundnuts, dates and fresh fruits and so when this question arose, there was no difficulty on his account. Mahatmaji saw our orthodoxy and told us that when we were engaged in public work of the kind we were doing in Champaran, we all became of one caste, namely, the caste of the co-workers, and it was not desirable for us to stick to the lifeless custom of not eating particular things touched by particular persons. At any rate so long as we were in Champaran, our work should not be allowed to suffer, our time should not be wasted and the expenses of establishment should not be permitted to mount up just for the sake of preserving our castes. And so for the first time we began to eat rice and dal [13] touched by others without distinction, although we happened to have amongst us Kayasthas, Rajputs, Agarwals, Goalas, Gujerati Banias, [14] and possibly some others whom I forget now. We discovered soon afterwards that this change in our habits was necessary and useful as without it we would have found great difficulty in carrying on the work which became more and more heavy and exacting.

The next question was about the servants—should we keep so many of them? Mahatmaji again told us that if we wanted to serve the country this dependence on servants should also go. In any case we could not afford to have so many servants in the camp both because it was expensive and because there was not sufficient accommodation. Besides, it was wholly unnecessary.

One after another the servants were sent away and only one kitchen servant was employed to clean and wash and help in sundry other ways. We were thrown upon our own resources for everything else. It thus became necessary for us to draw water for our use from the well, to wash our own clothes after bath, to wash our plates after meals and to clean the rooms. It was a novel experience to all of us and though it was irksome to begin with, we easily reconciled ourselves to it. It had a splendid effect on the ryots who used to assemble in their hundreds every day to give their statements.

The cook was also sent away afterwards when Srimati Kasturba Gandhi (Mahatmaji's wife) arrived. He told us that she would cook for all and that some of us would only have to assist her. It appeared to us to be hard on her to have to cook for so many of us, and when we protested, he silenced us by saying that she was used to cooking for larger numbers and there would be no difficulty. So some of us had to help her in the kitchen and we used to see how with our wood-fuel she would be busy in the kitchen fanning the fire which would smoke and cause tears in her and her assistant's eyes. Mahatmaji also used to help in feeding us, as he took it upon himself to serve out the food when we sat for dinner, particularly at the evening meal. He would take particular pleasure in doing so. It was a sight to see about a dozen of us seated with our plates, Mahatmaji serving out rice and *dal*, and Ba, as we soon learnt to call her, handing over the different dishes to him to serve. Before and after meals we were required to clean and wash our utensils and to wash the floor where we used to dine, and restore the whole place to a clean and tidy condition. I remember that there were occasions when we had to wash the cooking pots also during the absence or indisposition of the single servant who was retained for the purpose.

I remember a funny story. One morning I was busy cleaning a tiffin-carrier [15] at the well. It had been left unwashed for some days and it was taking time to make it quite clean and bright. Mahatmaji came to the well for water and seeing that I was hard at work, laughed his usual hearty laugh and said: "Well, is it not creditable that I have made High Court Vakils scrape and wash their pots?" And so it was. It used to be an interesting sight for the villagers to see us doing all this with our own hands. They knew many of us as Vakil Sahebs who had houses and establishments and servants and cooks of our own at our homes, but we were drudging like common folks. Many of them would offer to help us and do all that for us. But Mahatmaji said we were having a lesson in self-help and should not spoil it by taking service from villagers even when voluntarily offered. Were we not there to serve them? Why then should we take service from them?

But this was not all. There was a corresponding change in our food also. In the beginning Mahatmaji was living on groundnuts, dates and fresh fruits. Later on he began to take rice and boiled vegetables without salt and without any spices. Our food also became very simple. Although our vegetables were not merely boiled with water—there used to be some ghee [16] added—spices, except perhaps for turmeric (haldi) and salt were practically excluded. We thus used to have two simple and healthy meals, one at about 8:30 or 9:00 in the morning and the other at about 5:00 in the evening before sunset. In between we used sometimes to have some fruits or other things of the season but this was irregular and occasional. The principal meals were in the morning and evening. We ate nothing during the night. The result was that in spite of the hard work we had to put in, we preserved excellent health and our living was cheap.

Apart from occasional visits, which we had to pay to villages either with Mahatmaji or by ourselves, our routine used to be a full day's work. We used to rise early, Mahatmaji earliest of all.

We did not have congregational prayers then as we used to have later, wherever we happened to be with Mahatmaji. He would have his prayers while we were all asleep in the small hours of the morning and, after morning ablutions, would begin writing or reading. We would rise later, yet early enough to be ready for bath, etc. by about 6:30, and sit to work. We would have put in about two hours' work before breakfast between 8:00 and 9:00 and thereafter we would continue our work till it was time for the evening meal, with occasional breaks according to the exigencies of work during the afternoon. By the time the evening meal was finished the day's post would have arrived along with newspapers. About 6:30 or 7:00 P.M. we would go out with Mahatmaji for a walk of about 2 or 3 miles. This used to be the time when we would talk to Mahatmaji about various matters not necessarily connected with the enquiry and discuss items of news published in the papers. After returning we would again sit to work for an hour or more, according as the work of the day was light or heavy, and then retire about 9:00 or 10:00 at night to rise the next day and continue as on the day before. Mahatmaji would not waste a single minute of his time and his hard work used to help and inspire us when we were inclined to be lazy. . . .

7 INDIAN PROBLEMS

A STRIKE AT AHMEDABAD
by M. K. Gandhi

Toward the beginning of 1918 Gandhi received word of unrest on the part of the workers in the textile mills of Ahmedabad. He studied the situation and found that the case of the millhands was strong. He was—as he wrote—"in a most delicate situation" since he was a close friend of Ambalal Sarabhai, the principal millowner. He advised the millowners to agree to arbitrate the dispute, but they refused. So Gandhi advised the workers to go on strike, exacting from them a pledge not to return to work until either their terms were accepted or the millowners agreed to refer the dispute to arbitration.

Gandhi attended the daily meetings of the strikers under the shade of a tree on the bank of the Sabarmati River and reminded them of their pledge. It was here that Gandhi first became well acquainted with Sardar Vallabhbhai Patel, a rich Ahmedabad attorney, who was to be associated with him for the next three decades and to become Deputy Prime Minister of India.

FOR THE FIRST two weeks the millhands exhibited great courage and self-restraint and daily held monster meetings. On these

• Reprinted with permission from Gandhi's Autobiography (Washington: Public Affairs Press, 1948), pp. 526-29.

occasions I used to remind them of their pledge, and they would shout back to me the assurance that they would rather die than break their word.

But at last they began to show signs of flagging. Just as physical weakness in men manifests itself in irascibility, their attitude towards the blacklegs [1] became more and more menacing as the strike seemed to weaken, and I began to fear an outbreak of rowdyism on their part. The attendance at their daily meetings also began to dwindle by degrees, and despondency and despair were writ large on the faces of those who did attend. Finally the information was brought to me that the strikers had begun to totter. I felt deeply troubled and set to thinking furiously as to what my duty was in the circumstances. I had had experience of a gigantic strike in South Africa, but the situation that confronted me here was different. The mill-hands had taken the pledge at my suggestion. They had repeated it before me day after day, and the very idea that they might now go back upon it was to me inconceivable. Was it pride or was it my love for the laborers and my passionate regard for the truth that was at the back of this feeling—who can say?

One morning—it was at a mill-hands' meeting—while I was still groping and unable to see my way clearly, the light came to me. Unbidden and all by themselves the words came to my lips: "Unless the strikers rally," I declared to the meeting, "and continue the strike till a settlement is reached, or till they leave the mills altogether, I will not touch any food."

The laborers were thunderstruck. Tears began to course down Anasuyabehn's [2] cheeks. The laborers broke out, "Not you but we shall fast. It would be monstrous if you were to fast. Please forgive us for our lapse, we will now remain faithful to our pledge to the end."

"There is no need for you to fast," I replied. "It would be enough if you could remain true to your pledge. As you know we are without funds, and we do not want to continue our strike by living on public charity. You should therefore try to eke out a bare existence by some kind of labor, so that you may be able to remain unconcerned, no matter how long the strike may continue. As for my fast, it will be broken only after the strike is settled."

In the meantime Vallabhbhai [Patel] was trying to find some employment for the strikers under the Municipality, but there was not much hope of success there. Maganlal Gandhi suggested that, as we needed sand for filling the foundation of our weaving school in the Ashram, a number of them might be employed for that purpose. The laborers welcomed the proposal. Anasuya-behn led the way with a basket on her head and soon an endless stream of laborers carrying baskets of sand on their heads could be seen issuing out of the hollow of the riverbed. It was a sight worth seeing. The laborers felt themselves infused with a new strength, and it became difficult to cope with the task of paying out wages to them.

My fast was not free from a grave defect. For as I have already mentioned . . . I enjoyed very close and cordial relations with the millowners, and my fast could not but affect their decision. As a Satyagrahi I knew that I might not fast against them, but ought to leave them free to be influenced by the mill-hands' strike alone. My fast was undertaken not on account of a lapse of the mill-owners, but on account of that of the laborers in which, as their representative, I felt I had a share. With the millowners, I could only plead; to fast against them would amount to coercion. Yet in spite of my knowledge that my fast was bound to put pressure upon them, as in fact it did, I felt I could not help it. The duty to undertake it seemed to me to be clear.

I tried to set the millowners at ease. "There is not the slightest necessity for you to withdraw from your position," I said to them. But they received my words coldly and even flung keen, delicate bits of sarcasm at me, as indeed they had a perfect right to do.

The principal man at the back of the millowners' unbending attitude towards the strike was Sheth Ambalal. His resolute will and transparent sincerity were wonderful and captured my heart. It was a pleasure to be pitched against him. The strain produced by my fast upon the opposition, of which he was the head, cut me, therefore, to the quick. And then, Sarladevi, his wife, was attached to me with the affection of a blood-sister, and I could not bear to see her anguish on account of my action.

Anasuyabehn and a number of other friends and laborers shared the fast with me on the first day. But after some difficulty I was able to dissuade them from continuing it further.

The net result of it was that an atmosphere of goodwill was created all round. The hearts of the millowners were touched, and they set about discovering some means for a settlement. Anasuyabehn's house became the venue of their discussions. Sjt. Anandshankar Dhruva intervened and was in the end appointed arbitrator, and the strike was called off after I had fasted only for three days. The millowners commemorated the event by distributing sweets among the laborers, and thus a settlement was reached after 21 days' strike. . . .[8]

THE CONDITION OF LABOR
by M. K. Gandhi

TWO PATHS are open before India today, either to introduce the western principle of "Might is right" or to uphold the eastern principle that truth alone conquers, that truth knows no mishap, that the strong and the weak have alike a right to secure justice. The choice is to begin with the laboring class. Should the laborers obtain an increment in their wages by violence? Even if that be possible, they cannot resort to anything like violence, howsoever legitimate may be their claims. To use violence for securing rights may seem an easy path, but it proves to be thorny in the long run. Those who live by the sword die also by the sword. . . .

• An article published in *Young India*, June 1, 1921; reprinted with permission. Also in M. K. Gandhi, *Young India, 1919–1922* (New York: B. W. Huebsch, 1923), pp. 727-31.

What shall we do then? The laborers in Bombay made a fine stand. I was not in a position to know all the facts. But this much I could see that they could fight in a better way. The millowner may be wholly in the wrong. In the struggle between capital and labor, it may be generally said that more often than not the capitalists are in the wrong box. But when labor comes fully to realize its strength, I know it can become more tyrannical than capital. The millowners will have to work on the terms dictated by labor, if the latter could command intelligence of the former. It is clear, however, that labor will never attain to that intelligence. If it does, labor will cease to be labor and become itself the master. The capitalists do not fight on the strength of money alone. They do possess intelligence and tact.

The question before us is this: When the laborers, remaining what they are, develop a certain consciousness, what should be their course? It would be suicidal if the laborers rely upon their numbers or brute-force, i.e., violence. By so doing, they will do harm to industries in the country. If, on the other hand, they take their stand on pure justice and suffer in their person to secure it, not only will they always succeed but they will reform their masters, develop industries and both master and men will be as members of one and the same family. A satisfactory solution of the condition of labor must include the following:

1. The hours of labor must leave the workmen some hours of leisure.
2. They must get facilities for their own education.
3. Provision should be made for an adequate supply of milk, clothing and necessary education for their children.
4. There should be sanitary dwellings for the workmen.
5. They should be in a position to save enough to maintain themselves during their old age.

None of these conditions is satisfied today. For this both the parties are responsible. The masters care only for the service they get. What becomes of the laborer does not concern them. All their endeavors are generally confined to obtaining maximum service with minimum payment. The laborer, on the other hand, tries to hit upon all tricks whereby he can get maximum pay with minimum work. The result is that although the laborers get an increment there is no improvement in the work turned out. The relations between the two parties are not purified and the laborers do not make proper use of the increment they get.

A third party has sprung up between these two parties. It has become the laborer's friend. There is need for such a party. Only to the extent to which this party has disinterested friendship for the laborers can it befriend them.

A time has come now when attempts will be made to use labor as a pawn in more ways than one. The occasion demands consideration at the hands of those that would take part in politics. What will they choose? Their own interest or the service of labor and the nation? Labor stands in sore need of friends. It cannot proceed without a lead. What sort of men give this lead will decide the condition of labor.

Strikes, cessation of work and hartal [4] are wonderful things no doubt, but it is not difficult to abuse them. Workmen ought to organize themselves into strong Labor Unions, and on no account shall they strike work without the consent of these Unions. Strikes should not be risked without previous negotiations with the millowners. If the millowners resort to arbitration, the principle of *Panchayat* [5] should be accepted. And once the *Panch* [6] are appointed, their decision must be accepted by both the parties alike, whether they like it or not.

Readers, if you are interested in ameliorating the condition of labor, if you want to befriend the workman and serve him, you will see from the above that there is only one royal road before you, viz., to elevate the workmen by creating between the two parties family relationship. And to secure this end there is no path like Truth. Mere increase in wages should not satisfy you; you must also watch by what means they get it and how they spend it.

STRIKES

•

by M. K. Gandhi

STRIKES ARE the order of the day. They are a symptom of the existing unrest. All kinds of vague ideas are floating in the air. A vague hope inspires all, and great will be the disappointment if that vague hope does not take definite shape. The labor world in India, as elsewhere, is at the mercy of those who set up as advisers and guides. The latter are not always scrupulous, and not always wise even when they are scrupulous. The laborers are dissatisfied with their lot. They have every reason for dissatisfaction. They are being taught, and justly, to regard themselves as being chiefly instrumental in enriching their employers. And so it requires little effort to make them lay down their tools. The political situation too is beginning to affect the laborers of India. And there are not wanting labor leaders who consider that strikes may be engineered for political purposes.

In my opinion, it will be a most serious mistake to make use of labor strikes for such a purpose. I don't deny that such strikes can serve political ends. But they do not fall within the plan of non-violent non-cooperation. It does not require much effort of the intellect to perceive that it is a most dangerous thing to make political use of labor until laborers understand the political condition of the country and are prepared to work for the common good. This is hardly to be expected of them all of a sudden and until they have bettered their own condition so as to enable them to keep body and soul together in a decent manner. The greatest political contribution, therefore, that laborers can make is to

* An article published in Young India, February 16, 1921; reprinted with permission. Also in M. K. Gandhi, Young India, 1919–1922 (New York: B. W. Huebsch, 1923), pp. 736-41.

improve their own condition, to become better informed, to insist on their rights, and even to demand proper use by their employers of the manufactures in which they have had such an important hand. The proper evolution, therefore, would be for the laborers to raise themselves to the status of part proprietors. Strikes, therefore, for the present should only take place for the direct betterment of laborers' lot and, when they have acquired the spirit of patriotism, for the regulation of prices of their manufactures.

The conditions of a successful strike are simple. And when they are fulfilled, a strike need never fail.

1. The cause of the strike must be just.

2. There should be practical unanimity among the strikers.

3. There should be no violence used against non-strikers.

4. Strikers should be able to maintain themselves during the strike period without falling back upon Union funds and should therefore occupy themselves in some useful and productive temporary occupation.

5. A strike is no remedy when there is enough other labor to replace strikers. In that case, in the event of unjust treatment or inadequate wages or the like, resignation is the remedy.

6. Successful strikes have taken place even when all the above conditions have not been fulfilled, but that merely proves that the employers were weak and have a guilty conscience. We often make terrible mistakes by copying bad examples. The safest thing is not to copy examples of which we have rarely complete knowledge but to follow the conditions which we know and recognize to be essential for success.

It is the duty of every well wisher of the country, if we are to attain Swaraj during the year, not to precipitate any action that may even by a day retard the fulfillment of the great national purpose.

THE UNTOUCHABLES

•
by M. K. Gandhi

Gandhi was deeply concerned with the problem of untouchability almost as soon as he returned to India from South Africa. He increasingly considered the elimination of untouchability as part of the national campaign for freedom. In 1921, at Ahmedabad, he made the following memorable address before a convention of the untouchables—the Suppressed Class Conference.

I REGARD untouchability as the greatest blot on Hinduism. This idea was not brought home to me by my bitter experiences during the South African struggle. It is not due to the fact that I was once an agnostic. It is equally wrong to think, as some people do, that I have taken my views from my study of Christian religious literature. These views date as far back as the time when I was neither enamoured of, nor was acquainted with, the Bible or the followers of the Bible.

I was hardly yet twelve when this idea had dawned on me. A scavenger named Uka, an untouchable, used to attend our house for cleaning latrines. Often I would ask my mother why it was wrong to touch him, why I was forbidden to touch him. If I accidentally touched Uka, I was asked to perform the ablutions, and though I naturally obeyed, it was not without smilingly protesting that untouchability was not sanctioned by religion, that it was impossible that it should be so. I was a very dutiful and obedient child and so far as it was consistent with respect for parents, I often had tussles with them on this matter. I told

• Reprinted with permission from an article published in *Young India*, April 27, 1921. Also in M. K. Gandhi, *Young India, 1919–1922* (New York: B. W. Huebsch, 1923), pp. 472-77.

my mother that she was entirely wrong in considering physical contact with Uka as sinful.

While at school I would often happen to touch the "untouchables," and as I never would conceal the fact from my parents, my mother would tell me that the shortest cut to purification after the unholy touch was to cancel the touch by touching any Mussalman passing by. And simply out of reverence and regard for my mother I often did so, but never did so believing it to be a religious obligation. After some time we shifted to Porbandar, where I made my first acquaintance with Sanskrit. I was not yet put to an English school, and my brother and I were placed in charge of a Brahmin, who taught us *Ramraksha* and *Vishnu Punjar.*[7] The texts "*jale Vishnuh*" "*sthale Vishnuh*" (there is the Lord [present] in water, there is the Lord [present] in earth) have never gone out of my memory. . . . I could never believe then that there was any text in the *Ramraksha* pointing to the contact of the "untouchables" as a sin. . . .

The *Ramayana* used to be regularly read in our family. A Brahmin called Ladha Maharaj used to read it. He was stricken with leprosy, and he was confident that a regular reading of the *Ramayana* would cure him of leprosy, and, indeed he was cured of it. "How can the *Ramayana*," I thought to myself, "in which one who is regarded now-a-days as an untouchable took Rama across the Ganges in his boat, countenance the idea of any human beings being untouchable on the ground that they were polluted souls?" The fact that we addressed God as the "purifier of the polluted" and by similar appellations, shows that it is a sin to regard any one born in Hinduism as polluted or untouchable— that it is satanic to do so. I have hence been never tired of repeating that it is a great sin. I do not pretend that this thing had crystallized as a conviction in me at the age of twelve, but I do say that I did then regard untouchability as a sin. I narrate this story for the information of the *Vaishnavas* and Orthodox Hindus.

I have always claimed to be a *Sanatani*[8] Hindu. It was not that I am quite innocent of the scriptures. I am not a profound scholar of Sanskrit. I have read the *Vedas* and the *Upanishads* only in translations. Naturally therefore, mine is not a scholarly study of them. My knowledge of them is in no way profound, but I have studied them as I should do as a Hindu and I claim to have grasped their true spirit. By the time I had reached the age of 21, I had studied other religions also.

There was a time when I was wavering between Hinduism and Christianity. When I recovered my balance of mind, I felt that to me salvation was possible only through the Hindu religion and my faith in Hinduism grew deeper and more enlightened.

But even then I believed that untouchability was no part of Hinduism; and that, if it was, such Hinduism was not for me.

True, Hinduism does not regard untouchability as a sin. I do not want to enter into any controversy regarding the interpretation of the *shastras*.[9] It might be difficult for me to establish my point by quoting authorities from the *Bhagwat* [10] or *Manusmriti*. But I claim to have understood the spirit of Hinduism. Hinduism has sinned in giving sanction to untouchability. It has degraded us, made us the pariahs of the Empire. Even the Mussalmans caught the sinful contagion from us; and in South Africa, in East Africa and in Canada, the Mussalmans no less than Hindus came to be regarded as pariahs. All this evil has resulted from the sin of untouchability.

I may here recall my proposition, which is this: So long as the Hindus wilfully regard untouchability as part of their religion, so long as the mass of Hindus consider it a sin to touch a section of their brethren, Swaraj is impossible of attainment. Yudhish-thira [11] would not enter heaven without his dog. How can, then, the descendants of that Yudhishthira expect to obtain Swaraj, without the untouchables? What crimes, for which we condemn the Government as satanic, have not we been guilty or toward our untouchable brethren?

We are guilty of having suppressed our brethren; we make them crawl on their bellies; we have made them rub their noses on the ground; with eyes red with rage, we push them out of railway compartments—what more than this has British Rule done? What charge, that we bring against Dyer and O'Dwyer,[12] may not others, and even our own people, lay at our doors? We ought to purge ourselves of this pollution. It is idle to talk of Swaraj so long as we do not protect the weak and the helpless, or so long as it is possible for a single Swarajist to injure the feelings of any individual. Swaraj means that not a single Hindu or Muslim shall for a moment arrogantly think that he can crush with impunity meek Hindus or Muslims. Unless this condition is fulfilled, we will gain Swaraj only to lose it the next moment. We are no better than the brutes until we have purged ourselves of the sins we have committed against our weaker brethren.

But I have faith in me still. In the course of my peregrinations in India, I have realized that the spirit of kindness of which the Poet Tulsidas sings so eloquently, which forms the corner-stone of the Jain and Vaishnava religions, which is the quintessence of the *Bhagavat* and which every verse of the Gita is saturated with—this kindness, this love, this charity, is slowly but steadily gaining ground in the hearts of the masses of this country. . . .

If it can bring any comfort to you, my untouchable brethren, I would say that your question does not cause so much stir as it used to do formerly. That does not mean that I expect you to cease to have misgivings about the Hindus. How can they deserve to be not mistrusted having wronged you so much? Swami Vivekananda [13] used to say that the untouchables were not depressed, they were suppressed by the Hindus who in turn had suppressed themselves by suppressing them.

I suppose I was at Nellore [14] on the 6th of April. I met the untouchables there and I prayed that day as I have done today. I do want to attain *Moksha*.[15] I do not want to be reborn. But if I have to be reborn, I should be born an untouchable, so that I may share their sorrows, sufferings, and the affronts levelled at them, in order that I may endeavor to free myself and them from that miserable condition. I, therefore, prayed that, if I should be born again, I should do so not as a *Brahmin*, *Kshatriya*, *Vaishya*, or *Shudra*, but as an *Atishudra*.[16] . . .

I love scavengering.[17] In my Ashram, an eighteen-year-old Brahmin lad is doing the scavenger's work in order to teach the Ashram scavenger cleanliness. The lad is no reformer. He was born and bred in orthodoxy. He is a regular reader of the Gita and faithfully performs Sandhyavandana.[18] His pronunciation of Sanskrit verses is more faultless than mine. When he conducts the prayer, his soft sweet melodies melt one into love. But he felt that his accomplishments were incomplete until he had become also a perfect sweeper and that if we wanted the Ashram sweeper to do his work well, he must do it himself and set an example.

You should realize that you are cleaning Hindu society. You have therefore to purify your lives. You should cultivate the habits of cleanliness, so that no one may point his finger at you. Use alkali-ash or earth, if you cannot afford to use soap, to keep yourselves clean. Some of you are given to drinking and gambling which you must get rid of. You will point your finger at the Brahmins and say even they are given to these vices. But they are not looked upon as polluted and you are. You must not ask the Hindus to emancipate you as a matter of favor. Hindus must do so, if they want, in their own interest. You should, therefore, make them feel ashamed by your own purity and cleanliness. I believe that we shall have purified ourselves within the next five months. If my expectations are not fulfilled, I will think that, although my proposition was fundamentally correct, yet I was wrong in my calculation; and I will again say that I had erred in my calculation.

You claim to be Hindus; you read the Bhagavat; if, therefore, the Hindus oppress you, then you should understand that the fault does not lie in the Hindu religion but in those who profess it. In order to emancipate yourselves, you shall have to purify yourselves. You shall have to get rid of evil habits like drinking.

If you want to ameliorate your condition, if you want to obtain Swaraj, you should be self-reliant. I was told in Bombay that some of you are opposed to the N.C.O.[19] and believe that salvation is only possible through the British Government. Let me tell you that you will never be able to obtain redress by discarding Hindu Religion and courting the favor of a third party. Your emancipation lies in your own hands.

I have come in contact with the untouchables all over the country and I have observed that immense possibilities lie latent in them of which neither they nor the rest of the Hindus seem to be aware. Their intellect is of virginal purity. I ask you to learn spinning and weaving, and if you take them up as a profession, you will keep poverty from your doors. As regards your attitude towards the *Bhangis*,[20] I will repeat what I said at Godhra. I cannot understand why you should yourselves countenance the distinction between *Dheds*[21] and *Bhangis*. There is no difference between them. Even in normal times their occupation is as honorable as that of lawyers or Government servants. . . .

The Hindus are not sinful by nature; they are sunk in ignorance. Untouchability must be extinct in this very year. Two of the strongest desires that keep me in flesh and bone are the emancipation of the untouchables and the protection of the cow. When these two desires are fulfilled, there is Swaraj, and therein lies my own *Moksha*. May God give you strength to work out your salvation.

HINDUISM

by M. K. Gandhi

Gandhi could never disentangle his religious from his political interests, and when he was most deeply immersed in politics, he was often also most deeply concerned with religion. In 1921, in the midst of a major struggle with the British, he wrote an essay on Hinduism which was published in Young India.

•An article published in Young India, October 6, 1921; reprinted with permission. Also in C. F. Andrews, *Mahatma Gandhi's Ideas* (London: Allen and Unwin, 1929), pp. 35-42.

I CALL MYSELF a Sanatani Hindu because—

1. I believe in the Vedas, the Upanishads, the Puranas,[22] and all that goes by the name of Hindu Scriptures and therefore in Avataras (divine incarnations) and rebirth.

2. I believe in Varnashrama Dharma [23] in a sense strictly Vedic, but not in its present popular and crude sense.

3. I believe in "Cow Protection" in a much larger sense than the popular belief.

4. I do not disbelieve in "idol-worship."

5. I believe implicitly in the Hindu aphorism that no one truly knows the Scriptures who has not attained perfection in Innocence (Ahimsa), Truth (Satya), and Self-control (Brahmacharya), and who has not renounced all acquisition or possession of wealth.

6. I believe, along with every Hindu, in God and His Oneness, in rebirth and salvation.

That which distinguishes Hinduism from every other religion is its "Cow Protection," even more than its Varnashrama. Varnashrama is in my opinion inherent in human nature, and Hinduism has simply reduced it to a science. It attaches to birth. A man cannot change "Varna" by choice. Not to abide by Varna is to disregard the law of heredity.

I do not believe in the exclusive divinity of the Vedas. I believe the Bible, the Koran, and the Zend Avesta [24] to be as much divinely inspired as the Vedas. My belief in the Hindu Scriptures does not require me to accept every word and every sense as divinely inspired. Nor do I claim to have any first-hand knowledge of these wonderful books. But I do claim to know and feel the truths of the essential teaching of the Scriptures. I decline to be bound by any interpretation, however learned it may be, if it is repugnant to reason or moral sense.

I do not believe that interdining, or even intermarriage, necessarily deprives a man of the Caste status that his birth has given him. The four divisions, Brahmin, Kshattriya, Vaishya, Shudra, define a man's calling; they do not restrict or regulate social intercourse. The divisions define duties; they confer no privileges. It is, I hold, against the genius of Hinduism to arrogate to oneself a higher status, or assign to another a lower status. All are born to serve God's creation—a Brahmin with his knowledge, a Kshattriya with his power of protection, a Vaishya with his commercial ability, and a Shudra with his bodily labor.

This, however, does not mean that a Brahmin is absolved from bodily labor, or the duty of protecting himself and others. His birth makes a Brahmin predominantly a man of knowledge, the fittest by heredity and training to impart it to others. There is nothing, again, to prevent the Shudra from acquiring all the knowledge he wishes. Only he will best serve with his body, and need not envy others their special qualities for service. But a Brahmin who claims superiority by right of knowledge falls, and has no knowledge. And so with the others, who pride themselves upon their special qualities. Varnashrama implies self-restraint, conservation, and economy of energy.

Though, therefore, Varnashrama is not affected by interdining or intermarriage, Hinduism does most emphatically discourage these things.

Hinduism has reached the highest limit of self-restraint. It is undoubtedly a religion of renunciation of the flesh, so that the spirit may be set free. By restricting a Hindu's choice of a bride for his son to a particular group he exercises rare self-restraint.

Hinduism does not regard the married state as by any means essential for salvation. Marriage is a "fall" even as "birth" is a fall. Salvation is freedom from birth and hence from death also.

Prohibition against intermarriage and interdining is essential for a rapid evolution of the soul. But this self-denial is no test of Varna (Caste). A Brahmin may remain a Brahmin, though he may dine with his Shudra brother, provided he has not left off his duty of service by knowledge. It follows from what I have said above that restraint in matters of marriage and dining is not based upon notions of superiority. A Hindu who refuses to dine with another from a sense of superiority altogether misrepresents his Hindu religion.

Unfortunately, today Hinduism seems to consist merely in "eating" and "not eating." Hinduism is in danger of losing its substance; it is resolving itself into a matter of elaborate rules as to what and with whom to eat. Abstemiousness from meat is undoubtedly a great aid to the evolution of the spirit; but it is by no means an end in itself. Many a man eating meat and dining with everybody, but living in the fear of God, is nearer to his salvation than a man religiously abstaining from meat and many other things, but blaspheming God in every one of his acts.

The central fact of Hinduism, however, is "Cow Protection." "Cow Protection" to me is one of the most wonderful phenomena in all human evolution; for it takes the human being beyond his species. The cow to me means the entire sub-human world. Man through the cow is enjoined to realize his identity with all that lives. Why the cow was selected for apotheosis is obvious to me. The cow was in India the best companion. She was the giver of plenty. Not only did she give milk, but she also made agriculture possible. The cow is a poem of pity. One reads pity in the gentle animal. She is the "mother" to millions of Indian mankind. Protection of the cow means protection of the whole dumb creation of God. The ancient seer, whoever he was, began in India with the cow. The appeal of the lower order of creation is all the more forcible because it is speechless. "Cow Protection" is the gift of Hinduism to the world; and Hinduism will live so long as there are Hindus to protect the cow.

Hindus are enjoined to protect the cow by self-purification, by self-sacrifice. The present day "Cow Protection" has degenerated into a perpetual feud with the Mussalmans, whereas true cow protection means conquering the Mussalmans by our love.

A Mussalman friend sent me some time ago a book detailing the inhumanities practiced by us on the cow and her progeny; how we bleed her to take the last drop of milk from her; how we starve her to emaciation; how we ill-treat the calves; how we deprive them of their portion of milk; how cruelly we treat the oxen; how we castrate them; how we beat them; how we overload them. If they had speech they would bear witness to our crimes against them which would stagger the world. By every act of cruelty to our cattle we disown God and Hinduism; I do not know that the condition of the cattle in any other part of the world is so bad as in unhappy India. We may not blame the Englishman for this; we may not plead poverty in our defense. Criminal negligence is the only cause of the miserable condition of our cattle. Our cow-shelters, though they are an answer to our instinct of mercy, are a clumsy demonstration of its execution. Instead of being model dairy farms and great profitable national institutions they are merely depots for receiving decrepit cattle.

Hindus will be judged, not by their correct chanting of sacred texts, not by their pilgrimages, not by their most punctilious observance of Caste rules, but by their ability to protect the cow. Whilst professing the religion of "Cow Protection" we have enslaved the cow and her progeny and have become slaves ourselves.

I can no more describe my feeling for Hinduism than for my own wife. She moves me as no other woman in the world can. Not that she has no faults; I dare say she has many more than I see myself. But the feeling of an indissoluble bond is there. Even so I feel for and about Hinduism with all its faults and limitations. Nothing elates me so much as the music of the Gita or Tulsidas's Ramayana, the only two books in Hinduism I may be said really to know. When on one occasion I fancied I was taking my last breath the Gita was my solace.

I know the vice that is going on today in all the great Hindu shrines, but I love them in spite of their unspeakable failings. There is an interest which I take in them and in no other. I am a reformer through and through. But my zeal never leads me to the rejection of any of the essential things of Hinduism.

I have said I do not disbelieve in idol-worship. An idol does not excite any feeling of veneration in me. But I think that idol-worship is part of human nature. We hanker after symbolism. Why should one be more composed in a church than elsewhere? Images are an aid to worship. No Hindu considers an image to be God. I do not consider idol-worship sin.

It is clear from the foregoing that Hinduism is not an exclusive religion. In it there is room for the worship of all the prophets of the world. It is not a missionary religion in the ordinary sense of the term. It has no doubt absorbed many tribes in its fold, but this absorption has been of an evolutionary, imperceptible character. Hinduism tells everyone to worship God according to his own faith, and so it lives at peace with all the religions. . . .

"Untouchability" is repugnant to reason and to the instinct of pity or love. A religion that establishes the worship of the cow cannot possibly countenance or warrant a cruel and unhuman boycott of human beings; and I should be content to be torn to pieces rather than disown the suppressed classes. Hindus will certainly never deserve freedom, nor get it, if they allow their noble religion to be disgraced by the retention of the taint of untouchability; and, as I love Hinduism dearer than life itself, the taint has become for me an intolerable burden. Let us not deny God by denying to a fifth of our race the right of association on an equal footing.

A STUDENT'S FOUR QUESTIONS
by Mahadev Desai

During Gandhi's fast at Delhi in 1924, one of C. F. Andrews' students came to assist Andrews while Andrews was serving Gandhi as nurse and editor. This student, Ramachandran, was the son of an official in Travancore, and had studied with both Andrews and Rabindranath Tagore at Shantiniketan. Some questions arose in Ramachandran's mind about the differences in outlook between Tagore and Gandhi. Ramachandran was hesitant to

• An article published in Young India, November 13, 1924; reprinted with permission. Also in C. F. Andrews, Mahatma Gandhi's Ideas (London: Allen and Unwin, 1929), pp. 331-42.

talk to Gandhi about these matters, but after the fast was over Andrews arranged for him to have a morning with Gandhi. Mahadev Desai, Gandhi's personal secretary, was present during this interview, taking careful notes as usual.

AMONG THOSE who visited Delhi during the weeks of fasting, penance, and prayer there was a young student from Shantiniketan named Ramachandran. He is one of the pupils of Mr. Andrews, and had no difficulty in persuading his teacher to permit him to stay at Delhi for some time after the fast was over. In the end Mr. Andrews took Ramachandran upstairs and said to Gandhiji, "I have not even introduced Ramachandran as yet to you. But he has been all the while with us, helping us devotedly with true love. He wants to ask you some questions, and I shall be so glad if you could have a talk with him before he leaves tomorrow to go back to Shantiniketan." Gandhiji at once gave his consent.

"How is it," asked Ramachandran, "that many intelligent and eminent men, who love and admire you, hold that you have ruled out of the scheme of national regeneration all considerations of Art?"

"I am sorry," replied Gandhiji, "that in this matter I have been generally misunderstood. Let me explain. There are two aspects, the outward and the inward. It is purely a matter of emphasis with me. The outward has no meaning to me at all except in so far as it helps the inward. All true Art is the expression of the soul. The outward forms have value only in so far as they are the expression of the inner spirit of man."

Ramachandran hesitatingly suggested, "The great artists themselves have declared that Art is the translation of the urge and unrest in the soul of the artists into words, colors, shapes."

"Yes," said Gandhiji, "Art of that nature has the greatest possible appeal for me. But I know that many call themselves artists in whose works there is absolutely no trace of the soul's upward urge and unrest."

"Have you any instance in mind?"

"Yes," said Gandhiji, "take Oscar Wilde. I can speak of him

because I was in England at the time that he was being discussed
and talked about."

"I have been told," put in Ramachandran, "that Oscar Wilde
was one of the greatest literary artists of modern times."

"Yes, that is just my trouble. Wilde saw the highest Art only
in outward forms, and therefore succeeded in beautifying immorality. All true Art must help the soul to realize its inner self.
In my own case I find that I can do entirely without external
forms in my soul's realization. I can claim, therefore, that there
is truly sufficient Art in my life, though you might not see what
you call works of Art about me. My room may have blank walls;
and I may even dispense with the roof, so that I may gaze out
upon the starry heavens overhead that stretch in an unending ex-
panse of beauty. What conscious Art of man can give me the
scene that opens before me when I look up to the sky above with
all its shining stars? This, however, does not mean that I refuse to
accept the value of human productions of Art, but only that I
personally feel how inadequate these are compared with the eternal symbols of beauty in Nature."

"But the artists claim to see and to find Truth through outward
beauty," said Ramachandran. "Is it possible to see and find Truth
in that way?"

"I would reverse the order," Gandhiji immediately answered:
"I see and find beauty through Truth. All Truths, not merely true
ideas, but truthful faces, truthful pictures, truthful songs, are
highly beautiful. Whenever men begin to see Beauty in Truth,
then Art will arise."

"But cannot Beauty," Ramachandran asked, "be separated from
Truth and Truth from Beauty?"

"I should want to know exactly what is Beauty," Gandhiji replied. "If it is what people generally understand by that word,
then they are wide apart. Is a woman with fair features necessarily
beautiful?"

"Yes," replied Ramachandran without thinking.

"Even," asked Bapu, continuing his question, "if she may be of
an ugly character?"

Ramachandran hesitated. "But her face," he said, "in that case cannot be beautiful."

"You are begging the whole question," Gandhiji replied. "You now admit that mere outward form may not make a thing beautiful. To a true artist only that face is beautiful which, quite apart from its exterior, shines with the Truth within the soul. There is then, as I have said, no Beauty apart from Truth. On the other hand, Truth may manifest itself in forms which may not be outwardly beautiful at all. Socrates, we are told, was the most truthful man of his time, and yet his features are said to have been the ugliest in Greece. To my mind he was beautiful because all his life was a striving after Truth; and you may remember that his outward form did not prevent Phidias from appreciating the beauty of Truth in him, though as an artist he was accustomed to see Beauty in outward forms also!"

"But, Bapuji," said Ramachandran eagerly, "the most beautiful things have often been created by men whose lives were not beautiful."

"That," said Gandhiji, "only means that Truth and Untruth often co-exist; good and evil are often found together. In an artist also not seldom the right perception of things and the wrong co-exist. Truly beautiful creations only come when right perception is at work. If these moments are rare in life they are also rare in Art."

"Is there Truth, Bapuji, in things that are neither moral nor immoral in themselves? For instance, is there Truth in a sunset, or a crescent moon that shines amid the stars at night?"

"Indeed," replied Gandhiji, "these beauties are truthful inasmuch as they make me think of the Creator at the back of them. How could these be beautiful but for the Truth that is in the center of creation? When I admire the wonder of a sunset or the beauty of the moon, my soul expands in worship of the Creator. I try to see Him and His mercies in all these creations. But even the sunsets and sunrises would be mere hindrances if they did not help me to think of Him. Anything which is a hindrance to the flight of the soul is a delusion and a snare; even like the body, which often does actually hinder you in the path of salvation."

"Are you against all machinery, Bapuji?" asked Ramachandran.

"How can I be," he answered, smiling at Ramachandran's naive question, "when I know that even the body is a most delicate piece of machinery? The spinning-wheel itself is a machine. What I object to is the craze for machinery, not machinery as such. The craze is for what they call labor-saving machinery. Men go on 'saving labor' till thousands are without work and thrown on the open streets to die of starvation. I want to save time and labor, not for a fraction of mankind, but for all. I want the concentration of wealth, not in the hands of a few, but in the hands of all. Today machinery merely helps a few to ride on the backs of millions. The impetus behind it all is not the philanthropy to save labor but greed. It is against this constitution of things that I am fighting with all my might."

"Then, Bapuji," said Ramachandran, "you are fighting not against machinery as such, but against its abuses, which are so much in evidence today?"

"I would unhesitatingly say 'yes'; but I would add that scientific truths and discoveries should first of all cease to be the mere instruments of greed. Then laborers will not be overworked, and machinery, instead of becoming a hindrance, will be a help. I am aiming, not at the eradication of all machinery, but its limitation."

Ramachandran said: "When logically argued out that would seem to imply that all complicated power-driven machinery should go."

"It might have to go," admitted Gandhiji, "but I must make one thing clear. The supreme consideration is man. The machine should not tend to make atrophied the limbs of men. For instance, I would make intelligent exceptions. Take the case of the Singer Sewing Machine. It is one of the few useful things ever invented, and there is a romance about the device itself. Mr. Singer saw his wife laboring over the tedious process of sewing with her own hands, and simply out of his love for her he devised the sewing machine, in order to save her from unnecessary labor. He, however, saved not only her labor, but also the labor of everyone who could purchase a sewing machine."

"But, in that case," said Ramachandran, "there would have to be a factory for making these Singer Sewing Machines, and it would have to contain power-driven machinery of ordinary type."

"Yes," said Bapu, smiling at Ramachandran's eager opposition. "But I am Socialist enough to say that such factories should be nationalized. They ought only to be working under the most attractive conditions, not for profit, but for the benefit of humanity, love taking the place of greed as the motive-power. It is an alteration in the conditions of labor that I want. This mad rush for wealth must cease; and the laborer must be assured, not only of a living wage, but of a daily task that is not a mere drudgery. The machine will, under these conditions, be as much a help to the man working it as to the State. The present mad rush will cease, and the laborers will work (as I have said) under attractive and ideal conditions. This is but one of the exceptions I have in mind. The sewing machine had love at its back. The individual is the one supreme consideration. The saving of labor of the individual should be the object, and honest humanitarian considerations and not greed the motive-power. Thus, for instance, I would welcome any day a machine to straighten crooked spindles. Not that blacksmiths will cease to make supplies; they will continue to provide the spindles; but when the spindle gets wrong every spinner will have a machine of his own to get it straight. Therefore replace greed by love and everything will come right."

"The third question," said Ramachandran, "that I would like to ask you is whether you are against the institution of marriage."

"I shall have to answer this question at some length," said Bapu. "The aim of human life is deliverance. As a Hindu, I believe that Moksha, or deliverance, is freedom from birth, by breaking the bonds of the flesh, by becoming one with God. Now marriage is a hindrance in the attainment of this supreme object, inasmuch as it only tightens the bonds of flesh. Celibacy is a great help, inasmuch as it enables one to lead a life of full surrender to God. What is the object generally understood of marriage except a repetition of one's own kind? And why need you advocate marriage? It propagates itself. It requires no agency to promote its growth."

"But must you advocate celibacy and preach it to one and all?"

"Yes," said Gandhiji. Ramachandran looked perplexed. "Then you fear there will be an end of creation? No. The extreme logical result would be not extinction of the human species, but the transference of it to a higher plane."

"But may not an artist, or a poet, or a great genius leave a legacy of his genius to posterity through his own children?"

"Certainly not," said Bapu, with emphasis. "He will have more disciples than he can ever have children; and through those disciples all his gifts to the world will be handed down in a way that nothing else can accomplish. It will be the soul's marriage with the spirit; the progeny being the disciple, a sort of divine procreation. No! You must leave marriage to take care of itself. Repetition and not growth would be the result, for lust has come to play the most important part in marriage."

"Mr. Andrews," said Ramachandran, "does not like your emphasis on celibacy."

"Yes, I know," said Gandhiji. "That is the legacy of his Protestantism. Protestantism did many good things; but one of its few evils was that it ridiculed celibacy."

"That," rejoined Ramachandran, "was because it had to fight the abuses in which the clergy of the Middle Ages had sunk."

"But all that was not due to any inherent evil of celibacy," said Bapu. "It is celibacy that has kept Catholicism green up to the present day."

Ramachandran's next question was about the much-discussed "Spinning Franchise" which Gandhiji had enjoined, insisting that none should be a member of the National Congress who did not spin with his own hands. Ramachandran assured Gandhiji at the outset that he was a spinner, but had to confess that he, with three friends at Shantiniketan, only began spinning after they had heard of the fast. He also affirmed that he believed in universal spinning. But he could not understand how the Congress should compel its members to spin. Persuasion and not compulsion should be the method.

"I see," said Gandhiji, "you even go farther than Charlie Andrews. He would not have the Congress to compel its members; but he would fain become a member of a voluntary spinning association. You object to any such association whatsoever?"

Ramachandran sat silent.

"Well, then," replied Gandhiji, enjoying the argument. "I ask you, has the Congress any right to say that its members shall not drink? Will that be a restriction of the freedom of the individual, too? If the Congress exercised that right of enjoining abstinence from drinking there would be no objection. Why? Because the evils of drink are obvious. Well, I say that in India today, where millions are on the brink of starvation, it is perhaps a much worse evil to import foreign cloth. Think of the starving millions of Orissa. When I went there I saw the famine-stricken. Thanks to a kind superintendent who was in charge of an industrial home, I saw also their children, bright, healthy, and merry, working away at their carpets, baskets, etc. There was no spinning because these other things were much in vogue at the time. But on their faces there was the luster of joyful work. But when I came to the famine-stricken, what did I see? They were merely skin and bone, only waiting to die. They were then in that condition because they would under no circumstances work. Even though you had threatened to shoot them if they refused to work, I am sure they would have preferred to be shot rather than do any honest work. This aversion from work is a greater evil than drink itself. You can take some work out of a drunkard. A drunkard retains something of a heart. He has intelligence. These starved men, refusing to work, were like mere animals. Now, how can we solve the problem of getting work out of people like this? I see no way except that of universalizing spinning. Every yard of foreign cloth brought into India is one bit of bread snatched out of the mouths of these starving poor. If you could visualize, as I can, the supreme need of the hour, which is to give India's starving millions a chance to earn their bread with joy and gladness, you would not object to the Spinning Franchise."

Ramachandran still appeared doubtful, but changed the subject. "So, Bapuji," he said, resuming the first point in the conversation, "Beauty and Truth are not merely separate aspects of the same thing?"

"Truth," repeated Gandhiji, "is the first thing to be sought for, and Beauty and Goodness will then be added unto you. That is what Christ really taught in the Sermon on the Mount. Jesus was to my mind a supreme artist because he saw and expressed Truth; and so was Muhammad. Scholars say that the Koran is the most perfect composition in all Arabic literature. Because both of them strove first for Truth, therefore the grace of expression naturally came in. Yet neither Jesus nor Muhammad wrote on Art. That is the Truth and Beauty I crave for, live for, and would die for."

Ramachandran then reverted to his difficulties as to Gandhiji's logical position with regard to machinery. "If you make an exception of the Singer Sewing Machine and your spindle," he said, "where would these exceptions end?"

Gandhiji replied: "Just where they cease to help the individual and encroach upon his individuality. The machine should not be allowed to cripple the limbs of man."

"But I was not thinking just now of the practical side, Bapuji," said Ramachandran. "Ideally would you not rule out all machinery? When you except the sewing machine, will you not have to make an exception of the motor-car?"

"No," said Bapu, "because it does not satisfy any of the primary wants of man; for it is not the primary need of man to traverse distances with the rapidity of a motor-car. The needle, on the contrary, happens to be an essential thing in life—a primary need. Ideally, however, I would rule out all machinery, even as I would reject this very body, which is not helpful to salvation, and seek the absolute liberation of the soul. From that point of view I would reject all machinery; but machines will remain because, like the body, they are inevitable. The body itself, as I told you, is the purest piece of mechanism; but if it is a hindrance to the highest flights of the soul it has to be rejected!"

"Why is the body a necessary evil?" asked Ramachandran. "There I don't understand you. But let me return to my earlier point. May not, after all, some artists be able to see Truth itself in and through Beauty, rather than Beauty in and through Truth?"

"Some may," said Gandhiji, "but here too, just as elsewhere, I must think in terms of the millions. And to the millions we cannot give that training to acquire a perception of Beauty in such a way as to see Truth in it. Show them Truth first and they will see Beauty afterwards. The famine-stricken skeletons of men and women in Orissa haunt me in my waking hours and in my dreams. Whatever can be useful to those starving millions is beautiful to my mind. Let us give today first the vital things of life, and all the graces and ornaments of life will follow."

Here the long conversation ended, and early the next morning Ramachandran started on his way back to Shantiniketan, rich with Bapu's blessings, wondering how far the teaching of his own Gurudev,[25] Rabindranath Tagore, would harmonize with that which he had just heard, and how far there was a fundamental difference between them.

8 SEDITION
(1919–1924)

A "HIMALAYAN MISCALCULATION"
by M. K. Gandhi

The first nation-wide civil disobedience campaign in India was launched by Gandhi on April 6, 1919 in protest against the Rowlatt Act, which continued in time of peace restrictions on civil liberties that had been imposed during the World War. Thousands rose to Gandhi's call for non-violent protest and did not resist arrest or punishment. In several places, however, Indians resorted to mob violence, killing, looting, and sabotage, and the British took harsh reprisals, including the terrible Amritsar massacre on April 13. The excesses committed by Indians were to Gandhi like "a rapier run through my body," and at length convinced him that the people of India needed further training before they would be ready to practice satyagraha. Confessing that he had been guilty of "Himalayan miscalculation," he called off the movement on April 18.

NEWS WAS RECEIVED that the Rowlatt Bill had been published as an Act. That night I fell asleep while thinking over the question. Towards the small hours of the morning I woke up somewhat

• Reprinted with permission from *Gandhi's Autobiography* (Washington: Public Affairs Press, 1948), pp. 562-63, 565-66, 573-77.

earlier than usual. I was still in that twilight condition between sleep and consciousness when suddenly the idea broke upon me— it was as if in a dream. Early in the morning I related the whole story to Rajagopalachari.[1]

"The idea came to me last night in a dream that we should call upon the country to observe a general *hartal*. Satyagraha is a process of self-purification, and ours is a sacred fight, and it seems to me to be in the fitness of things that it should be commenced with an act of self-purification. Let all the people of India, therefore, suspend their business on that day and observe the day as one of fasting and prayer. The Musalmans may not fast for more than one day; so the duration of the fast should be 24 hours. It is very difficult to say whether all the provinces would respond to this appeal of ours or not, but I feel fairly sure of Bombay, Madras, Bihar and Sindh. I think we should have every reason to feel satisfied even if all these places observe the *hartal* fittingly."

Rajagopalachari was at once taken up with my suggestion. Other friends too welcomed it when it was communicated to them later. I drafted a brief appeal. The date of the *hartal* was first fixed on the 30th of March 1919, but was subsequently changed to 6th April. The people thus had only a short notice of the *hartal*. As the work had to be started at once, it was hardly possible to give longer notice.

But who knows how it all came about? The whole of India from one end to the other, towns as well as villages, observed a complete *hartal* on that day. It was a most wonderful spectacle. . . .

Needless to say the *hartal* in Bombay was a complete success. Full preparation had been made for starting civil disobedience. Two or three things had been discussed in this connection. It was decided that civil disobedience might be offered in respect of such laws only as easily lent themselves to being disobeyed by the masses. The salt tax was extremely unpopular and a powerful movement had been for some time past going on to secure its repeal. I therefore suggested that the people might prepare salt from sea-water in their own houses in disregard of the salt laws. My other suggestion was about the sale of proscribed literature. Two of my books, viz., *Hind Swaraj* and *Sarvodaya* (Gujarati adaptation of Ruskin's *Unto This Last*), which had been already proscribed, came handy for this purpose. To print and sell them openly seemed to be the easiest way of offering civil disobedience. A sufficient number of copies of the books was therefore printed, and it was arranged to sell them at the end of the monster meeting that was to be held that evening after the breaking of the fast.

On the evening of the 6th an army of volunteers issued forth accordingly with this prohibited literature to sell it among the people. Both Shrimati Sarojini Devi [2] and I went out in cars. All the copies were soon sold out. The proceeds of the sale were to be utilized for furthering the civil disobedience campaign. Both these books were priced at four annas per copy, but I hardly remember anybody having purchased them from me at their face value merely. Quite a large number of people simply poured out all the cash that was in their pockets to purchase their copy. Five and ten rupee notes just flew out to cover the price of a single copy, while in one case I remember having sold a copy for fifty rupees! It was duly explained to the people that they were liable to be arrested and imprisoned for purchasing the proscribed literature. But for the moment they had shed all fear of jail-going.

It was subsequently learnt that the Government had conveniently taken the view that the books that had been proscribed by it had not in fact been sold, and that what we had sold was not held as coming under the definition of proscribed literature. The reprint was held by the Government to be a new edition of the books that had been proscribed, and to sell them did not constitute an offense under the law. This news caused general disappointment. . . .

. . . I proceeded to Ahmedabad. I learnt that an attempt had been made to pull up the rails near the Nadiad railway station, that a Government officer had been murdered in Viramgam, and that Ahmedabad was under martial law. The people were terror-stricken. They had indulged in acts of violence and were being made to pay for them with interest.

A police officer was waiting at the station to escort me to Mr. Pratt, the Commissioner. I found him in a state of rage. I spoke to him gently, and expressed my regret for the disturbances. I suggested that martial law was unnecessary, and declared my readiness to cooperate in all efforts to restore peace. I asked for permission to hold a public meeting on the grounds of the Sabarmati Ashram. The proposal appealed to him, and the meeting was held, I think, on Sunday, the 13th of April, and martial law was withdrawn the same day or the day after. Addressing the meeting, I tried to bring home to the people the sense of their wrong, declared a penitential fast of three days for myself, appealed to the people to go on a similar fast for a day, and suggested to those who had been guilty of acts of violence to confess their guilt.

I saw my duty as clear as daylight. It was unbearable for me to find that the laborers, amongst whom I had spent a good deal of my time, whom I had served, and from whom I had expected better things, had taken part in the riots, and I felt I was a sharer in their guilt.

Just as I suggested to the people to confess their guilt, I suggested to the Government to condone the crimes. Neither accepted my suggestion.

The late Sir Ramanbhai and other citizens of Ahmedabad came to me with an appeal to suspend Satyagraha. The appeal was needless, for I had already made up my mind to suspend Satyagraha so long as people had not learnt the lesson of peace. The friends went away happy.

There were, however, others who were unhappy over the decision. They felt that, if I expected peace everywhere and regarded it as a condition precedent to launching Satyagraha, mass Satyagraha would be an impossibility. I was sorry to disagree with them. If those amongst whom I worked, and whom I expected to be prepared for non-violence and self-suffering, could not be non-violent, Satyagraha was certainly impossible. I was firmly of opinion that those who wanted to lead the people to Satyagraha ought to be able to keep the people within the limited non-violence expected of them. I hold the same opinion even today.

nost immediately after the Ahmedabad meeting I went to
ad. It was here that I first used the expression of "Himalayan
miscalculation" which obtained such a wide currency afterwards.
Even at Ahmedabad I had begun to have a dim perception of my
mistake. But when I reached Nadiad and saw the actual state of
things there and heard reports about a large number of people
from Kheda district [3] having been arrested, it suddenly dawned
upon me that I had committed a grave error in calling upon the
people in the Kheda district and elsewhere to launch upon civil
disobedience prematurely, as it now seemed to me. I was addressing a public meeting. My confession brought down upon me
no small amount of ridicule. But I have never regretted having
made that confession. For I have always held that it is only when
one sees one's own mistakes with a convex lens, and does just the
reverse in the case of others, that one is able to arrive at a just
relative estimate of the two. I further believe that a scrupulous
and conscientious observance of this rule is necessary for one who
wants to be a Satyagrahi.

Let us now see what that Himalayan miscalculation was. Before one can be fit for the practice of civil disobedience one must
have rendered a willing and respectful obedience to the state laws.
For the most part we obey such laws out of fear of the penalty for
their breach, and this holds good particularly in respect of such
laws as do not involve a moral principle. For instance, an honest,
respectable man will not suddenly take to stealing, whether there
is a law against stealing or not, but this very man will not feel any
remorse for failure to observe the rule about carrying head-lights
on bicycles after dark. Indeed it is doubtful whether he would
even accept advice kindly about being more careful in this respect.
But he would observe any obligatory rule of this kind, if only to
escape the inconvenience of facing a prosecution for a breach of
the rule. Such compliance is not, however, the willing and spon-
taneous obedience that is required of a Satyagrahi. A Satyagrahi
obeys the laws of society intelligently and of his own free will,
because he considers it to be his sacred duty to do so. It is only
when a person has thus obeyed the laws of society scrupulously

that he is in a position to judge as to which particular rules are good and just and which unjust and iniquitous. Only then does the right accrue to him of the civil disobedience of certain laws in well-defined circumstances. My error lay in my failure to observe this necessary limitation. I had called on the people to launch upon civil disobedience before they had thus qualified themselves for it, and this mistake seemed to me of Himalayan magnitude. As soon as I entered the Kheda district, all the old recollections of the Kheda Satyagraha [4] struggle came back to me, and I wondered how I could have failed to perceive what was so obvious. I realized that before a people could be fit for offering civil disobedience, they should thoroughly understand its deeper implications. That being so, before re-starting civil disobedience on a mass scale, it would be necessary to create a band of well-tried, pure-hearted volunteers who thoroughly understood the strict conditions of Satyagraha. They could explain these to the people, and by sleepless vigilance keep them on the right path.

With these thoughts filling my mind I reached Bombay, raised a corps of Satyagrahi volunteers through the Satyagraha Sabha [5] there, and with their help commenced the work of educating the people with regard to the meaning and inner significance of Satyagraha. This was principally done by issuing leaflets of an educative character bearing on the subject.

But whilst this work was going on, I could see that it was a difficult task to interest the people in the peaceful side of Satyagraha. The volunteers too failed to enlist themselves in large numbers. Nor did all those who actually enlisted take anything like a regular systematic training, and as the days passed by, the number of fresh recruits began gradually to dwindle instead of to grow. I realized that the progress of the training in civil disobedience was not going to be as rapid as I had at first expected.

THREE SEDITIOUS ARTICLES

During the disturbances surrounding the hartals in April 1919 two local Congress Party leaders were deported from the Punjab and, as a result, an Indian mob raged through the streets of Amritsar in that province and three Englishmen were killed. Two days later General R. E. H. Dyer arrived in Amritsar and issued an order prohibiting public meetings. On April 13, in defiance of the ban, a large but peaceful crowd gathered in the Jallianwalla Bagh, a vacant lot with few exits. General Dyer, without giving the crowd any warning to disperse, ordered his troops to open fire on the crowd. The firing continued for about ten minutes and approximately 379 persons were killed and 1,137 wounded. Other stern measures were taken throughout the Punjab. These included General Dyer's famous "crawling order," to the effect that any Indian passing through a street in Amritsar where an Englishwoman had been beaten up by an Indian mob must crawl on all fours. C. F. Andrews wrote, "No one can understand Mahatma Gandhi's attitude towards Great Britain and the British Empire unless he has come to realize that 'Amritsar' was the critical event which changed Mahatma Gandhi from a whole-hearted supporter into a pronounced opponent."

In 1920 the Congress Party, under Gandhi's leadership, decided to boycott the elections to be held under the new Montagu-Chelmsford constitutional reforms, which accorded severely limited self-government on the provincial level. At the same time the Congress launched a second nation-wide non-cooperation movement with the goal of securing full self-government for India, within the Empire or outside it if necessary. So far as practicable Indians were urged to boycott various government activities such as schools and law courts. Gandhi, in a symbolic gesture, returned to the Viceroy the Kaisar-i-Hind Gold Medal which had been conferred on him for his humanitarian work in South Africa.

The civil disobedience campaign continued until 1922. Thousands were thrown into jail and some violence occurred, but Swaraj seemed little nearer. Late in 1921 many Congress leaders urged that the pressure be stepped up by organizing non-violent mass demonstrations of non-cooperation throughout the country. Gandhi, fearing that such a movement might get out of control, persuaded them to confine it to one district, Bardoli, near Bombay, so that he could personally supervise the operation. On February 1, 1922 he informed the Viceroy, Lord Reading, that mass non-cooperation was about to start in Bardoli. On February 5, at a town called Chauri Chaura about 800 miles from Bardoli, an Indian mob burned the city hall and killed several constables. Gandhi thereupon suspended the civil disobedience movement in Bardoli and elsewhere. Many of his associates, including Nehru, accepted this decision with great reluctance, while some people maintained that he had shrewdly used the Chauri Chaura incident as an excuse to call off a campaign that was flagging in any case.

Shortly afterward Gandhi was arrested and tried for sedition. The evidence against him included three articles, reproduced below, which he had published in Young India in 1921–22. The first article refers to the arrest in September 1921 of one of Gandhi's close associates, Mohammed Ali, for attempting to persuade Moslems not to serve in the British Army. Gandhi also mentions two major Indian grievances, namely, the harsh reprisals taken by the British in the Punjab and the severe terms imposed by the Allies upon Turkey after World War I. Indian Moslems protested against the latter in what was known as the Khilafat movement (in defense of the Mohammedan Caliphate). Gandhi supported this movement and sought, in this period with great success, to promote close cooperation between Hindus and Moslems in the struggle against the British.

TAMPERING WITH LOYALTY
• by M. K. Gandhi

His EXCELLENCY the Governor of Bombay had warned the public sometime ago, that he "meant business," that he was not going to tolerate the speeches that were being made. In his note on the Ali Brothers and others he has made clear his meaning. The Ali Brothers are to be charged with having tampered with the loyalty of the sepoy [6] and with having uttered sedition. I must confess that I was not prepared for the revelation of such hopeless ignorance on the part of the Governor of Bombay. It is evident that he has not followed the course of Indian history during the past twelve months. He evidently does not know that the National Congress began to tamper with the loyalty of the sepoy in September last year, that the Central Khilafat Committee began it earlier still, for I must be permitted to take the credit or the odium of suggesting that India had a right openly to tell the sepoy and everyone who served the Government in any capacity whatsoever, that he participated in the wrongs done by the Government. The Conference at Karachi merely repeated the Congress declaration in terms of Islam, but speaking for Hinduism and speaking for nationalism I have no hesitation in saying that it is sinful for anyone, either as soldier or civilian, to serve this Government which has proved treacherous to the Mussalmans of India and which had been guilty of the inhumanities of the Punjab. I have said this from many a platform in the presence of sepoys. And if I have not asked individual sepoys to come out, it has not been due to want of will but of ability to support them.

• Published in Young India September 19, 1921; reprinted with permission. Also in M. K. Gandhi, Young India, 1919–1922 (New York: B. W. Huebsch, 1923), Appendix, pp. 9-11.

I have not hesitated to tell the sepoy that, if he could leave the service and support himself without the Congress or the Khilafat aid, he should leave at once. And I promise that, as soon as the spinning wheel finds an abiding place in every home and Indians begin to feel that weaving gives anybody any day an honorable livelihood, I shall not hesitate, at the peril of being shot, to ask the Indian sepoy individually to leave his service and become a weaver. For, has not the sepoy been used to hold India under subjection, has he not been used to murder innocent people at Jallianwala Bagh, has he not been used to drive away innocent men, women and children during that dreadful night at Chandpur,[7] has he not been used to subjugate the proud Arab of Mesopotamia, has he not been utilized to crush the Egyptians? How can any Indian having a spark of humanity in him and any Mussalman having any pride in his religion feel otherwise than as the Ali Brothers have done? The sepoy has been used more often as a hired assassin than as a soldier defending the liberty or the honor of the weak and the helpless. The Governor has pandered to the basest in us by telling us what would have happened in Malabar [8] but for the British soldier or sepoy. I venture to inform His Excellency that Malabar Hindus would have fared better without the British bayonets, that Hindus and Mussalmans would have jointly appeased the Moplahs, that possibly there being no Khilafat question there would have been no Moplah riot at all, that at the worst supposing that Mussalmans had common cause with the Moplahs, Hinduism would have relied upon its creed of non-violence and turned every Mussalman into a friend, or Hindu valor would have been tested and tried. The Governor of Bombay has done a disservice to himself and his cause (whatever it might be) by fomenting Hindu-Mussalman disunion, and has insulted the Hindus as well, by letting them infer from his note, that Hindus are helpless creatures unable to die for or defend their hearth, home or religion. If however the Governor is right in his assumptions, the sooner the Hindus die out the better for humanity. But let me remind His Excellency that he has pronounced the greatest condemnation upon British rule, in that it finds Indians today devoid of enough manliness to defend themselves against looters, whether they are Moplahs, Mussalmans or infuriated Hindus of Arrah.[9]

His Excellency's reference to the sedition of Ali Brothers is only less pardonable than his reference to the tampering. For he must know that sedition has become the creed of the Congress. Every Non-cooperator is pledged to preach disaffection towards the Government established by law. Non-cooperation, though a religious and strictly moral movement, deliberately aims at the overthrow of the Government, and it is therefore legally seditious in terms of the Indian Penal Code. But this is no new discovery. Lord Chelmsford knew it. Lord Reading knows it. It is unthinkable that the Governor of Bombay does not know it. It was common cause that so long as the movement remained non-violent nothing would be done to interfere with it.

But it may be urged that the Government has a right to change its policy when it finds that the movement is really threatening its very existence as a system. I do not deny its right. I object to the Governor's note, because it is so worded as to let the unknowing public think that tampering with the loyalty of the sepoy and sedition were fresh crimes committed by the Ali Brothers and brought for the first time to His Excellency's notice.

However, the duty of the Congress and Khilafat workers is clear. We ask for no quarter; we expect none from the Government. We did not solicit the promise of immunity from prison so long as we remained non-violent. We may not now complain, if we are imprisoned for sedition. Therefore our self-respect and our pledge require us to remain calm, unperturbed and non-violent. We have our appointed course to follow. We must reiterate from a thousand platforms the formula of the Ali Brothers regarding the sepoys, and we must spread disaffection openly and systematically till it pleases the Government to arrest us. And this we do not by way of angry retaliation but because it is our Dharma. We must wear Khadi even as the Brothers have worn it, and spread the Gospel of Swadeshi. The Mussalmans must collect for Smyrna Relief and the Angora Government. We must spread like the Ali Brothers the Gospel of Hindu-Muslim Unity and of non-violence for the purpose of attaining Swaraj and the redress of the Khilafat and the Punjab wrongs.

We have almost reached the crisis. It is well with a patient who survives a crisis. If on the one hand we remain firm as a rock in the presence of danger, and on the other observe the greatest self-restraint, we shall certainly attain our end this very year.

A PUZZLE AND ITS SOLUTION
• by M. K. Gandhi

LORD READING is puzzled and perplexed. Speaking in reply to the addresses from the British Indian Association and the Bengal National Chamber of Commerce at Calcutta, His Excellency said: "I confess that when I contemplate the activities of a section of the community, I find myself still, notwithstanding persistent study ever since I have been in India, puzzled and perplexed. I ask myself what purpose is served by flagrant breaches of the law for the purpose of challenging the Government and in order to compel arrest?" The answer was partly given by Pandit Motilal Nehru [10] when he said on being arrested that he was being taken to the house of freedom. We seek arrest because the so-called freedom is slavery. We are challenging the might of this Government because we consider its activity to be wholly evil. We want to overthrow the Government. We want to compel its submission to the people's will. We desire to show that the Government exists to serve the people, not the people the Government. Free life under the Government has become intolerable, for the price exacted for

• Published in *Young India* December 15, 1921; reprinted with permission. Also in M. K. Gandhi, *Young India, 1919–1922* (New York: B. W. Huebsch, 1923), Appendix, pp. 11-15.

the retention of freedom is unconscionably great. Whether we are one or many, we must refuse to purchase freedom at the cost of our self-respect or our cherished convictions. I have known even little children become unbending when an attempt has been made to cross their declared purpose, be it ever so flimsy in the estimation of their parents.

Lord Reading must clearly understand that the Non-cooperators are at war with the Government. They have declared rebellion against it in as much as it has committed a breach of faith with the Mussalmans, it has humiliated the Punjab and it insists upon imposing its will upon the people and refuses to repair the breach and repent of the wrong done in the Punjab.

There were two ways open to the people, the way of armed rebellion and the way of peaceful revolt. Non-cooperators have chosen, some out of weakness, some out of strength, the way of peace, i.e., voluntary suffering.

If the people are behind the sufferers, the Government must yield or be overthrown. If the people are not with them, they have at least the satisfaction of not having sold their freedom. In an armed conflict the more violent is generally the victor. The way of peace and suffering is the quickest method of cultivating public opinion, and therefore when victory is attained it is for what the world regards as Truth. Bred in the atmosphere of law courts, Lord Reading finds it difficult to appreciate the peaceful resistance to authority. His Excellency will learn by the time the conflict is over that there is a higher court than courts of justice and that is the court of conscience. It supersedes all other courts.

Lord Reading is welcome to treat all the sufferers as lunatics who do not know their own interest. He is entitled therefore to put them out of harm's way. It is an arrangement that entirely suits the lunatics and it is an ideal situation if it also suits the Government. He will have cause to complain if having courted imprisonment, Non-cooperators fret and fume or "whine for favors" as Lalaji [11] puts it. The strength of a Non-cooperator lies in his going to jail uncomplainingly. He loses his case if having courted imprisonment he begins to grumble immediately his courtship is rewarded.

The threats used by His Excellency are unbecoming. This is a fight to the finish. It is a conflict between the reign of violence and of public opinion. Those who are fighting for the latter are determined to submit to any violence rather than surrender their opinion.

SHAKING THE MANES

• by M. K. Gandhi

How CAN THERE BE any compromise whilst the British Lion continues to shake his gory claws in our faces? Lord Birkenhead [12] reminds us that Britain has lost none of her hard fibre. Mr. Montagu [13] tells us in the plainest language that the British are the most determined nation in the world, who will brook no interference with their purpose. Let me quote the exact words telegraphed by Reuter:

"If the existence of our Empire were challenged, the discharge of responsibilities of the British Government to India prevented and demands were made in the very mistaken belief that we contemplated retreat from India, then India would not challenge with success the most determined people in the world, who would once again answer the challenge with all the vigor and determination at its command."

Both Lord Birkenhead and Mr. Montagu little know that India is prepared for all the hard fibre that can be transported across the seas and that her challenge was issued in the September of 1920 at Calcutta that India would be satisfied with nothing less

• Published in *Young India* February 23, 1922; reprinted with permission. Also in M. K. Gandhi, *Young India, 1919–1922* (New York: B. W. Huebsch, 1923), Appendix, pp. 15-16.

than Swaraj and full redress of the Khilafat and the Punjab wrongs. This does involve the existence of the Empire and if the present custodians of the British Empire are not satisfied with its quiet transformation into a true Commonwealth of free nations, each with equal rights and each having the power to secede at will from an honorable and friendly partnership, all the determination and vigor of "the most determined people in the world" and the "hard fibre" will have to be spent in India in a vain effort to crush the spirit that has risen and that will neither bend nor break. It is true that we have no "hard fibre." The rice-eating puny millions of India seem to have resolved upon achieving their own destiny without any further tutelage and without arms. In the Lokamanya's language it is their "birthright," and they will have it in spite of the "hard fibre" and in spite of the vigor and determination with which it may be administered. India cannot and will not answer this insolence with insolence, but if she remains true to her pledge, her prayer to God to be delivered from such a scourge will certainly not go in vain. No empire intoxicated with red wine of power and plunder of weaker races has yet lived long in this world, and this British Empire, which is based upon organized exploitation of physically weaker races of the earth and upon a continuous exhibition of brute force, cannot live if there is a just God ruling the universe. Little do these so-called representatives of the British nation realize that India has already given many of her best men to be dealt with by the British "hard fibre." Had Chauri Chaura not interrupted the even course of the national sacrifice, there would have been still greater and more delectable offerings placed before the Lion, but God has willed it otherwise. There is nothing, however, to prevent all those representatives in Downing Street and Whitehall from doing their worst. I am aware that I have written strongly about the insolent threat that has come from across the seas, but it is high time that the British people were made to realize that the fight that was commenced in 1920 is a fight to the finish, whether it lasts one month or one year or many months or many years, and whether the representatives of Britain re-enact all the in-

describable orgies of the Mutiny days with redoubled force or
whether they do not. I shall only hope and pray that God will give
India sufficient humility and sufficient strength to remain non-
violent to the end. Submission to the insolent challenges that
are cabled out on due occasions is now an utter impossibility.

THE GREAT TRIAL
by K. P. K. Menon

Lord Reading, the Viceroy of India, had considerable respect
for Gandhi, whom he interviewed in 1921, and of whom he wrote:
"His religious and moral views are admirable and indeed are on
a remarkably high altitude, though I must confess that I find it
difficult to understand his practice of them in politics." Lord
Reading was under great pressure from the home government in
London to place Gandhi under arrest, but hesitated to do so until
Gandhi should commit some overt act. At length, however, he
gave the order. Gandhi was arrested on March 10, 1922, together
with S. G. Banker, the printer of Young India. Only the day
before he had published an article in Young India entitled "If
I Am Arrested." At the preliminary hearing on March 11, Gandhi
pleaded guilty to writing seditious articles. He gave his age as
fifty-three and his profession as "farmer and weaver." He was kept
in jail for a week until the trial, which was held at Ahmedabad
on March 18 before Justice C. N. Broomfield.

AT THE CIRCUIT HOUSE at Shahi Bag, the trial of Mr. Gandhi and
Mr. Banker commenced on Saturday noon, 18th March 1922,

• Abridged and reprinted from K. P. K. Menon, editor, The Great Trial of
Mahatma Gandhi and Mr. Banker (Madras: Ganesh, 1922). Also found, in
slightly abridged form, in Ronald Duncan, editor, Selected Writings of
Mahatma Gandhi (Boston: Beacon Press, 1951), pp. 137-47.

before Mr. C. N. Broomfield, I. C. S.,[14] District and Sessions Judge of Ahmedabad.

Sir J. T. Strangman with Rao Bahadur Girdharlal conducted the prosecution, while the accused were undefended. The Judge took his seat at 12 noon, and said there was a slight mistake in the charges framed, which he corrected. The charges were then read out by the Registrar, the offense being in three articles published in the Young India of September 29th, December 15th, of 1921 and February 23rd, 1922. The offending articles were then read out: first of them was "Tampering with Loyalty"; the second, "A Puzzle and Its Solution"; and the last was "Shaking the Manes."

The Judge said the law required that the charge should not only be read out, but explained. In this case, it would not be necessary for him to say much by way of explanation. The charge in each case was that of bringing or attempting to bring into hatred or contempt or exciting or attempting to excite disaffection towards His Majesty's Government, established by law in British India. Both the accused were charged with the three offences under Section 124A, contained in the articles read out, written by Mr. Gandhi and printed by Mr. Banker. The words "hatred and contempt" were words the meaning of which was sufficiently obvious. The word "disaffection" was defined under the section, where they were told that disaffection included disloyalty and feelings of enmity. . . . The charges having been read out, the Judge . . . asked Mr. Gandhi whether he pleaded guilty or claimed to be tried.

Mr. Gandhi: "I plead guilty to all the charges. . . ."

The Judge: "Mr. Banker, do you plead guilty, or do you claim to be tried?"

Mr. Banker: "I plead guilty."

Sir J. T. Strangman then wanted the Judge to proceed with the trial fully, but the Judge said he did not agree with what had been said by the Counsel. The Judge said that from the time he knew he was going to try the case, he had thought over the question of sentence, and he was prepared to hear anything that the

Counsel might have to say, or Mr. Gandhi wished to say, on the sentence. He honestly did not believe that the mere recording of evidence in the trial which Counsel had called for would make a difference to them, one way or the other. He, therefore, proposed to accept the pleas.

Mr. Gandhi smiled at this decision.

The Judge said nothing further remained but to pass sentence, and before doing so, he liked to hear Sir J. T. Strangman. He was entitled to base his general remarks on the charges against the accused and on their pleas.

Sir J. T. Strangman: The first point, he said, he wanted to make out, was that the matter which formed the subject of the present charges formed a part of the campaign to spread disaffection openly and systematically to render government impossible and to overthrow it. The earliest article that was put in from *Young India* was dated 25th May 1921, which said that it was the duty of a non-cooperator to create disaffection towards the Government. The Counsel then read out portions of articles written by Mr. Gandhi in the *Young India*. . . .

Sir J. T. Strangman said he wanted to show that these articles were not isolated. They formed part of an organized campaign, but so far as *Young India* was concerned, they would show that from the year 1921. The Counsel then read out extracts from the paper, dated June 8th, on the duty of a non-cooperator, which was to preach disaffection towards the existing Government and preparing the country for civil disobedience. Then in the same number, there was an article on disobedience. Then in the same number there was an article on "Disaffection—a virtue" or something to that effect. Then there was an article on 28th July 1921, in which it was stated that "we have to destroy the system." Again, on 30th September 1921, there was an article headed "Punjab Prosecutions," where it was stated that a non-cooperator worth his name should preach disaffection. That was all so far as *Young India* was concerned. They were earlier in date than the article, "Tampering with Loyalty," and it was referred to the Government of Bombay. Continuing, he said the accused was a man of high educational qualifications and evidently from his writings a recognized leader. The harm that was likely to be caused was considerable. They were the writings of an educated man, and not the writings of an obscure man, and the court must consider to what the results of a campaign of the nature disclosed in the writings must inevitably lead. They had examples before them in the last few months. He referred to the occurrences in Bombay last November and Chauri Chaura, leading to murder and destruction of property, involving many people in misery and misfortune. It is true that in the course of those articles they would find non-violence was insisted upon as an item of the campaign and as an item of the creed. But what was the use of preaching non-violence when he preached disaffection towards government or openly instigated others to overthrow it? The answer to that question appeared to him to come from Chauri Chaura, Madras and Bombay. These were circumstances which he asked the court to take into account in sentencing the accused, and it would be for the court to consider those circumstances which involve sentences of severity.

As regards the second accused, his offense was lesser. He did the publication and he did not write. His offence nevertheless was a serious one. His instructions were that he was a man of means and he asked the court to impose a substantial fine in addition to such term of imprisonment as might be inflicted. He quoted Section 10 of the Press Act as bearing on the question of fine. When making a fresh declaration, he said a deposit of Rs. 1,000 to Rs. 10,000 was asked in many cases.

Court: "Mr. Gandhi, do you wish to make a statement on the question of sentence?"

Mr. Gandhi: "I would like to make a statement."

Court: "Could you give it in writing to put it on record?"

Mr. Gandhi: "I shall give it as soon as I finish reading it."

Before reading his written statement, Mr. Gandhi spoke a few words as introductory remarks to the whole statement. He said:

"Before I read this statement, I would like to state that I entirely endorse the learned Advocate-General's remarks in connection with my humble self. I think that he was entirely fair to me in all the statements that he has made, because it is very true and I have no desire whatsoever to conceal from this court the fact that to preach disaffection towards the existing system of government has become almost a passion with me, and the learned Advocate-General is also entirely in the right when he says that my preaching of disaffection did not commence with my connection with *Young India*, but that it commenced much earlier; and in the statement that I am about to read it will be my painful duty to admit before this court that it commenced much earlier than the period stated by the Advocate-General. It is the most painful duty with me, but I have to discharge that duty knowing the responsibility that rests upon my shoulders.

"I wish to endorse all the blame that the learned Advocate-General has thrown on my shoulders in connection with the Bombay occurrences, Madras occurrences and the Chauri Chaura occurrences. Thinking over these deeply and sleeping over them night after night, it is impossible for me to dissociate myself from the diabolical crimes of Chauri Chaura or the mad outrages of Bombay. He is quite right when he says that as a man of responsibility, a man having received a fair share of education, having had a fair share of experience of this world, I should have known the consequences of every one of my acts. I knew that I was playing with fire. I ran the risk, and if I was set free, I would still do the same. I have felt it this morning that I would have failed in my duty, if I did not say what I said here just now.

"I wanted to avoid violence. Non-violence is the first article of my faith. It is also the last article of my creed. But I had to make my choice. I had either to submit to a system which I considered had done an irreparable harm to my country, or incur the risk of the mad fury of my people bursting forth, when they understood the truth from my lips. I know that my people have sometimes gone mad. I am deeply sorry for it and I am therefore here to submit not to a light penalty but to the highest penalty. I do not ask for mercy. . . ."

The written statement was then read:

"I owe it perhaps to the Indian public and to the public in England, to placate which this prosecution is mainly taken up, that I should explain why from a staunch loyalist and cooperator I have become an uncompromising disaffectionist and non-cooperator. To the court too I should say why I plead guilty to the charge of promoting disaffection towards the Government established by law in India.

"My public life began in 1893 in South Africa in troubled weather. My first contact with British authority in that country was not of a happy character. I discovered that as a man and an Indian I had no rights. More correctly, I discovered that I had no rights as a man, because I was an Indian.

"But I was not baffled. I thought that this treatment of Indians was an excrescence upon a system that was intrinsically and mainly good. I gave the Government my voluntary and hearty cooperation, criticizing it freely where I felt it was faulty but never wishing its destruction.

"Consequently when the existence of the Empire was threatened in 1899 by the Boer challenge, I offered my services to it, raised a volunteer ambulance corps and served at several actions that took place for the relief of Ladysmith.[15] Similarly in 1906, at the time of the Zulu revolt, I raised a stretcher-bearer party and served till the end of the "rebellion." On both these occasions I received medals and was even mentioned in dispatches. For my work in South Africa I was given by Lord Hardinge a Kaisar-i-Hind gold medal. When the war broke out in 1914 between England and Germany, I raised a volunteer ambulance corps in London consisting of the then resident Indians in London, chiefly students. Its work was acknowledged by the authorities to be valuable. Lastly, in India, when a special appeal was made at the War Conference in Delhi in 1918 by Lord Chelmsford for recruits, I struggled at the cost of my health to raise a corps in Kheda [16] and the response was being made when the hostilities ceased and orders were received that no more recruits were wanted. In all these efforts at service I was actuated by the belief that it was possible by such services to gain a status of full equality in the Empire for my countrymen.

"The first shock came in the shape of the Rowlatt Act, a law designated to rob the people of all real freedom. I felt called upon to lead an intensive agitation against it. Then followed the Punjab horrors beginning with the massacre at Jallianwala Bagh and culminating in crawling orders, public floggings and other indescribable humiliations. I discovered too that the plighted word of the Prime Minister to the Mussulmans of India regarding the integrity of Turkey and the holy places of Islam was not likely to be fulfilled. But in spite of the forebodings and the grave warnings of friends, at the Amritsar Congress in 1919, I fought for cooperation in working the Montagu-Chelmsford reforms, hoping that the Prime Minister would redeem his promise to the Indian Mussulmans, that the Punjab wound would be healed and that the reforms, inadequate and unsatisfactory though they were, marked a new era of hope in the life of India.

"But all that hope was shattered. The Khilafat promise was not to be redeemed. The Punjab crime was whitewashed and most culprits went not only unpunished but remained in service and in some cases continued to draw pensions from the Indian revenue, and in some cases were even rewarded. I saw too that not only did the reforms not mark a change of heart, but they were only a method of further draining India of her wealth and of prolonging her servitude.

"I came reluctantly to the conclusion that the British connection had made India more helpless than she ever was before, politically and economically. A disarmed India has no power of resistance against any aggressor if she wanted to engage in an armed conflict with him. So much is this the case that some of our best men consider that India must take generations before she can achieve Dominion status. She has become so poor that she has little power of resisting famines. Before the British advent, India spun and wove in her millions of cottages just the supplement she needed for adding to her meagre agricultural resources. This cottage industry, so vital for India's existence, has been

ruined by incredibly heartless and inhuman processes as described
by English witnesses. Little do town dwellers know how the semi-
starved masses of India are slowly sinking to lifelessness. Little
do they know that their miserable comfort represents the brokerage they get for the work they do for the foreign exploiter, that
the profits and the brokerage are sucked from the masses. Little do
they realize that the Government established by law in British
India is carried on for this exploitation of the masses. No sophis-
try, no jugglery in figures can explain away the evidence that the
skeletons in many villages present to the naked eye. I have no
doubt whatsoever that both English and the town dwellers of
India will have to answer, if there is a God above, for this crime
against humanity which is perhaps unequalled in history. The
law itself in this country has been used to serve the foreign exploiter. My unbiased examination of the Punjab Martial Law
cases has led me to believe that at least 95 per cent of convictions
were wholly bad. My experience of political cases in India leads
me to the conclusion that in nine out of ten the condemned men
were totally innocent. Their crime consisted in the love of their
country. In 99 cases out of a hundred justice has been denied to
Indians as against Europeans in the courts of India. This is not
an exaggerated picture. It is the experience of almost every Indian
who has had anything to do with such cases. In my opinion, the
administration of the law is thus prostituted consciously or unconsciously for the benefit of the exploiter.

"The greatest misfortune is that Englishmen and their Indian
associates in the administration of the country do not know that
they are engaged in the crime I have attempted to describe. I
am satisfied that many Englishmen and Indian officials honestly
believe that they are administering one of the best systems devised
in the world and that India is making steady though slow progress.
They do not know that a subtle but effective system of terrorism
and an organized display of force on the one hand, and the dep-
rivation of all powers of retaliation or self-defense on the other,
have emasculated the people and induced in them the habit of
simulation. This awful habit has added to the ignorance and the

self-deception of the administrators. Section 124A under which I am happily charged is perhaps the prince among the political sections of the Indian Penal Code designed to suppress the liberty of the citizen. Affection cannot be manufactured or regulated by law. If one has no affection for a person or system, one should be free to give the fullest expression to his disaffection, so long as he does not contemplate, promote or incite to violence. But the section under which Mr. Banker and I are charged is one under which mere promotion of disaffection is a crime. I have studied some of the cases tried under it, and I know that some of the most loved of India's patriots have been convicted under it. I consider it a privilege, therefore, to be charged under that section. I have endeavored to give in their briefest outline the reasons for my disaffection. I have no personal ill-will against any single administrator, much less can I have any disaffection toward the King's person. But I hold it to be a virtue to be disaffected towards a government which in its totality has done more harm to India than any previous system. India is less manly under the British rule than she ever was before. Holding such a belief, I consider it to be a sin to have affection for the system. And it has been a precious privilege for me to be able to write what I have in the various articles tendered in evidence against me.

"In fact, I believe that I have rendered a service to India and England by showing in non-cooperation the way out of the unnatural state in which both are living. In my humble opinion, non-cooperation with evil is as much a duty as is cooperation with good. But in the past, non-cooperation has been deliberately expressed in violence to the evil doer. I am endeavoring to show to my countrymen that violent non-cooperation only multiplies evil and that as evil can only be sustained by violence, withdrawal of support of evil requires complete abstention from violence. Non-violence implies voluntary submission to the penalty for non-cooperation with evil. I am here, therefore, to invite and submit cheerfully to the highest penalty that can be inflicted upon me for what in law is a deliberate crime and what appears to me to be the highest duty of a citizen. The only course open to you, the Judge, is either to resign your post and thus dissociate yourself from evil, if you feel that the law you are called upon to administer is an evil and that in reality I am innocent; or to inflict on me the severest penalty if you believe that the system and the law you are assisting to administer are good for the people of this country and that my activity is therefore injurious to the public weal."

Mr. Banker: "I only want to say that I had the privilege of printing these articles and I plead guilty to the charge. I have got nothing to say as regards the sentence."

The Judge: "Mr. Gandhi, you have made my task easy in one way by pleading guilty to the charge. Nevertheless, what remains, namely, the determination of a just sentence, is perhaps as difficult a proposition as a judge in this country could have to face. The law is no respecter of persons. Nevertheless, it will be impossible to ignore the fact that you are in a different category from any person I have ever tried or am likely to have to try. It would be impossible to ignore the fact that, in the eyes of millions of your countrymen, you are a great patriot and a great leader. Even those who differ from you in politics look upon you as a man of high ideals and of noble and even saintly life. I have to deal with you in one character only. It is not my duty and I do not presume to judge or criticize you in any other character. It is my duty to judge you as a man subject to the law, who by his own admission has broken the law and committed what to an ordinary man must appear to be grave offence against the State. I do not forget that you have consistently preached against violence and that you have on many occasions, as I am willing to believe, done much to prevent violence. But having regard to the nature of your political teaching and the nature of many of those to whom it was addressed, how you could have continued to believe that violence would not be the inevitable consequence, it passes my capacity to understand.

"There are probably few people in India who do not sincerely regret that you should have made it impossible for any government to leave you at liberty. But it is so. I am trying to bal-

ance what is due to you against what appears to me to be necessary in the interest of the public, and I propose in passing sentence
to follow the precedent of a case in many respects similar to this
case that was decided some 12 years ago, I mean the case against
Bal Gangadhar Tilak [17] under the same section. The sentence
that was passed upon him as it finally stood was a sentence of simple imprisonment for six years. You will not consider it unreasonable, I think, that you should be classed with Mr. Tilak, i.e., a
sentence of two years' simple imprisonment on each count of
the charge; six years in all, which I feel it my duty to pass upon
you; and I should like to say in doing so that, if the course of
events in India should make it possible for the Government to
reduce the period and release you, no one will be better pleased
than I."

The Judge to Mr. Banker: "I assume you have been to a large
extent under the influence of your chief. The sentence that I
propose to pass upon you is simple imprisonment for six months
on each of the first two counts, that is to say, simple imprisonment for one year and a fine of a thousand rupees on the third
count, with six months' simple imprisonment in default."

Mr. Gandhi said: "I would say one word. Since you have done
me the honor of recalling the trial of the late Lokamanya Bal
Gangadhar Tilak, I just want to say that I consider it to be the
proudest privilege and honor to be associated with his name. So
far as the sentence itself is concerned, I certainly consider that
it is as light as any judge would inflict on me, and so far as the
whole proceedings are concerned, I must say that I could not
have expected greater courtesy."

A minute passed after the pronouncement of the sentence. The
Judge . . . got up, bowed and departed. Then followed the last
scene—the farewell. Friends and followers, one after another, both
men and women, passed before him. He had a kind word or a
cutting joke to everybody. The leave-taking nearly took one hour.
The military officers with an automobile were waiting for Gandhi.
They were not only courteous to him, but were respectful and
deferential. At about two o'clock, Gandhi entered the car with his

devoted wife, Pandit Malaviya, Banker, and Mrs. Naidu. The eager crowds standing in front of the court-house attempted to shout, "Mahatma Gandhi *ki jai*," but stopped at his request. He was taken to Sabarmati prison.

MRS. GANDHI'S MESSAGE
• by Kasturbai Gandhi

MY DEAR Countrymen and Countrywomen,

My dear husband has been sentenced today to six years simple imprisonment. While I cannot deny that this heavy sentence has to some extent told upon me, I have consoled myself with the thought that it is not beyond our powers to reduce that sentence and release him by our own exertions long before his term of imprisonment is over.

I have no doubt that, if India wakes up and seriously undertakes to carry out the constructive program of the Congress, we shall succeed not only in releasing him, but also in solving to our satisfaction all the three issues for which we have been fighting and suffering for the last 18 months or more.

The remedy, therefore, lies with us. If we fail, the fault will be ours. I, therefore, appeal to all men and women who feel for me and have regard for my husband to wholeheartedly concentrate on the constructive program and make it a success.

Among all the items of the program, he laid the greatest emphasis on the spinning wheel and *khaddar*. Our success in these will not only solve the economic problem of India in relation to the masses, but also free us from our political bondage. In-

• Published in *Young India* March 23, 1922; reprinted with permission. Also in M. K. Gandhi, *Young India, 1919–1922* (New York: B. W. Huebsch, 1923), pp. 1066-67.

dia's first answer, then, to Mr. Gandhi's conviction should be that:

(a) All men and women give up their foreign cloth and adopt khaddar and persuade others to do so.
(b) All women make it a religious duty to spin and produce yarn every day and persuade others to do so.
(c) All merchants cease trading in foreign piece-goods.

Kasturbai Gandhi

MIDNIGHT OPERATION AT SASSOON HOSPITAL

by V. S. Srinivasa Sastri

Gandhi entered Yeravda Central Jail on March 20, 1922. After being confined there for almost two years, he developed acute appendicitis, and was suddenly transferred to the Sassoon Hospital in nearby Poona on January 10, 1924. V. S. Srinivasa Sastri, who described this operation, was head of the Servants of India Society.

DR. V. B. GOKHALE came to me at about 8:45 P.M. just as I was finishing my dinner and told me how the Yeravda authorities had removed Mr. Gandhi to the Sassoon Hospital where he was in charge. He was about to be operated upon for appendicitis. As the case was serious, the patient had been asked whether he would like any doctor friends of his to be sent for. He had mentioned Dr. Dalal of Bombay and Dr. Jivraj Mehta who was in Baroda. Both had been wired to; and attempts had been made, but in

• Reprinted with permission from Chandrashanker Shukla, editor, *Gandhiji As We Know Him* (Bombay: Vora, 1945), pp. 55-60.

vain, to get at Dr. Dalal by means of the phone. Meanwhile, in view of the patient's temperature and pulse, it had been decided to perform the operation immediately, and he was asked whether he would like to have any friends brought to see him. He mentioned me, Dr. Phatak of the Non-cooperation Party, and Mr. N. C. Kelkar. Dr. Gokhale and I started at once and took Dr. Phatak on the way, Mr. Kelkar being away at Satara. On my entering the room we greeted each other, and I enquired how he felt as to the operation. He answered firmly that the doctors had come to a definite conclusion, and that he was content to abide by it. In reply to further inquiry he said that he had full confidence in the medical men about him, and that they had been very kind and very careful. Should there arise any public agitation, he added, then it should be made known that he had no complaint whatsoever to make against the authorities, and that so far as the care of his body went their treatment left nothing to be desired.

Then I enquired if Mrs. Gandhi had been informed of his condition. He said that she did not know the latest developments, but she knew that for some time he had not been well, and he expected to hear from her. He then made enquiries of my wife and of my colleagues in the Servants of India Society, viz., Messrs. Devadhar, Joshi, Patwardhan and Kunzru. "Have your frequent journeys out of India benefited your health?" asked the Mahatma.

Dr. Phatak then read a draft statement to be signed by Mr. Gandhi conveying his consent to the operation. After hearing it once, Mr. Gandhi put on his spectacles and read it himself. Then he said he would like the wording changed, and asked Col. Maddock who was in the room what he thought. The Colonel said that, since Mr. Gandhi knew best how to put it in appropriate language, his own suggestion would not be of much value. Then he [Gandhi] dictated a longish statement which I took down in pencil. It was addressed to Col. Maddock who was to perform the operation. The letter acknowledged the exceeding kindness and attention which he had received from Col. Maddock, the Surgeon-General, and other medical officers and attendants, and stated that he had the utmost confidence in Col. Maddock. It proceeded to thank the Government for their consideration in allowing him to send for his own doctors, but as they could not be got in spite of the best attempts made by Col. Maddock, and as delay would in the opinion of the Colonel involve serious risk, Mr. Gandhi requested him to perform the operation at once. When it was finished I read it out to him once. Then he called Col. Maddock to his side, and I read it again at his desire. Col. Maddock was quite satisfied and remarked: "Of course, you know best how to put it in proper language." He then drew up his knees in posture for signing the paper which he did in pencil. His hand shook very much, and I noticed that he did not dot the "i" at the end. He remarked to the doctor: "See how my hand trembles. You will have to put this right." Col. Maddock answered: "Oh, we will put tons and tons of strength into you."

As the operation room was being got ready, the doctors went out, and I found myself nearly alone with the Mahatma. After a remark or two of a purely personal nature I asked him whether he had anything particular to say. I noticed a touch of eagerness as he replied, as though he was waiting for an opportunity to say something. "If there is an agitation," he said, "for my release after the operation, which I do not wish, let it be on proper lines. My quarrel with the Government is there and will continue so long as the originating causes exist. Of course there can't be any conditions. If Government think they have kept me long enough, they may let me go. That would be honorable. If they think that I am an innocent man and that my motives have been good, that while I have a deep quarrel with the Government I love Englishmen and have many friends amongst them, they may release me. But it must not be on false issues. Any agitation must be kept on proper non-violent lines. Perhaps I have not expressed myself quite well, but you had better put it in your own inimitable style." I mentioned the motions of which notice had been given in the Assembly, and added that though Government might in other circumstances have opposed it, I expected that they would take a different line.

I then pressed him again for a message to his people, his followers or the country. He was surprisingly firm on this subject. He said he was a prisoner of Government and he must observe the prisoner's code of honor scrupulously. He was supposed to be civilly dead. He had no knowledge of outside events, and he could not have anything to do with the public. He had no message.

"How is it then that Mr. Mahomed Ali communicated a message as from you the other day?" The words were scarcely out of my mouth when I regretted them. But recall was impossible. He was obviously astonished at my question and exclaimed: "Mr. Mahomed Ali! A message from me!" Luckily at this point the nurse came in with some articles of apparel for him, and signalled me to depart. In a few minutes he was shifted to the operation room. I sat outside marvelling at the exhibition I had witnessed of highmindedness, forgiveness, chivalry and love transcending ordinary human nature; and what mercy it was that the non-cooperation movement should have had a leader of such serene vision and sensitiveness to honor! The Surgeon-General and the Inspector-General of Prisons were also there. I could see from their faces how anxious they were at the tremendous responsibility that lay on them. They said that the patient had borne the operation very well indeed, that some pus had come out, and that it was a matter of congratulation that the operation had not been delayed any longer. The patient had morphia and was expected to sleep soundly for some time longer, when we dispersed. I learnt from the doctor this morning that the patient's condition was thoroughly satisfactory.

AFTER THE OPERATION

by Mahadev Desai

GOD IN HIS infinite mercy has spared to us our Bapu. These
have been days which will live in our annals. . . .

I have had the privilege of being with Bapu these ten days,
though not of serving him. That privilege is being entirely mo-
nopolized by the hospital nurses. One of them is an Englishwoman of long experience. He cannot help smiling as she ap-
proaches him. One day, she comes talking about her pet dogs, and
draws Bapu into a conversation about the different varieties of
dogs and their usefulness. Another day, she talks about her experience in English and African hospitals, and tells him how she
has lived throughout her life the lesson that her doctors taught
her of never trying to be popular. A third day she decorates the
room with the finest flowers and asks Bapu to admire her work.
There was another nurse much younger, but equally fond of
Bapu, who prided herself on having Mr. Gandhi as her first
"private" patient after passing out as a trained nurse. "Nursing
is not always a joy, at times it is a task," she used to say, "but it
has been a pure joy and a privilege to nurse Mr. Gandhi. The
doctor comes and tells me, 'You did not use to print your reports
like this ever before,' and I tell him straightway, 'Nor had I such
a patient before.'" Another day she told me, "My friends were
chaffing me for getting so fond of Mr. Gandhi; I told them they
would do the same if they had the privilege of serving him."

And the Surgeon's love for him is as undisguised as that of the
nurses. The Civil Surgeon has had letters and telegrams pouring

• Reprinted with permission from C. F. Andrews, *Mahatma Gandhi: His
Own Story* (New York: Macmillan, 1930), pp. 358-62.

in on him to congratulate him for the way in which he was serving Mahatmaji, and it is not without a blush that he says, "How am I to reply to all of them? Shall I do it through the Press?"

I do not know if any one attending Bapu has the slightest consciousness that he is serving a state prisoner. For he is still under a guard. A compelling love chokes all other consciousness.

But why? Even he who has to look upon him as a prisoner seemed scarcely different in his manner from the rest. Col. Murray, the Yeravda Superintendent, came to see Bapu the other day. "Do you think, Mr. Gandhi, I have neglected you? No. I thought I should not disturb you. And as I see you now after some days I find you very much better. The Colonel also assures me you are quickly improving. Your friends remember you. Mr. Gani especially asked me to tell you that he still gets up at four o'clock for prayers. Every one of them is happy, and misses you—I hope they do so permanently." "Thank you, Col. Murray," said Bapu, "but I assure you nothing will please me better than to be up and doing and under your kind care once again at Yeravda." You never could tell, if you did not know him, that a jail superintendent was speaking to one of his prisoners, and you could almost visualize the atmosphere of love created by Bapu in his prison-cell at Yeravda. . . .

And need I say anything concerning the torrents of love that have taken their course to Poona from all the parts of India? Devadas, who should be privileged to be with his father all the time, has to content himself by attending to the numerous letters and telegrams coming day and night enquiring after Bapu's health. But the telegrams and letters do not exhaust these acts of affection. One day residents of far off Tanjore write to say that they did their devotions in a particular temple for Mahatmaji, Hindus from Shiyali, Tirupur, and Dindigul, vie in their love with their Mussalman brethren of Nagore who send special food that has been blessed for him to take. A Parsi sister writes offering her blood if the surgeons thought it necessary to put blood in Mahatmaji; while an English lady writes detailed instructions about Bapu's diet, and Mrs. Gokhale from Bombay writes to say that she will spin an extra couple of hours every day, now that Mahat-maji cannot spin.

One of the constant visitors at the hospital is an Englishman, an old military pensioner, who makes it a point to come every other day with a bouquet of flowers, and gets into Bapu's room unobstructed by any one. It is simply impossible to stop him. Impatiently he rushes to Bapu, shakes his hand, and delivers his message of cheer in a few seconds and walks away. "Cheer up!" he cries "I see that you are very much better than yesterday. I know you must get better. How old are you? Fifty-five. Oh it is nothing. You know I am 82. Get better, please do." One day he stopped and asked, "Can I do anything for you, Mr. Gandhi?" "No," said Bapu. "Please pray for me." "That I will, but tell me if I can do anything for you. Please do tell me. Trust me to be your brother." To which Bapu replies with a smile, "Believe me, I have amongst my friends a number of Englishmen whom I re-gard as more than my brothers." The man is deeply touched, moves out assuring us that he prays thrice every day that Mr. Gandhi may live up to his own age, and also telling us that many Englishmen pray for him, and many officers enquire after him.

The picture would be incomplete if I did not say a word about the illustrious leaders who are now flocking to Poona to see their leader. They did not come until now, as they knew it would not be well to disturb him. A man like Mr. Jayakar [18] says, "I will now come, but will only have a sight of him at a distance; for I must not do anything to tire him in his present weakness." And Pandit Jawaharlal [Nehru] assures Devadas that he will come last of all. The big brother, Shawkat Ali, comes, and insists lovingly that Mahatmaji should not talk to him for fear of his becoming too tired. Pandit Motilal Nehru has no heart to get away without bidding him good-bye a second time, and deliberately misses a train. Lajpat Rai comes, eager to have a talk with him, but stands aside, almost in spite of himself, so that he may not draw him into a talk with him. He visits him again before leaving Poona. There is something in him which is struggling to find expression. Probably it checks the tears, or the tears check it. But ultimately it succeeds and bursts out. Bapu with his inimitable smile says, "Lalaji, the joke is too big for my stomach. I would have a hearty laugh, but for the wound and the stitches." Lalaji, who would have departed otherwise with a heavy heart, goes away with a much lighter heart, not without assuring others also, that we may not be sad now, but rejoice that God in His infinite mercy has blessed us by preserving the life of the one whom we all love best in the world.

Although the operation was successful, an abscess developed and Gandhi was released from prison unconditionally. Since Hindu-Moslem rioting had increased, he went to Delhi and there on September 18, 1924 he began a fast of twenty-one days as an act of penance for the sins of his people. This has been called "The Great Fast," and was reported in articles by C. F. Andrews in Young India, October 9, 16, 1924.

9 GANDHI AND TAGORE

THE POET'S ANXIETY
by M. K. Gandhi

Rabindranath Tagore was perhaps Gandhi's most famous
Indian contemporary, who traveled widely and was well known
abroad. Born in 1861, and thus eight years older than Gandhi,
Tagore became a noted novelist and poet, and received the Nobel
Prize for literature in 1913. He founded and presided over Shantiniketan, a religious community and school in Bengal. Tagore
was referred to, by Gandhi and others, simply as The Poet and
also as Gurudev—a great teacher.

John Haynes Holmes once compared Tagore and Gandhi as
follows: "As different as Erasmus and Luther, these two men,
each in his own distinctive way, labor to bring in that new period
of world history which must mark an epoch in the annals of mankind." Although Gandhi and Tagore were great enough men to
remain good friends all of their lives—and had the services of C. F.
Andrews to act as an intermediary between them for a quarter of
a century—they had their sharp differences. Andrews felt that
there was, between these two men, a "difference of temperament

• Published in Young India June 1, 1921; reprinted with permission. Also in
M. K. Gandhi, Young India, 1919–1922 (New York: B. W. Huebsch, 1923),
pp. 608-13.

so wide that it was extremely difficult to arrive at a common intellectual understanding, though the moral ties of friendship remained entirely unbroken."

During the early satyagraha campaign, Tagore detected excesses
and frankly told Gandhi so in three different letters. Gandhi answered these publicly in the columns of Young India on June 1,
1921. Tagore in a sense replied in a manifesto entitled "The Call
of Truth" published in the Modern Review in October 1921.
Gandhi promptly answered this article in Young India on October
13, 1921.

THE POET OF ASIA, as Lord Hardinge called Dr. Tagore, is
fast becoming, if he has not already become, the Poet of the
world. Increasing prestige has brought him increasing responsibility. His greatest service to India must be his poetic interpretation of India's message to the world. The Poet is therefore sincerely anxious that India should deliver no false or feeble message
in her name. He is naturally jealous of his country's reputation.
He says he has striven hard to find himself in tune with the present movement. He confesses that he is baffled. He can find nothing for his lyre in the din and the bustle of Non-cooperation. In
three forceful letters he has endeavored to give expression to his
misgivings, and he has come to the conclusion that Non-cooperation is not dignified enough for the India of his vision, that it is
a doctrine of negation and despair. He fears that it is a doctrine
of separation, exclusiveness, narrowness and negation.

No Indian can feel anything but pride in the Poet's exquisite
jealousy of India's honor. It is good that he should have sent to
us his misgivings in language at once beautiful and clear.

In all humility, I shall endeavor to answer the Poet's doubts.
I may fail to convince him or the reader who may have been
touched by his eloquence, but I would like to assure him and
India that Non-cooperation in conception is not any of the things
he fears, and he need have no cause to be ashamed of his country
for having adopted Non-cooperation. If, in actual application, it

appears in the end to have failed, it will be no more the fault of the doctrine, than it would be of Truth, if those who claim to apply it in practice do not appear to succeed. Non-cooperation may have come in advance of its time. India and the world must then wait, but there is no choice for India save between violence and Non-cooperation.

Nor need the Poet fear that Non-cooperation is intended to erect a Chinese wall between India and the West. On the contrary, Non-cooperation is intended to pave the way to real, honorable and voluntary cooperation based on mutual respect and trust. The present struggle is being waged against compulsory cooperation, against one-sided combination, against the armed imposition of modern methods of exploitation masquerading under the name of civilization.

Non-cooperation is a protest against an unwitting and unwilling participation in evil.

The Poet's concern is largely about the students. He is of opinion that they should not have been called upon to give up Government schools before they had other schools to go to. Here I must differ from him. I have never been able to make a fetish of literary training. My experience has proved to my satisfaction that literary training by itself adds not an inch to one's moral height and that character-building is independent of literary training. I am firmly of opinion that the Government schools have unmanned us, rendered us helpless and Godless. They have filled us with discontent, and providing no remedy for the discontent, have made us despondent. They have made us what we were intended to become—clerks and interpreters. A Government builds its prestige upon the apparently voluntary association of the governed. And if it was wrong to cooperate with the Government in keeping us slaves, we were bound to begin with those institutions in which our association appeared to be most voluntary. The youth of a nation are its hope. I hold that, as soon as we discovered that the system of Government was wholly, or mainly evil, it became sinful for us to associate our children with it.

It is no argument against the soundness of the proposition laid down by me that the vast majority of the students went back after the first flush of enthusiasm. Their recantation is proof rather of the extent of our degradation than of the wrongness of the step. Experience has shown that the establishment of national schools has not resulted in drawing many more students. The strongest and the truest of them came out without any national schools to fall back upon, and I am convinced that these first withdrawals are rendering service of the highest order.

But the Poet's protest against the calling out of the boys is really a corollary to his objection to the very doctrine of Noncooperation. He has a horror of everything negative. His whole soul seems to rebel against the negative commandments of religion. I must give his objection in his own inimitable language. "R in support of the present movement has often said to me that passion for rejection is a stronger power in the beginning than the acceptance of an ideal. Though I know it to be a fact, I cannot take it as a truth. . . . Brahmavidya [1] in India has for its object *Mukti* (emancipation), while Buddhism has *Nirvana* (extinction). *Mukti* draws our attention to the positive and *Nirvana* to the negative side of truth. Therefore, he emphasized the fact of *duhkha* (misery) which had to be avoided and the Brahmavidya emphasized the fact of *Ananda* (joy) which had to be attained." In these and kindred passages, the reader will find the key to the Poet's mentality. In my humble opinion, rejection is as much an ideal as the acceptance of a thing. It is as necessary to reject untruth as it is to accept truth. All religions teach that two opposite forces act upon us and that the human endeavor consists in a series of eternal rejections and acceptances. Non-cooperation with evil is as much a duty as cooperation with good. I venture to suggest that the Poet has done an unconscious injustice to Buddhism in describing *Nirvana* as merely a negative state. I make bold to say that *Mukti* (emancipation) is as much a negative state as *Nirvana*. Emancipation from or extinction of the bondage of the flesh leads to *Ananda* (eternal bliss). Let me close this part of my argument by drawing attention to the fact that the final word of the Upanishads (Brahmavidya) is *Not. Neti* [2] was the best description the authors of the Upanishads were able to find for Brahman.

I therefore think that the Poet has been unnecessarily alarmed at the negative aspect of Non-cooperation. We had lost the power of saying "no." It had become disloyal, almost sacrilegious to say "no" to the Government. This deliberate refusal to cooperate is like the necessary weeding process that a cultivator has to resort to before he sows. Weeding is as necessary to agriculture as sowing. Indeed, even whilst the crops are growing, the weeding fork, as every husbandman knows, is an instrument almost of daily use. The nation's Non-cooperation is an invitation to the Government to cooperate with it on its own terms as is every nation's right and every good government's duty. Non-cooperation is the nation's notice that it is no longer satisfied to be in tutelage. The nation has taken to the harmless (for it), natural and religious doctrine of Non-cooperation in the place of the unnatural and irreligious doctrine of violence. And if India is ever to attain the Swaraj of the Poet's dream, she will do so only by Non-violent Non-cooperation. Let him deliver his message of peace to the world, and feel confident that India, through her Non-cooperation, if she remains true to her pledge, will have exemplified his message. Non-cooperation is intended to give the very meaning to patriotism that the Poet is yearning after. An India prostrate at the feet of Europe can give no hope to humanity. An India awakened and free has a message of peace and goodwill to a groaning world. Non-cooperation is designed to supply her with a platform from which she will preach the message.

THE CALL OF TRUTH

by Rabindranath Tagore

... THE MOVEMENT, which has now succeeded the Swadeshi agitation, is ever so much greater and has moreover extended its influence all over India. Previously, the vision of our political leaders had never reached beyond the English-knowing classes, because the country meant for them only that bookish aspect of it which is to be found in the pages of the Englishman's history. Such a country was merely a mirage born of vaporings in the English language, in which flitted about thin shades of Burke and Gladstone, Mazzini and Garibaldi. Nothing resembling self-sacrifice or true feeling for their countrymen was visible. At this juncture, Mahatma Gandhi came and stood at the cottage door of the destitute millions, clad as one of themselves, and talking to them in their own language. Here was the truth at last, not a mere quotation out of a book. So the name of Mahatma, which was given to him, is his true name. Who else has felt so many men of India to be of his own flesh and blood? At the touch of Truth the pent-up forces of the soul are set free. As soon as true love stood at India's door, it flew open; all hesitation and holding back vanished. Truth awakened truth.

Stratagem in politics is a barren policy—this was a lesson of which we were sorely in need. All honor to the Mahatma, who made visible to us the power of Truth. But reliance on tactics is so ingrained in the cowardly and the weak, that, in order to eradicate it, the very skin must be sloughed off. Even today, our worldly-wise men cannot get rid of the idea of utilizing the Mahatma as a secret and more ingenious move in their political gam-

• Reprinted from *The Modern Review* (Calcutta), October 1921, pp. 423-33. Only a portion of the essay is reproduced here.

ble. With their minds corroded by untruth, they cannot understand what an important thing it is that the Mahatma's supreme
love should have drawn forth the country's love. The thing that
has happened is nothing less than the birth of freedom. It is the
gain by the country of itself. In it there is no room for any
thought, as to where the Englishman is, or is not. This love is
self-expression. It is pure affirmation. It does not argue with negation; it has no need for argument.

Some notes of the music of this wonderful awakening of India
by love, floated over to me across the seas. It was a great joy to
me to think that the call of this festivity of awakening would
come to each one of us; and that the true *shakti* [3] of India's spirit,
in all its multifarious variety, would at last find expression. This
thought came to me because I have always believed that in such
a way India would find its freedom. . . .

So, in the expectation of breathing the buoyant breezes of this
new found freedom, I came home rejoicing. But what I found
in Calcutta when I arrived depressed me. An oppressive atmosphere seemed to burden the land. Some outside compulsion
seemed to be urging one and all to talk in the same strain, to work
at the same mill. When I wanted to inquire, to discuss, my well-
wishers clapped their hands over my lips saying: "not now, not
now. Today, in the atmosphere of the country, there is a spirit
of persecution, which is not that of armed force, but something
still more alarming, because it is invisible." I found, further, that
those who had their doubts as to the present activities, if they
happened to whisper them out, however cautiously, however
guardedly, felt some admonishing hand clutching them within.
There was a newspaper which one day had the temerity to disap-
prove, in a feeble way, of the burning of [foreign] cloth. The
very next day the editor was shaken out of his balance by the
agitation of his readers. How long would it take for the fire which
was burning cloth to reduce his paper to ashes? The sight that
met my eye was, on the one hand, people immensely busy; on
the other, intensely afraid. What I heard on every side was, that
reason, and culture as well, must be closured. It was only necessary

to cling to an unquestioning obedience. Obedience to whom? To some *mantra*, some unreasoned creed?

And why this obedience? Here again comes that same greed, our spiritual enemy. There dangles before the country the bait of getting a thing of inestimable value, dirt cheap and in double-quick time. It is like the faqir with his goldmaking trick. With such a lure men cast so readily to the winds their independent judgment and wax so mightily wroth with those who will not do likewise. So easy is it to overpower, in the name of outside freedom, the inner freedom of man. The most deplorable part of it is that so many do not even honestly believe in the hope that they swear by. "It will serve to make our countrymen do what is necessary"—say they. Evidently, according to them, the India which once declared: "In truth is victory, not in untruth"—that India would not have been fit for Swaraj. . . .

The Mahatma has won the heart of India with his love; for that we have all acknowledged his sovereignty. He has given us a vision of the *shakti* of truth; for that our gratitude to him is unbounded. We read about truth in books; we talk about it; but it is indeed a red-letter day when we see it face to face. Rare is the moment, in many a long year, when such good fortune happens. We can make and break Congresses every other day. It is at any time possible for us to stump the country preaching politics in English. But the golden rod which can awaken our country in Truth and Love is not a thing which can be manufactured by the nearest goldsmith. To the wielder of that rod our profound salutation! But if, having seen truth, our belief in it is not confirmed, what is the good of it all? Our mind must acknowledge the truth of the intellect, just as our heart does the truth of love. No Congress or other outside institution succeeded in touching the heart of India. It was roused only by the touch of love. Having had such a clear vision of this wonderful power of Truth, are we to cease to believe in it, just where the attainment of *Swaraj* is concerned? Has the truth, which was needed in the process of awakening, to be got rid of in the process of achievement?

. . . From our master, the Mahatma—may our devotion to him

never grow less!—we must learn the truth of love in all its purity, but the science and art of building up *Swaraj* is a vast subject. Its pathways are difficult to traverse and take time. For this task, aspiration and emotion must be there, but no less must study and thought be there likewise. For it, the economist must think, the mechanic must labor, the educationist and statesman must teach and contrive. In a word, the mind of the country must exert itself in all directions. Above all, the spirit of inquiry throughout the whole country must be kept intact and untrammelled, its mind not made timid or inactive by compulsion, open or secret. . . .

Consider the burning of cloth, heaped up before the very eyes of our motherland shivering and ashamed in her nakedness. What is the nature of the call to do this? Is it not another instance of a magical formula? The question of using or refusing cloth of a particular manufacture belongs mainly to economic science. The discussion of the matter by our countrymen should have been in the language of economics. If the country has really come to such a habit of mind that precise thinking has become impossible for it, then our very first fight should be against such a fatal habit, to the temporary exclusion of all else if need be. Such a habit would clearly be the original sin from which all our ills are flowing. But far from this, we take the course of confirming ourselves in it by relying on the magical formula that foreign cloth is "impure." Thus economics is bundled out and a fictitious moral dictum dragged into its place.

Untruth is impure in any circumstances, not merely because it may cause us material loss, but even when it does not; for it makes our inner nature unclean. This is a moral law and belongs to a higher plane. But if there be anything wrong in wearing a particular kind of cloth, that would be an offense against economics, or hygiene, or aesthetics, but certainly not against morality. Some urge that any mistake which brings sorrow to body or mind is a moral wrong. To which I reply that sorrow follows in the train of every mistake. A mistake in geometry may make a road too long, or a foundation weak, or a bridge dangerous. But mathematical mistakes cannot be cured by moral maxims. If a student makes a mistake in his geometry problem and his exercise book is torn up in consequence, the problem will nevertheless remain unsolved until attacked by geometrical methods. But what if the school-master comes to the conclusion that unless the exercise books are condemned and destroyed, his boys will never realize the folly of their mistakes? If such conclusion be well-founded, then I can only repeat that the reformation of such moral weakness of these particular boys should take precedence over all other lessons, otherwise there is no hope of their becoming men in the future.

The command to burn our foreign clothes has been laid on us. I, for one, am unable to obey it. Firstly, because I conceive it to be my very first duty to put up a valiant fight against this terrible habit of blindly obeying orders, and this fight can never be carried on by our people being driven from one injunction to another. Secondly, I feel that the clothes to be burnt are not mine, but belong to those who most sorely need them. If those who are going naked should have given us the mandate to burn, it would, at least, have been a case of self-immolation and the crime of incendiarism would not lie at our door. But how can we expiate the sin of the forcible destruction of clothes which might have gone to women whose nakedness is actually keeping them prisoners, unable to stir out of the privacy of their homes?

I have said repeatedly and must repeat once more that we cannot afford to lose our mind for the sake of any external gain. Where Mahatma Gandhi has declared war against the tyranny of the machine which is oppressing the whole world, we are all enrolled under his banner. But we must refuse to accept as our ally the illusion-haunted magic-ridden slave-mentality that is at the root of all the poverty and insult under which our country groans. Here is the enemy itself, on whose defeat alone *Swaraj* within and without can come to us.

The time, moreover, has arrived when we must think of one thing more, and that is this. The awakening of India is a part of the awakening of the world. The door of the New Age has been flung open at the trumpet blast of a great war. We have read in

the Mahabharata how the day of self-revelation had to be preceded by a year of retirement. The same has happened in the
world today. Nations had attained nearness to each other without
being aware of it, that is to say, the outside fact was there, but it
had not penetrated into the mind. At the shock of the war, the
truth of it stood revealed to mankind. The foundation of modern,
that is Western, civilization was shaken; and it has become evident that the convulsion is neither local nor temporary, but has
traversed the whole earth and will last until the shocks between
man and man, which have extended from continent to continent,
can be brought to rest, and a harmony be established. . . .

THE GREAT SENTINEL

•

by M. K. Gandhi

THE BARD of Shantiniketan has contributed to the *Modern
Review* a brilliant essay on the present movement. It is a series
of word pictures which he alone can paint. It is an eloquent protest against authority, slave mentality or whatever description one
gives of blind acceptance of a passing mania whether out of fear
or hope. It is a welcome and wholesome reminder to all workers
that we must not be impatient, we must not impose authority
no matter how great. The poet tells us summarily to reject
anything and everything that does not appeal to our reason
or heart. If we would gain Swaraj, we must stand for Truth as
we know it at any cost. A reformer who is enraged because his
message is not accepted must retire to the forest to learn how to
watch, wait and pray. With all this one must heartily agree, and
the Poet deserves the thanks of his countrymen for standing up

• Published in *Young India*, October 13, 1921; reprinted with permission.
Also in M. K. Gandhi, *Young India, 1919–1922* (New York: B. W. Huebsch,
1923), pp. 668-75.

for Truth and Reason. There is no doubt that our last state will be worse than our first, if we surrender our reason into somebody's keeping. And I would feel extremely sorry to discover that the country had unthinkingly and blindly followed all I had said or done. I am quite conscious of the fact that blind surrender to love is often more mischievous than a forced surrender to the lash of the tyrant. There is hope for the slave of the brute, none for that of love. Love is needed to strengthen the weak, love becomes tyrannical when it exacts obedience from an unbeliever. To mutter a *mantra* without knowing its value is unmanly. It is good, therefore, that the Poet has invited all who are slavishly *mimicking* the call of the *charkha* [4] boldly to declare their revolt. His essay serves as a warning to us all who in our impatience are betrayed into intolerance or even violence against those who differ from us. I regard the Poet as a sentinel warning us against the approach of enemies called Bigotry, Lethargy, Intolerance, Ignorance, Inertia, and other members of that brood.

But whilst I agree with all that the Poet has said as to the necessity of watchfulness lest we cease to think, I must not be understood to endorse the proposition that there is any such blind obedience on a large scale in the country today. I have again and again appealed to reason, and let me assure him that if happily the country has come to believe in the spinning wheel as the giver of plenty, it has done so after laborious thinking, after great hesitation. I am not sure that even now educated India has assimilated the truth underlying the *charkha*. He must not mistake the surface dirt for the substance underneath. Let him go deeper and see for himself, whether the *charkha* has been accepted from blind faith or from reasoned necessity.

I do indeed ask the poet and the page to spin the wheel as a sacrament. When there is war, the poet lays down the lyre, the lawyer his law reports, the schoolboy his books. The poet will sing the true note after the war is over, the lawyer will have occasion to go to his law books when people have time to fight among themselves. When a house is on fire, all the inmates go out, and each one takes up a bucket to quench the fire. When all about me are dying for want of food, the only occupation permissible to me is to feed the hungry. It is my conviction that India is a house on fire because its manhood is being daily scorched, it is dying of hunger because it has no work to buy food with. Khulna [5] is starving not because the people cannot work, but because they have no work. The Ceded Districts [6] are passing successively through a fourth famine. Orissa is a land suffering from chronic famines. Our cities are not India. India lives in her seven and a half lacs of villages, and the cities live upon the villages. They do not bring their wealth from other countries. The city people are brokers and commission agents for the big houses of Europe, America and Japan. The cities have cooperated with the latter in the bleeding process that has gone on for the past two hundred years. It is my belief based on experience that India is daily growing poorer. The circulation about her feet and legs has almost stopped. And if we do not take care, she will collapse altogether.

To a people famishing and idle, the only acceptable form in which God can dare appear is work and promise of food as wages. God created man to work for his food, and said that those who ate without work were thieves. Eighty per cent of India are compulsorily thieves half the year. Is it any wonder if India has become one vast prison? Hunger is the argument that is driving India to the spinning wheel. The call of the spinning wheel is the noblest of all. Because it is the call of love. And love is Swaraj. The spinning wheel will "curb the mind" when the time is spent on necessary physical labor can be said to do so. We must think of millions who are today less than animals, who are almost in a dying state. The spinning wheel is the reviving draught for the millions of our dying countrymen and countrywomen. "Why should I who have no need to work for food, spin?" may be the question asked. Because I am eating what does not belong to me. I am living on the spoliation of my countrymen. Trace the course of every piece that finds its way into your pocket, and you will realize the truth of what I write. Swaraj has no meaning for the millions if they do not know how to employ their enforced idle-

ness. The attainment of this Swaraj is possible within a short time
and it is so possible only by the revival of the spinning wheel.

I do want growth. I do want self-determination. I do want
freedom, but I want all these for the soul. I doubt if the steel
age is an advance upon the flint age. I am indifferent. It is the evolution of the soul to which the intellect and all our faculties have
to be devoted. I have no difficulty in imagining the possibility of
a man armored after the modern style making some lasting and
new discovery for mankind, but I have less difficulty in imagining
the possibility of a man having nothing but a bit of flint and a
nail for lighting his path or his matchlock ever singing new hymns
of praise and delivering to an aching world a message of peace
and good will upon earth. A plea for the spinning wheel is a plea
for recognizing the dignity of labor.

I claim that in losing the spinning wheel we lost our left lung.
We are therefore suffering from galloping consumption. The
restoration of the wheel arrests the progress of the fell disease.
There are certain things which all must do in certain climes. The
spinning wheel is the thing which all must turn in the Indian
clime for the transition stage at any rate and the vast majority
must for all time.

It was our love of foreign cloth that ousted the wheel from its
position of dignity. Therefore I consider it a sin to wear foreign
cloth. I must confess that I do not draw a sharp or any distinction between economics and ethics. Economics that hurt the
moral well-being of an individual or a nation are immoral and
therefore sinful. Thus the economics that permit one country to
prey upon another are immoral. It is sinful to buy and use articles made by sweated labor. It is sinful to eat American wheat
and let my neighbor the grain dealer starve for want of custom.
Similarly it is sinful for me to wear the latest finery of Regent
Street, when I know that if I had but worn the things woven by
the neighboring spinners and weavers, that would have clothed
me, and fed and clothed them. On the knowledge of my sin
bursting upon me, I must consign the foreign garments to the
flames and thus purify myself, and thenceforth rest content with

the rough *Khadi* made by my neighbors. On knowing that my neighbors may not, having given up the occupation, take kindly to the spinning wheel, I must take it up myself and thus make it popular.

I venture to suggest to the Poet that the clothes I ask him to burn must be and are his. If they had to his knowledge belonged to the poor or the ill-clad, he would long ago have restored to the poor what was theirs. In burning my foreign clothes I burn my shame. I must refuse to insult the naked by giving them clothes they do not need, instead of giving them work which they sorely need. I will not commit the sin of becoming their patron, but on learning that I had assisted in impoverishing them, I would give them a privileged position and give them neither crumbs nor cast off clothing, but the best of my food and clothes and associate myself with them in work.

Nor is the scheme of Non-cooperation or Swadeshi an exclusive doctrine. My modesty has prevented me from declaring from the house top that the message of Non-cooperation, Non-violence and Swadeshi is a message to the world. It must fall flat, if it does not bear fruit in the soil where it has been delivered. At the present moment India has nothing to share with the world save her degradation, pauperism and plagues. Is it her ancient Shastras that we would send to the world? Well, they are printed in many editions, and an incredulous and idolatrous world refuses to look at them, because we, the heirs and custodians, do not live them. Before, therefore, I can think of sharing with the world, I must possess. Our Non-cooperation is neither with the English nor with the West. Our Non-cooperation is with the system the English have established, with the material civilization and its attendant greed and exploitation of the weak. Our Non-cooperation is a retirement within ourselves. Our Non-cooperation is a refusal to cooperate with the English administrators on their own terms. We say to them, "Come and cooperate with us on our terms, and it will be well for us, for you and the world." We must refuse to be lifted off our feet. A drowning man cannot save others. In order to be fit to save others, we must try to save ourselves. Indian nationalism is not exclusive, nor aggressive, nor destructive. It is health-giving, religious and therefore humanitarian. India must learn to live before she can aspire to die for humanity. The mice which helplessly find themselves between the cat's teeth acquire no merit from their enforced sacrifice.

True to his poetical instinct the Poet lives for the morrow and would have us do likewise. He presents to our admiring gaze the beautiful picture of the birds early in the morning singing hymns of praise as they soar into the sky. These birds had their day's food and soared with rested wings in whose veins new blood had flown during the previous night. But I have had the pain of watching birds who for want of strength could not be coaxed even into a flutter of their wings. The human bird under the Indian sky gets up weaker than when he pretended to retire. For millions it is an eternal vigil or an eternal trance. It is an indescribably painful state which has to be experienced to be realized. I have found it impossible to sooth suffering patients with a song from Kabir.[7] The hungry millions ask for one poem—invigorating food. They cannot be given it. They must earn it. And they can earn it only by the sweat of their brow. . . .

THE TWO OUTSTANDING FIGURES

by Jawaharlal Nehru

TAGORE AND GANDHI have undoubtedly been the two outstanding and dominating figures of India in this first half of the twentieth century. It is instructive to compare and contrast them. No two persons could be so different from one another in their make-up or temperaments. Tagore, the aristocratic artist, turned

• Reprinted with permission from Jawaharlal Nehru, The Discovery of India (New York: John Day, 1946), pp. 342-43.

democrat with proletarian sympathies, represented essentially the cultural tradition of India, the tradition of accepting life in the fullness thereof and going through it with song and dance. Gandhi, more a man of the people, almost the embodiment of the Indian peasant, represented the other ancient tradition of India, that of renunciation and asceticism. And yet Tagore was primarily the man of thought, Gandhi of concentrated and ceaseless activity. Both, in their different ways, had a world outlook, and both were at the same time wholly India. They seemed to represent different but harmonious aspects of India and to complement one another.

I OWE MUCH
by M. K. Gandhi

In 1931 in Calcutta was published a beautiful "Golden Book of Tagore" in celebration of his seventieth birthday. Gandhi was one of the sponsors of this volume. His message led the pages of tributes from world figures.

IN COMMON with thousands of his countrymen I owe much to one who by his poetic genius and singular purity of life has raised India in the estimation of the world. But I owe also more. Did he not harbor in Shantiniketan the inmates of my Ashram who had preceded me from South Africa? The other ties and memories are too sacred to bear mention in a public tribute.

· Reprinted from *The Golden Book of Tagore* (Calcutta, 1931).

A MEASURE OF THEIR STATURE

• by K. R. Kripalani

Tagore died in 1941. K. R. Kripalani, in an essay on the two men, gives a fitting description of their last contacts.

THEIR LAST MEETING—the most touching and beautiful of all their meetings—took place in Shantiniketan in February 1940, when "this great soul in a beggar's garb," to quote the poet's description of him, came to see him. A few months later when Tagore lay in Calcutta, hovering between life and death, Gandhi sent his personal secretary, Mahadev Desai, to see him. As Mahadev Desai handed to him Gandhi's letter, the poet's hands shook with emotion and tears trickled down his cheeks. He who never wept in sorrow wept in joy. The friendship of these two to the end, despite the many differences that seemed to divide them, will be remembered by their countrymen as an undying testimony to their greatness. Had one of them been a little less great, they would have fallen out. It was so easy to misunderstand each other, with their sensibilities and their ways of living so sharply in contrast, their fields of activity so widely separated, and each surrounded by admirers, not as tolerant and understanding as the masters. That they did not do so is a measure of their stature.

• Reprinted with permission from K. R. Kripalani, *Gandhi, Tagore and Nehru* (Bombay: Hind Kitabs, 1947), pp. 24-25.

10 THE SALT MARCH
(1930)

TOWARD DANDI

by H. S. L. Polak

In the years following 1922 the nationalist movement was at a low ebb. In 1924, after his convalescence and release from prison, Gandhi conducted a dramatic twenty-one-day fast to promote Hindu-Moslem unity, but he did not consider the time ripe for a revival of civil disobedience. In 1927 the British government appointed the Simon Commission to make recommendations for further political reform in India, but as the Commission contained no Indian members it was boycotted by Indian nationalists. In 1928, in the Bardoli district near Bombay, a satyagraha campaign against a tax increase won support throughout the country and achieved its aim by non-violent means. Many in the Congress were pressing for action on a wider scale; some even advocated armed rebellion. Gandhi, however, was cautious. At his suggestion, late in 1928 the Congress resolved that unless within one year the British agreed to give India a constitution and Dominion status, a third nation-wide civil disobedience movement would be launched. When the British failed to meet its terms the Congress, in December 1929, at last announced that its goal was full inde-

• Reprinted with permission from H. S. L. Polak, *Mahatma Gandhi: The Man and His Mission* (Madras: Natesan, 8th ed., 1931[?]), pp. 106-16.

pendence. It fixed January twenty-sixth as National Independence Day, and in effect authorized Gandhi to decide the time and method of a new campaign of civil disobedience.

The manufacture of salt was a government monopoly. Accordingly Gandhi decided to inaugurate the campaign by leading a march to the sea in order to take salt illegally from its waters— an action which symbolized the Indians' refusal to recognize the authority of the government. On March 2, 1930 Gandhi warned the Viceroy, Lord Irwin, of his intentions, saying, "If my letter makes no appeal to your heart, on the eleventh day of this month I shall proceed with such co-workers of the Ashram as I can take, to disregard the provisions of the Salt Laws. I regard this tax to be the most iniquitous of all from the poor man's standpoint. As the Independence movement is essentially for the poorest in the land, the beginning will be made with this evil." The Viceroy's secretary replied: "His Excellency . . . regrets to learn that you contemplate a course of action which is clearly bound to involve violation of the law and danger to the public peace." Accordingly the famous march was begun.

TRUE TO HIS DECLARATION, just a little before daybreak on the morning of the 12th, Mahatma Gandhi with his 79 volunteers, all students of the Vidyapith,[1] left the Ashram on a campaign of civil disobedience. Their destination was the village of Dandi on the sea coast near Jalalpur [2] where Gandhi was to break the law regarding the manufacture of salt. Streams of Khaddar-clad men and women had flowed to the Ashram all night through to have a darshan [3] of Mahatmaji and witness the great march. Among those were journalists and cameramen from far and near and correspondents of some British papers as well.

"The scenes that preceded, accompanied and followed this great national event," wrote the Bombay Chronicle, "were so enthusiastic, magnificent and soul-stirring that indeed they beggar description. Never was the wave of patriotism so powerful in the hearts of mankind, as it was on this great occasion which is bound to go down to the chapters of the history of India's national freedom as a great beginning of a Great Movement. . . ."

Mahatmaji with a gentle smile betokening his undying faith in the justice of the cause he was pursuing and in the success of the great campaign he had embarked upon, began at the head of the procession to march with quick steps and unfaltering. The pace was a trifle too fast for his health and age, wrote the correspondent: "He was carrying a long stick in his hand obviously for support. The whole army was marching in a perfectly disciplined manner. The agile general in the front was indeed a source of inspiration to all. The army passed all along the distance of ten miles up to Aslali between the densely packed rows of people who were standing in their places for hours together, eager for the 'darshan' of India's great General. Ahmedabad had had on the occasion one of its hugest processions during living memory. With the possible exception of children and decrepits, every resident of the city must have watched the great procession which was at least two miles in length. Those who could not find a standing place in the streets through which the army marched had made use of housetops and galleries, open walls and trees and every conceivable place they could get hold of. The whole city seemed to be *enfete* on this historic occasion. The cries of 'Gandhi-ki-Jai' were rending the skies all along the march. . . ."

As the procession marched through village after village, Mahatmaji spoke at all the halting stations, urging the people to take to Khaddar, to stop drinking, to give up cooperation with Government and join the ranks of the Satyagrahis. At Aslali he told his followers that he would either die on the way or else keep away from the Ashram until Swaraj had been won. This was an expression of despair, said his critics; while his own followers were moved to their depths. "I have no intention of returning to the Ashram until I succeed in getting the salt tax repealed," said Mr. Gandhi. He exhorted villagers to take to the spinning wheel, to look to the sanitation of the village and to treat the untouchables with brotherly love. He urged them to join his movement to break the salt monopoly of Government, as this would be a step forward on the way to Swaraj. Volunteers were enrolling themselves in the hundreds in the cause of civil disobedience and the headmen of several villages were resigning their jobs and joining the campaign. The arrest of Mr. Gandhi was supposed to be imminent and Mahatmaji, as might be expected, was well prepared for it and he gave instruction that his place should be taken up by Abbas Tyabjee,[4] the aged friend, who had stood by Gandhi through all the years of Non-cooperation. The fight threatened to be well nigh grim; and as Sir P. C. Ray said, "Mahatma Gandhi's historic march was like the exodus of Israelites under Moses. Until the Seer seized the promised land, he won't turn his back." . . .

Gandhi and his party reached Dandi on the morning of the 5th April. Mrs. Sarojini Naidu had also gone there to see the Mahatma. Interviewed by the Associated Press immediately after his arrival at Dandi, Gandhiji said: "God be thanked for what may be termed the happy ending of the first stage in this, for me at least, the final struggle for freedom. I cannot withhold my compliments from the Government for the policy of complete non-interference adopted by them throughout the march. After the graceless and childish performance in the matter of Mr. Vallabhai's arrest and imprisonment and equally unprovoked arrest and imprisonment of Mr. Sen Gupta,[5] I was wholly unprepared for this exemplary non-interference. I am not so foolish as to imagine that the Government has suddenly lost their proved capacity for provoking popular resentment and then punishing with frightfulness. I wish I could believe this non-interference was due to any real change of heart or policy. The wanton disregard shown by them to popular feeling in the Legislative Assembly and their high-handed action leave no room for doubt that the policy of heartless exploitation of India is to be persisted in at any cost, and so the only interpretation I can put upon this non-interference is that the British Government, powerful though it is, is sensitive to world opinion which will not tolerate repression of extreme political agitation which civil disobedience undoubtedly is, so long as disobedience remains civil and therefore necessarily non-violent.

"It remains to be seen whether the Government will tolerate as they have tolerated the march, the actual breach of the salt laws by countless people from tomorrow. I expect extensive popular response to the resolution of the Working Committee (of the Indian National Congress). I have seen nothing to warrant the cancellation of the notice I have already issued that all Committees and organizations throughout the length and breadth of the land are free, if they are prepared to commence from tomorrow Civil Disobedience in respect of the salt laws. God willing, I expect with my companions (volunteers) to commence actual Civil Disobedience at 6:30 tomorrow morning. Sixth April has been to us since its culmination in Jallianwala massacre a day for penance and purification. We therefore commence it with prayer and fasting. I hope the whole of India will observe the National Week commencing from tomorrow in the spirit in which it was conceived. I am positive that the greater the dedication to the country's cause and the greater the purification, the speedier will be the glorious end for which the millions of India consciously or unconsciously are striving."

Gandhi's prayer on the morning of the 6th was more than usually solemn. In the course of his speech he observed that if he was arrested, they should take orders from Mr. Abbas Tyabjee and if he, too, was removed, from Mrs. Sarojini Naidu. He paid a tribute to both these leaders and asked the volunteers implicitly to obey them. Gandhiji concluded his address by asking the visitors not to offer Satyagraha that day, but to do so the next day. He considered his offer of Civil Disobedience as a great Yagna [6] and he evidently did not want demonstrations, proceeding out of motives other than spiritual, to be associated with this great movement.

Soon after prayers, Mr. Gandhi with his 84 volunteers of the Gujerat Vidyapith [7] and Saheth Punjabhai [8] of Ahmedabad, proceeded exactly at 6 in the morning for a bath in the sea. A large crowd accompanied the party. Gandhi was walking at a slow pace in grave solemnity and entered the water of the sea amidst loud cries of "Mahatma Gandhi-ki-jai."

Gandhi was leaning on Miss Abbas Tyabji's shoulder, and was accompanied by Mrs. Sarojini Naidu. Then Gandhi and his volunteers proceeded to break the salt law by picking up the salt lying on the seashore. Mrs. Sarojini Naidu hailed the Mahatma by calling him "law-breaker." No policemen appeared on the scene when Gandhi and his volunteers broke the salt law.

Immediately after breaking the salt law, Mr. Gandhi issued the following press statement: "Now that the technical or ceremonial breach of the salt law has been committed, it is now open to any one who would take the risk of prosecution under the salt law to manufacture salt wherever he wishes and wherever it is convenient. My advice is that workers should everywhere manufacture salt, and where they know how to prepare clean salt, make use of it and instruct the villagers likewise, telling the villager at the same time that he runs the risk of being prosecuted. In other words, the villagers should be fully instructed as to the incidence of the salt tax, and the manner of breaking the laws and regulations connected with it so as to have the salt tax repealed.

"It should be made absolutely clear to the villagers that the breach is open, and in no way stealthy. This condition being known, they may manufacture salt or help themselves to the salt manufactured by Nature in creeks and pits near the seashore, use it for themselves and their cattle, and sell it to those who will buy it, it being well understood that all such people are committing a breach of the salt law and running the risk of a prosecution, or even without a prosecution, are to be subjected by so-called salt officers to harassment.

"This war against the salt tax should be continued during the National Week, that is, up to the 13th April. Those who are not engaged in this sacred work should themselves do vigorous propaganda for the boycott of foreign cloth and the use of Khaddar. They should also endeavor to manufacture as much Khaddar as possible. As to this and the prohibition of liquor, I am preparing a message for the women of India who, I am becoming more and more convinced, can make a larger contribution than men towards the attainment of Independence, I feel that they will be worthier interpreters of non-violence than men, not because they are weak as men, in their arrogance, believe them to be, but because they have greater courage of the right type, and immeasurably greater spirit of self-sacrifice."

Being asked what he would do during the national week, Mr. Gandhi said, "I have a lot of work to do." He however laughingly added, "I shall encourage illicit manufacture of salt."

A PINCH OF SALT
• by Louis Fischer

HAD GANDHI gone by train or automobile to make salt, the effect would have been considerable. But to walk for twenty-four days and rivet the attention of all India, to trek across a country-side saying, "Watch, I am about to give a signal to the nation," and then to pick up a pinch of salt in publicized defiance of the mighty government and thus become a criminal, that required imagination, dignity, and the sense of showmanship of a great artist. It appealed to the illiterate peasant and it appealed to a sophisticated critic and sometime fierce opponent of Gandhi's like Subhas Chandra Bose [9] who compared the Salt March to "Napoleon's march to Paris on his return from Elba."

The act performed, Gandhi withdrew from the scene. India had its cue. Gandhi had communicated with it by lifting up some grains of salt.

The next act was an insurrection without arms. Every villager on India's long seacoast went to the beach or waded into the sea with a pan to make salt. The police began mass arrests. Ramdas, third son of Gandhi, with a large group of ashramites, was ar-

• Reprinted with permission from Louis Fischer, *The Life of Mahatma Gandhi* (New York: Harper, 1950), pp. 268-69.

rested. Pandit Malaviya and other moderate cooperators resigned from the Legislative Assembly. The police began to use violence. Civil resisters never resisted arrest; but they resisted the confiscation of the salt they had made, and Mahadev Desai reported cases where such Indians were beaten and bitten in the fingers by constables. Congress Volunteers openly sold contraband salt in cities. Many were arrested and sentenced to short prison terms. In Delhi, a meeting of fifteen thousand persons heard Pandit Malaviya appeal to the audience to boycott foreign cloth; he himself bought some illegal salt after his speech. The police raided the Congress party headquarters in Bombay where salt was being made in pans on the roof. A crowd of sixty thousand assembled. Hundreds were handcuffed or their arms fastened with ropes and led off to jail. In Ahmedabad, ten thousand people obtained illegal salt from Congress in the first week after the act at Dandi. They paid what they could; if they had no money they got it free. The salt lifted by Gandhi from the beach was sold to a Dr. Kanuga, the highest bidder, for 1,600 rupees. Jawaharlal Nehru, the president of the Congress, was arrested in Allahabad under the Salt Acts and sentenced to six months' imprisonment. The agitation and disobedience spread to the turbulent regions of the Maharashtra and Bengal. In Calcutta, the Mayor, J. M. Sengupta, read seditious literature aloud at a public meeting and urged non-wearing of foreign textiles. He was put in prison for six months. Picketing of liquor shops and foreign cloth shops commenced throughout India. Girls and ladies from aristocratic families and from families where purdah [10] had been observed came out into the streets to demonstrate. . . .

A SPRING HAD BEEN RELEASED

by Jawaharlal Nehru

THE SIXTH of April was the first day of the National Week, which is celebrated annually in memory of the happenings in 1919, from Satyagraha Day to Jallianwala Bagh. On that day Gandhiji began the breach of the salt laws at Dandi beach, and three or four days later permission was given to all Congress organizations to do likewise and begin civil disobedience in their own areas.

It seemed as though a spring had been suddenly released; all over the country, in town and village, salt manufacture was the topic of the day, and many curious expedients were adopted to produce salt. We knew precious little about it, and so we read it up where we could and issued leaflets giving directions; we collected pots and pans and ultimately succeeded in producing some unwholesome stuff, which we waved about in triumph and often auctioned for fancy prices. It was really immaterial whether the stuff was good or bad; the main thing was to commit a breach of the obnoxious salt law, and we were successful in that, even though the quality of our salt was poor. As we saw the abounding enthusiasm of the people and the way salt-making was spreading like a prairie fire, we felt a little abashed and ashamed for having questioned the efficacy of this method when it was first proposed by Gandhiji. And we marveled at the amazing knack of the man to impress the multitude and make it act in an organized way.

• Reprinted with permission from Jawaharlal Nehru, *Toward Freedom* (New York: John Day, 1941), pp. 159-60.

ARREST AT MIDNIGHT

by Haridas T. Muzumdar

While mass civil disobedience was being carried out through-out India, Gandhi carefully avoided participating further in the activity. He set up a temporary ashram at Camp Karadi, a mango grove midway between Dandi and the sea, from which he kept in close contact with developments throughout the country. Meanwhile he and the male members of his ashram were trying to educate nearby villagers to stop preparing an alcoholic toddy. Then, early in the morning on May 5, Gandhi was arrested.

NEAR THE COTTAGE of reeds is a plain cot out in the open, under the blue canopy of the Indian sky. Not far from the cot on one side there is a young man sleeping on the ground; on the other side of the cot is a young Indian lady (stopping over for the day) sleeping on the ground. Farther away both to the right and to the left are mango trees under which are sleeping groups of young men. Still farther away in the background is a modest school building in front of which about forty men, young and old, are sleeping. It is 12:45 A.M.

Of a sudden a tramping of feet is heard, disturbing the quiet repose of Karadi Camp. Two English officers—(1) the District Magistrate of Surat and (2) the District Superintendent of Police—and an Indian police officer, all three armed with pistols, along with thirty odd Indian policemen armed with rifles, enter the Camp through the gates in front of the school building. They make straight for the cottage of reeds and surround the cot.

• Reprinted with permission from Haridas T. Muzumdar, *Gandhi Versus the Empire* (New York: Universal Publishing Co., 1932), pp. 33-37.

Two flashlights are directed upon the face of the occupant of the cot.

The Mahatma, half-clad, weary of limb, having had less than two hours' rest, sleepily turns from one side to the other in order to dodge the dazzling light. Suddenly the words "Please wake up!" strike his ears. He is up in his bed. Gazing at the police party surrounding him, he takes in the situation all at once. He decides to break his silence.

Mahatma Gandhi: "Have you come to arrest me?"

The District Magistrate: "Yes. Your name is Mohandas Karamchand Gandhi?"

Mahatma Gandhi (getting off the bed): "Do you mind waiting until I brush my teeth and wash my face?"

The District Superintendent of Police (stiffly looking at his time-piece): "You may brush your teeth."

While the Mahatma is getting washed, a bell is rung at the school building. All the inmates of the Camp are immediately up and seen surrounding the police party. They make efforts to get inside the police cordon and after a while succeed in going near the Mahatma. They are steadfastly gazing at their beloved leader.

Mahatma Gandhi (still brushing his teeth): "Mr. District Magistrate, may I know the charge on which I am arrested? Is it Section 124-A of the Indian Penal Code?"

District Magistrate: "No, not under Section 124. I have a written order."

Mahatma Gandhi (his ablutions now finished): "Would you mind reading it to me?"

District Magistrate (with the stiff formality of which only an Englishman is capable): "Whereas the Governor-in-Council views with alarm the activities of Mohandas Karamchand Gandhi, he directs that the said Mohandas Karamchand Gandhi should be placed under restraint under Regulation XXV of 1827, and suffer imprisonment during the pleasure of the government: and that he be immediately removed to the Yeravda Central Jail."

Mahatma Gandhi (disappointed that it was not Section 124-A): "Thank you! (Turning to his grandson): Please make up my bedding. (Turning to Mr. V. G. Desai, Acting Commandant of the Non-Violent Battalion): Please take charge of the important papers from my satchels. (Turning to one of his other awestruck followers): Please get me two *taklis* (hand-spindles) and some slivers."

District Magistrate and District Superintendent of Police (in unison, their eyes fixed upon their time-pieces): "Please hurry up, please hurry up!"

It is now one o'clock. The darkness thickens.

Mahatma Gandhi (surrounded by his loyal band of Satyagrahists, i.e., Civil Resisters): "Punditji, please recite the hymn describing the qualities of a Vaishnava. [The famous hymn with which the Great March was commenced on the 12th of March, 1930, with which the violation of the Salt Act was undertaken on the 6th of April, 1930.]"

The Mahatma stands up, his eyes closed, his head bent in mute reverence, while Pundit Khare recites the hymn. At the end of the hymn Punditji leads the congregational worship in which all, including the thirty odd Indian policemen, participate. The two English officers are standing stiffly, watch in hand, during the singing of the Vaishnava hymn.

Pundit Khare (seated on the ground, mono-string musical instrument in hand): "Oh Rama! Lord of the Dynasty of Raghus! Thou, an ideal king, an ideal husband of the ideal wife Sita, Thou art verily the Redeemer of the fallen and the sinful!"

The congregation repeats this verse each time after Punditji sings it. The joyous chanting purifies the countryside—white clouds are seen hovering overhead.

District Magistrate and District Superintendent of Police (in unison, their eyes fixed upon their time-pieces, a bit nervously): "Please hurry up, please hurry up!"

One by one the Civil Resisters bow down before the Mahatma, touching his feet most reverently, and bid him farewell most tenderly and affectionately.

The young lady (touching the Mahatma's feet): "Have you any message for Kasturba?"

Mahatma Gandhi (gently patting the young lady's back): "No, I have no message for her. Tell her she is a brave girl."

The Mahatma surrenders himself into police custody. His two satchels and the small bundle of bedding are taken in charge by a police constable. The police party makes for the motor lorry. Tranquillity-incarnate, the Mahatma walks with steady steps in the direction of the gates. He is accompanied on the one side by the District Magistrate and on the other by the District Superintendent of Police—the eyes of both these officers are glued to their time-pieces. It is ten minutes past one. The policemen occupy the three police lorries. The Mahatma steps into the special lorry, casting a wistful glance at his Camp and his followers. The District Magistrate, watch in hand, gets into the same lorry. The District Superintendent of Police, watch in hand, also gets into the same lorry. And lo! the lorries are whisked away. A pall of darkness falls over the whole world.

Watches in hand, I take it, these English officers conducted the Mahatma to the railway train and helped him get into the special carriage reserved for the Gandhi party. The Gujarat Mail bound for Bombay was detained at 6:40 A.M. but for a moment at Borivli (a suburb of Bombay) where the Mahatma was made to alight. The passengers on the train paid their homage to the imprisoned Soul of India by loud shouts of "Mahatma Gandhi Ki Jai" (Victory to Mahatma Gandhi). The Mahatma was escorted to a high-powered grey car with bright pink blinds which were pulled down. The automobile with its precious cargo of barely a hundred pounds of flesh and bones arrived at its destination, the Yeravda Central Jail, Poona, at 10:30 A.M.

DHARASANA SALT RAID

by Webb Miller

Just before Gandhi's arrest on May 5, 1930, at Karadi, near Dandi, he announced his intention of raiding the Dharasana Salt Works about 150 miles north of Bombay. With Gandhi in jail, Mrs. Sarojini Naidu—close associate of Gandhi and Indian poetess —assumed the leadership and went to the site with 2,500 volunteers. Webb Miller, well-known foreign correspondent for the United Press, heard about this projected salt raid on May 21, and wrote the following eye-witness account.

AFTER WITNESSING two serious riots at the Wadala salt pans in the suburbs of Bombay, I received on the evening of May 20, 1930, an important tip from a friendly Gandhi sympathizer. He told me they were planning the biggest demonstration yet at Dharasana, about a hundred and fifty miles north of Bombay.

"Sarojini Naidu, the famous Indian poetess, is leading a non-violent demonstration against the big salt pans near Dharasana. The nearest railway station is Dungri. It is an isolated spot and you will have to take your own food and water. You'd better telegraph Mme. Naidu to provide transportation from Dungri, otherwise you will have to walk many miles. Be sure to take an adequate supply of bottled water, because the water from native sources is unhealthy for white men."

. . . Dungri consisted of a little huddle of native huts on the dusty plain. There were no means of transportation because Mme. Naidu had not received my telegram. I could find nobody who

* Reprinted with permission from Webb Miller, *I Found No Peace* (New York: Simon and Schuster, 1936), pp. 190, 192-96.

spoke English. By repeatedly pronouncing the word "Dharasana" and pointing questioningly around the horizon, I got directions and set off across country on foot through cactus hedges, millet fields, and inch-deep dust, inquiring my way by signs.

After plodding about six miles across country lugging a pack of sandwiches and two quart bottles of water under a sun which was already blazing hot, inquiring from every native I met, I reached the assembling place of the Gandhi followers. Several long, open, thatched sheds were surrounded by high cactus thickets. The sheds were literally swarming and buzzed like a beehive with some 2,500 Congress or Gandhi men dressed in the regulation uniform of rough homespun cotton *dhotis* and triangular Gandhi caps, somewhat like American overseas soldiers' hats. They chattered excitedly and when I arrived hundreds surrounded me, with evidences of hostility at first. After they learned my identity, I was warmly welcomed by young college-educated, English-speaking men and escorted to Mme. Naidu. The famous Indian poetess, stocky, swarthy, strong-featured, barelegged, dressed in rough, dark homespun robe and sandals, welcomed me. She explained that she was busy martialing her forces for the demonstration against the salt pans and would talk with me more at length later. She was educated in England and spoke English fluently.

Mme. Naidu called for prayer before the march started and the entire assemblage knelt. She exhorted them: "Gandhi's body is in jail but his soul is with you. India's prestige is in your hands. You must not use any violence under any circumstances. You will be beaten but you must not resist; you must not even raise a hand to ward off blows." Wild, shrill cheers terminated her speech.

Slowly and in silence the throng commenced the half-mile march to the salt deposits. A few carried ropes for lassoing the barbed-wire stockade around the salt pans. About a score who were assigned to act as stretcher-bearers wore crude, hand-painted red crosses pinned to their breasts; their stretchers consisted of blankets. Manilal Gandhi, second son of Gandhi, walked among the foremost of the marchers. As the throng drew near the salt pans they commenced chanting the revolutionary slogan, "In-quilah zindabad," [11] intoning the two words over and over.

The salt deposits were surrounded by ditches filled with water and guarded by four hundred native Surat police in khaki shorts and brown turbans. Half a dozen British officials commanded them. The police carried *lathis*—five-foot clubs tipped with steel. Inside the stockade twenty-five native riflemen were drawn up.

In complete silence the Gandhi men drew up and halted a hundred yards from the stockade. A picked column advanced from the crowd, waded the ditches, and approached the barbed-wire stockade, which the Surat police surrounded, holding their clubs at the ready. Police officials ordered the marchers to disperse under a recently imposed regulation which prohibited gatherings of more than five persons in any one place. The column silently ignored the warning and slowly walked forward. I stayed with the main body about a hundred yards from the stockade.

Suddenly, at a word of command, scores of native police rushed upon the advancing marchers and rained blows on their heads with their steel-shod *lathis*. Not one of the marchers even raised an arm to fend off the blows. They went down like tenpins. From where I stood I heard the sickening whacks of the clubs on un-protected skulls. The waiting crowd of watchers groaned and sucked in their breaths in sympathetic pain at every blow.

Those struck down fell sprawling, unconscious or writhing in pain with fractured skulls or broken shoulders. In two or three minutes the ground was quilted with bodies. Great patches of blood widened on their white clothes. The survivors without breaking ranks silently and doggedly marched on until struck down. When every one of the first column had been knocked down stretcher-bearers rushed up unmolested by the police and carried off the injured to a thatched hut which had been ar-ranged as a temporary hospital.

Then another column formed while the leaders pleaded with them to retain their self-control. They marched slowly toward the police. Although every one knew that within a few minutes he would be beaten down, perhaps killed, I could detect no signs of wavering or fear. They marched steadily with heads up, without the encouragement of music or cheering or any possibility that they might escape serious injury or death. The police rushed out and methodically and mechanically beat down the second column. There was no fight, no struggle; the marchers simply walked forward until struck down. There were no outcries, only groans after they fell. There were not enough stretcher-bearers to carry off the wounded; I saw eighteen injured being carried off simultaneously, while forty-two still lay bleeding on the ground awaiting stretcher-bearers. The blankets used as stretchers were sodden with blood.

At times the spectacle of unresisting men being methodically bashed into a bloody pulp sickened me so much that I had to turn away. The western mind finds it difficult to grasp the idea of nonresistance. I felt an indefinable sense of helpless rage and loathing, almost as much against the men who were submitting unresistingly to being beaten as against the police wielding the clubs, and this despite the fact that when I came to India I sympathized with the Gandhi cause.

Several times the leaders nearly lost control of the waiting crowd. They rushed up and down, frantically pleading with and exhorting the intensely excited men to remember Gandhi's instructions. It seemed that the unarmed throng was on the verge of launching a mass attack upon the police. The British official in charge, Superintendent Robinson of Surat, sensed the imminence of an outbreak and posted his twenty-five riflemen on a little knoll ready to fire. He came to me, inquired my identity, and said: "You'd better move aside out of the line of shooting. We may be forced to open fire into the crowd." While we were talking one of the Gandhiites, a young university student, ran up to Robinson, his face contorted by rage, tore open his cotton smock, exposing his bare breast, and shrieked: "Shoot me, shoot me! Kill me, it's for my country!" The leaders managed to calm the crowd.

The Gandhi men altered their tactics, marched up in groups of twenty-five and sat on the ground near the salt pans, making no effort to draw nearer. Led by a coffee-colored Parsi sergeant of police named Antia, a hulking, ugly-looking fellow, detachments of police approached one seated group and called upon them to disperse under the non-assemblage ordinance. The Gandhi followers ignored them and refused even to glance up at the *lathis* brandished threateningly above their heads. Upon a word from Antia the beating recommenced coldly, without anger. Bodies toppled over in threes and fours, bleeding from great gashes on their scalps. Group after group walked forward, sat down, and submitted to being beaten into insensibility without raising an arm to fend off the blows.

Finally the police became enraged by the nonresistance, sharing, I suppose, the helpless rage I had already felt at the demonstrators for not fighting back. They commenced savagely kicking the seated men in the abdomen and testicles. The injured men writhed and squealed in agony, which seemed to inflame the fury of the police, and the crowd again almost broke away from their leaders. The police then began dragging the sitting men by the arms or feet, sometimes for a hundred yards, and throwing them into ditches. One was dragged to the ditch where I stood; the splash of his body doused me with muddy water. Another policeman dragged a Gandhi man to the ditch, threw him in, then belabored him over the head with his *lathi*. Hour after hour stretcher-bearers carried back a stream of inert, bleeding bodies.

I went to see Mme. Naidu, who was directing the subleaders in keeping the crowds from charging the police. While we were talking one of the British officials approached her, touched her on the arm, and said: "Sarojini Naidu, you are under arrest." She haughtily shook off his hand and said: "I'll come, but don't touch me." The crowd cheered frantically as she strode with the British officer across the open space to the barbed-wire stockade, where she was interned. Later she was sentenced to prison. Manilal Gandhi was also arrested.

In the middle of the morning V. J. Patel arrived. He had been leading the Swaraj movement since Gandhi's arrest, and had just resigned as President of the Indian Legislative Assembly in protest against the British. Scores surrounded him, knelt, and kissed his feet. He was a venerable gentleman of about sixty with white flowing beard and mustache, dressed in the usual undyed, coarse homespun smock. Sitting on the ground under a mango tree, Patel said: "All hope of reconciling India with the British Empire is lost forever. I can understand any government's taking people into custody and punishing them for breaches of the law, but I cannot understand how any government that calls itself civilized could deal as savagely and brutally with nonviolent, un-resisting men as the British have this morning."

By eleven the heat reached 116 in the shade and activities of the Gandhi volunteers subsided. I went back to the temporary hospital to examine the wounded. They lay in rows on the bare ground in the shade of an open, palm-thatched shed. I counted 320 injured, many still insensible with fractured skulls, others writhing in agony from kicks in the testicles and stomach. The Gandhi men had been able to gather only a few native doctors, who were doing the best they could with the inadequate facil-ities. Scores of the injured had received no treatment for hours and two had died. The demonstration was finished for the day on account of the heat. . . .

11 THE ROUND TABLE CONFERENCE (1931)

THE REAL CONFERENCE
• by Mahadev Desai

In November 1930 the first Round Table Conference met in London to discuss a new constitution for India. Although this body contained some Indian members there were no representatives of the Congress. In January 1931 Gandhi and several other top Congress leaders were released from prison. There followed conversations between Gandhi and the Viceroy, Lord Irwin, leading to the Gandhi-Irwin agreement of March 5. Lord Irwin promised to release the other political prisoners, who numbered 100,000 or more, and Gandhi promised that the Congress would call off civil disobedience and send representatives to the second Round Table Conference, which met in London from September 14 to December 1. The conference failed to agree on a constitution, but Gandhi's stay in England did much to enlist sympathy there for the Indian cause. In fact, he regarded his unofficial contacts with the British people as "the real conference."

Gandhi gladly accepted an invitation to stay at Kingsley House,

• Reprinted with permission from C. Rajagopalachar[i] and J. C. Kumarappa, editors, *The Nation's Voice* (Ahmedabad: Navajivan, 1932), pp. 125-26, 220, 158-59, 197-98.

a social settlement in the London slums, and also had an office in Knightsbridge, nearer the conference headquarters. He visited many well-known personalities, including the King and Queen, Bernard Shaw, the Dean of Canterbury, Mme. Maria Montessori, Harold Laski, and General Smuts, who said of their days in South Africa, "I did not give you such a bad time as you gave me." Winston Churchill refused to see Gandhi, as did the Pope a few months later. Gandhi's relations with the press were excellent; when questioned about his habit of wearing a loincloth, he replied, "You people wear plus-fours, mine are minus fours." He made many trips outside London and addressed numerous public meetings.

Gandhi had little time for sleep in London. Here is a typical day's schedule: 1 A.M., reach Kingsley Hall; 1:45, finish the spinning quota of 160 yards of yarn; 1:50, write diary of preceding twenty-four hours; 2:00-3:45, sleep; 3:45-5:00, wash and prayer; 5:00-6:00, rest; 6:00-7:00, interview while walking; 7:00-8:00, morning ablutions and bath; 8:00-8:30, breakfast; 8:30-9:15, auto journey to office; 9:15-10:45, interviews with a journalist, an artist, a Sikh member of the Round Table Conference, and a merchant; 10:45-11:00, journey to St. James's Palace; 11 A.M. to 1 P.M., attend Round Table Conference; 1:00-2:45, speak at American journalists' luncheon; 3:00-5:30, conference with Moslems; 5:00-7:00, conference with Secretary of State for India; 7:00-7:30, return to Kingsley Hall for prayer and evening meal; 8:00-9:10, conference of temperance workers; 9:10-9:45, in transit; 9:45-12:00, conference with Nawah of Bhopal; 12:30 A.M., return to Kingsley Hall.

FRIENDS HAVE BEEN remonstrating with him against staying at this place [Kingsley Hall] so distant from the palaces and hotels. English friends have been forthcoming ready to offer their houses in the neighborhood of St. James' Palace, but Gandhiji is clear that he must not leave the home of the humble folk which has become his real home. He may have an office where he can receive and meet friends—and some Indian friends have placed their houses at his disposal for the purpose—but he cannot afford to miss the friends in the East End who meet him and bid him good morning when he is out for a walk, nor can he miss the little ones who surround him and have an occasional chat. In fact, a special meeting with these people was a thing he most enjoyed. He felt as though he was in the midst of the children of the Ashram, answering their simple but penetrating and puzzling inquiries and spreading through them his message of truth and love. "What is your language, Mr. Gandhi?" they ask, and Gandhiji takes them through the etymology of common words in English and Indian vernaculars and shows them that we are after all children of the same Father. He tells them stories of his childhood and explains how it is better by far not to hit back than to return a blow for a blow. He tells them why he wears the sort of clothes he wears and he also tells them why he lives amongst them. . . .

The child who has given Gandhiji the pet name of "Uncle Gandhi" is a boy of three in the Children's House attached to Kingsley Hall. Ever since the children saw Gandhiji, he has been in their days and their dreams "Now, tell me, mummy, what does Gandhi eat, and why does he not wear shoes?" and so on and so forth. One day the mother said: "No, look here, you mustn't say 'Gandhi,' but 'Mr. Gandhi.' You know Mr. Gandhi is a very good man." "I am sorry, mummy," says the little tot making amends, "I will call him 'Uncle Gandhi.'" . . . So the name caught on, and on his birthday the little children sent to "Dear Uncle Gandhi" birthday presents in the shape of a toy dog and sweets, and wished "you had a birthday cake with icing and a bird on it. Please will you come here on your birthday and we will have a band and play music about 'daisy' and 'away in a manger' and light candles?"

Bernard Shaw had long been wanting to see Gandhiji, and it was not without considerable hesitation that he came. He sat with Gandhiji for close on an hour, interrogating him on a bewildering variety of topics—ethnographical, religious, social, political, and economic—and his talk was illumined by his sparkling wit and sardonic humor. "I knew something about you and felt something in you of a kindred spirit. We belong to a very small community on earth," said he. Whilst his other questions were of universal importance, he could not help asking a question about the Round Table Conference. "Does not the Round Table Conference try your patience?" he asked, and Gandhiji had to confess with sorrow: "It requires more than the patience of a Job. The whole thing is a huge camouflage and the harangues that we are treated to are meant only to mark time. Why not, I ask them, make a clean breast and announce your policy and let us make our choice? But it does not seem to be in the English political nature to do so. It must go by round about and tortuous ways!"

[Louis Fischer writes this account of their meeting: "George Bernard Shaw also paid his respects. With unusual modesty he gave the palm to Gandhi and called himself 'Mahatma Minor.' 'You and I,' he said, 'belong to a very small community on earth.' They touched on a score of subjects and Shaw's humor immensely amused 'Mahatma Major,' but it cannot be said that Gandhi liked the playwright's love of the word that shocks. Neither had Tolstoy." •

[Shaw was driven from his interview with Gandhi by the Indian journalist, T. A. Raman. When he asked Shaw for his impressions, the playwright said, "Why, that is not a man, that is a PHENOMENON. You must really give me some time to recover from the shock." • •]

Some will say the reception at Buckingham Palace was an important event. Well, with all respect to Their Majesties, I cannot say so. Do these receptions mean anything? Do Their Majesties meet people in the real sense of the term? Do they transact any business? Can they? Or is it not more or less like a pantomime show? And yet, some will say, Gandhiji went there. Why did he? If it were so meaningless, why did he not abstain from it? Shall

• Reprinted with permission from Louis Fischer, *The Life of Mahatma Gandhi* (New York: Harper, 1950), p. 282.
• • Reprinted with permission from T. A. Raman, *What Does Gandhi Want?* (London: Oxford, 1942), p. 83.

I try to give the readers an inkling of his state of mind? He described it at the Friends' meeting: "I am here," he said, "in an embarrassing position. I have come as the guest of this nation and not as the elected representative of my own nation. I must, therefore, walk warily and I cannot tell you how warily I am walking. Do you think I relished the Prime Minister's minatory speech in the Minorities Committee? I would have repudiated it there and then, but I sat mum. I came home and wrote a letter of gentle reproach. And now, this week I am faced with a moral problem. I have an invitation to attend His Majesty's reception. I am feeling so heart-sick and sore over the happenings in India that I have no heart in attending such functions, and if I had come in my own right I should not have hesitated to come to a decision. But, as I am a guest, I am hesitating; I can do nothing hastily. I have every moment to consider the morality of the thing and not the legality." And, it is the morality of the thing that decided him to go, and when he did so, he wrote a courteous letter to the Lord Chamberlain thanking him for the invitation and intimating to him that he and his companion (who had also been invited) would attend the reception in their usual dress. He usually excuses himself from all social functions, but he had to make an exception in favor of this as in some others, as he would do nothing which would be regarded in the nature of a discourtesy. He would not refrain from doing anything that might be turned against him.

[When asked once if he was sufficiently dressed for his talk with the King, Gandhi replied, "The King had enough on for both of us." •]

When we were going to Eton one of the first questions that Gandhi had asked was whether Eton was not the school where Jawaharlal [Nehru] was educated. "It was at Harrow," I said, "and not Eton," and I am not exaggerating, if I say, that part of Gandhiji's interest in the Eton visit was lost because of that knowledge. The reader will now understand why Gandhiji was

• Reprinted with permission from H. S. L. Polak, H. N. Brailsford, and Lord Pethick-Lawrence, *Mahatma Gandhi* (London: Odhams, 1949), p. 191.

looking forward to a visit to Cambridge. It is the Cambridge of Jawaharlal and Charlie Andrews, and when the latter took him out for his morning walk, Gandhiji insisted on being taken through the vast quadrangle of Trinity College where Jawaharlal was educated. . . .

88 KNIGHTSBRIDGE, LONDON

by Agatha Harrison

Agatha Harrison, an English Friend, was a member of the small group of interpreters of Gandhi in England which included the Henry Polaks and Horace Alexander. It became formalized as the India Conciliation Group, with Carl Heath as chairman and Miss Harrison as secretary. Miss Harrison met C. F. Andrews at the time of the Round Table Conference and they became close friends until his death in 1940. As an authority on women in industry, especially in the Orient, she visited India several times. Her description of Gandhi's "office" in London during the Round Table Conference is especially memorable.

. . . MR. GANDHI was prevailed upon to have a *pied à terre* nearer to St. James's Palace. and 88 Knightsbridge was taken.

I do not think Mr. Gandhi was ever really happy about this arrangement. He would acknowledge its convenience, but the cost of it all was an ever-present anxiety. For you cannot be in Knightsbridge without paying its price, and this price represented to Mr. Gandhi food for starving people in India. The only time the two devoted friends, C. F. Andrews and Mr. Gandhi, had a difference of opinion in these days was over this house. Mr. An-

• Reprinted with permission from *The Christian Century*, Vol. 50, No. 1, January 4, 1933, pp. 15-17.

drews felt, naturally, that no expense should be spared to con-
serve the strength and time of his friend for the momentous work
he was called on to do; Mr. Gandhi continued to worry about the
money. He insisted on going back to Bow for his scanty hours
of sleep, but at other times when the Conference was not in session, Mr. Gandhi was to be found at 88. . . .

It is almost impossible to describe our household. Perhaps the
best way is to tell of some of the chief actors in that drama.
First and foremost is the Mahatma.

Personally, I find it difficult to make a critical estimate of this
man. For when you meet absolute honesty and directness of purpose in a tangled world, you are in the presence of something that
silences criticism. I can see how difficult he makes the path of
governments, for real sincerity and directness are embarrassing,
and I sometimes wished he could make more allowance for this.
He is the most disconcerting person to work with, but very human
and lovable. How he can work in the midst of so much turmoil is
amazing. He is rarely alone. The only time I saw him left by himself was after the famous session at the end of the Conference
when the Prime Minister had announced the policy of the government (later incorporated in a White Paper) and Mr. Gandhi
had given his serious answer foreshadowing what lay ahead. He
came back to 88 immediately after, and sat by the fire spinning
in silence. Watching him from the other end of the room, I was
reminded of Atlas carrying an intolerable burden on frail shoulders.

The Mahatma does not believe in closed doors. The most important talks were carried on with a variety of men and women
listening. Cables and letters could be seen lying about—he trusts
people entirely. Just before Mr. Gandhi left for India he asked me
if I would take on an impossible task—that of working as a free
lance on "the mutual understanding" between our two countries.
This conversation started with Mr. Gandhi, Horace Alexander
and me, but soon a group of people was sitting around while
arrangements, financial and otherwise, were carried on, and the

Mahatma questioned me closely on how I lived and at what cost! . . .

The picture would not be complete without mention of the two detectives attached by the government to guard the frail body of Mr. Gandhi. This particular pair are generally detailed to shadow royalty. Though accustomed to watch for the sinister side of life, their work now took a different turn. They grew to love "the little man" as they affectionately called him; he became their friend for whom they would do any service. They also lent a willing hand to the rest of us when we were extra busy.

Before Mr. Gandhi left London, when asked by a government official if there was anything more he could do for him, Mr. Gandhi requested that his two detectives might go with him as far as Brindisi. When asked why, the Mahatma replied, "Because they are part of my family." This request was granted, and they accompanied him across the continent. . . .

In the pockets of these men, going about their strange work, are the watches sent them from India with the inscription: "With love from M. K. Gandhi." What a tale these detectives could unfold if reminiscences of the doings of a criminal investigation officer were allowed to be written!

Out of all the memories that crowd these days, it is difficult to make a selection. Some stand out. The evening prayers when the room would be crowded with people eager to learn more about this man's way of life. The early mornings when Mr. Gandhi arrived, and you felt as though a torchlike "something" had come into the house. He would spring out of his car and be up in his room sitting by the fire spinning, in a flash. In every corner of the room were famous sculptors and artists trying to get a model or picture of this elusive man. Strewn around were letters and cables needing immediate attention; members of the Conference seated on the floor, anxious to get his opinion before the Conference session; men and women from all over the world waiting for a word from him; C. F. Andrews and Horace Alexander quietly working in the midst of it all; Mrs. Cheesman patiently waiting to take some important letter. And in the centre of all this the imperturbable Mahatma. Then finding it was time for the Conference, he would dart out to his car; followed by panting detectives and some of his staff clutching the famous spinning wheel and the green rush basket containing his food.

Another outstanding memory is the evening when Bishop Fisher [1] of America bridged the Atlantic by telephone from Chicago, begging the Mahatma to come to the States. Mr. Gandhi insisted on taking this call himself, though C. F. Andrews and I stood by in case he could not hear, as he so rarely uses the telephone. The press waited outside eager to catch what was said. But Mr. Gandhi soon ended this expensive conversation, for again his mind was worried about the cost, and what the money meant in terms of starving people.

There were amusing incidents. Mirabehn [2] for example, finding that someone had taken the special celery saved for Mr. Gandhi's lunch, and trying to find the culprit. They laughingly blamed C. F. Andrews for this.

Indescribable days, filled to the brim with hard work, vital interest and laughter, and a surge of people that came and went. I wish we had kept a visitors' book that there might be a record of the politicians, religious leaders, and men and women of every shade of opinion who crowded the passages of 88. Did our country realize the significance of this figure in its midst? . . .

APPEAL TO AMERICA

by M. K. Gandhi

On September 13, 1931, two days after Gandhi arrived in England, the Columbia Broadcasting System arranged for him to deliver a radio address to the American people. Gandhi did not write

• Reprinted with permission from Haridas T. Muzumdar, *Gandhi Versus the Empire* (New York: Universal Publishing Co., 1932), pp. 166-70.

out his speech in advance; his remarks were completely extemporaneous. He approached the microphone with curiosity and trepidation and asked, "Do I have to speak into that thing?" He was already on the air and these were the first words his listeners on the other side of the Atlantic heard. Three minutes before his time was to be up, a note was passed to him saying that his voice would be cut off in New York in three minutes. Unruffled, he began to bring his impromptu speech to a conclusion. After the engineer signaled for him to stop, he commented, "Well, that's over." These words, too, somehow were carried across the Atlantic. The American press reproduced great portions of this speech on the following day, although the British press largely ignored it.

IN MY OPINION, the Indian struggle [for freedom] bears in its consequences not only upon India [and England] but upon the whole world. It contains one-fifth of the human race. It represents one of the most ancient civilizations. It has traditions handed down from tens of thousands of years, some of which, to the astonishment of the world, remain intact. No doubt the ravages of time have affected the purity of that civilization as they have that of many other cultures and many institutions.

If India is to revive the glory of her ancient past, she can only do so when she attains her freedom. The reason for the struggle having drawn the attention of the world I know does not lie in the fact that we Indians are fighting for our liberty, but in the fact that the means adopted by us for attaining that liberty are unique and, as far as history shows us, have not been adopted by any other people of whom we have any record.

The means adopted are not violence, not bloodshed, not diplomacy as one understands it nowadays, but they are purely and simply truth and non-violence. No wonder that the attention of the world is directed toward this attempt to lead a successful bloodless revolution. Hitherto, nations have fought in the manner of the brute. They have wreaked vengeance upon those whom they have considered to be their enemies.

We find in searching national anthems adopted by great nations that they contain imprecations upon the so-called enemy. They have vowed destruction and have not hesitated to take the name of God and seek divine assistance for the destruction of the enemy. We in India have endeavored to reverse the process. We feel that the law that governs brute creation is not the law that should guide the human race. That law is inconsistent with human dignity.

I, personally, would wait, if need be, for ages rather than seek to attain the freedom of my country through bloody means. I feel in the innermost recesses of my heart, after a political experience extending over an unbroken period of close upon thirty-five years, that the world is sick unto death of blood-spilling. The world is seeking a way out, and I flatter myself with the belief that perhaps it will be the privilege of the ancient land of India to show the way out to the hungering world.

I have, therefore, no hesitation whatsoever in inviting all the great nations of the earth to give their hearty cooperation to India in her mighty struggle. It must be a sight worth contemplating and treasuring, that of millions of people giving themselves to suffering without retaliation in order that they might vindicate the dignity and honor of the nation.

I have called that suffering a process of self-purification. It is my certain conviction that no man loses his freedom except through his own weakness. I am painfully conscious of our own weaknesses. We represent in India all the principal religions of the earth, and it is a matter of deep humiliation to confess that we are a house divided against itself, that we Hindus and Mussalmans are flying at one another. It is a matter of still deeper humiliation to me that we Hindus regard several millions of our own kith and kin as too degraded even for our touch. I refer to the so-called "untouchables."

These are no small weaknesses in a nation struggling to be free. And hence you will find that in this struggle through self-purification we have assigned a foremost place to the removal of this curse of untouchability and the attainment of unity amongst all the different classes and communities of India representing the different creeds.

It is along the same lines that we seek to rid our land of the curse of drink. Happily for us, intoxicating drinks and drugs are confined to comparatively a very small number of people, largely factory hands and the like. Fortunately for us, the drink and drug curse is accepted as a curse. It is not considered to be the fashion for a man or a woman to drink or to take intoxicating drugs. All the same, it is an uphill fight that we are fighting in trying to remove this evil from our midst.

For it is a matter of regret, deep regret, for me to have to say that the existing government has made of this evil a source of very large revenue, amounting to nearly twenty-five crores of rupees [about $85,000,000]. But I am thankful to be able to say that the women of India have risen to the occasion in combatting it by peaceful means, that is, by fervent appeal to those who are given to the drink habit to give it up, and by an equally fervent appeal to the liquor dealers. A great impression has been created upon those who are addicted to these two evil habits.

I wish that it were possible for me to say that in this, at least, we were receiving the hearty cooperation of the rulers. If we could only have received that cooperation, [even] without any legislation, I dare say that we would have achieved this reform and banished intoxicating drink and drugs from our afflicted land.

There is a force which has a constructive effect and which has been put forth by the nation during this struggle. That is the great care for the semi-starved millions scattered throughout the 700,000 villages dotted over a surface of 1,900 miles long and 1,500 miles broad. It is a painful phenomenon that these simple villagers, through no fault of their own, have nearly six months in the year idleness upon their hands. The time was not very long ago when every village was self-sufficient in regard to the two primary human wants, food and clothing.

Unfortunately for us, the East India Company, by means which I would prefer not to describe, destroyed that supplementary village industry as well as the livelihood of millions of spinners who had become famous through the cunning of their deft fingers for drawing the finest thread, such as has never yet been drawn by any modern machinery. These village spinners found themselves one fine morning with their noble occupation gone. And from that day forward India has become progressively poor.

No matter what may be said to the contrary, it is a historical fact that before the advent of the East India Company, these villagers were not idle, and he who wants may see today that these villagers are idle. It, therefore, requires no great effort or learning to know that these villagers must starve if they cannot work for six months in the year.

May I not, then, on behalf of these semi-starved millions, appeal to the conscience of the world to come to the rescue of a people dying to regain its liberty?

EXCURSION TO LANCASHIRE

by Mahadev Desai

When C. F. Andrews was making preparations for Gandhi's visit to England, he wrote Gandhi that he must "meet Lancashire face to face as I myself am just going to do." Lancashire, a textile area, was in the midst of a great depression, partly because of the Indian boycott on foreign cloth. After Andrews visited Lancashire and saw the distress due to widespread unemployment, he pleaded with Gandhi to call off the boycott. Gandhi refused to do so, but promised Andrews that he would visit the Lancashire workers when he arrived in the British Isles. Gandhi made good his promise and, despite the risks involved, took the journey to Lancashire.

• Reprinted with permission from C. Rajagopalachari and J. C. Kumarappa, editors, The Nation's Voice (Ahmedabad: Navajivan, 1932), pp. 207-11, 213.

In some of the manufacturing areas of Lancashire the manufacturers have concentrated on cotton fabrics exclusively for export to India. "We were prepared for courtesy, which we expect from all gentlemen, we were even prepared for a little bitterness which distress and misunderstanding often create; but we found instead a warmth of affection for which we were not prepared. I shall treasure the memory of these days to the end of my earthly existence." In these words Gandhiji summed up his gratefulness for having been given the opportunity of meeting the Lancashire employers and working people. The warmth of reception could only be equalled by what Gandhiji has been familiar with in the towns and villages of India. There were no public meetings, but what was better was a heart-to-heart chat with various groups of employers and employed who placed before Gandhiji all the facts in their possession, and even at the risk of having to repeat the same reply in substance, Gandhiji met all groups and declined to interview none.

After having given all of them a patient hearing, it was no happiness to Gandhiji to tell them that he could bring them very little comfort. They had come with great expectations perhaps, but Gandhiji had, with great sorrow, to make it clear to them that he was called to undertake a task to which he and his country were unequal. "My nationalism is not so narrow that I should not feel for your distress or gloat over it. I do not want my country's happiness at the sacrifice of any other country's happiness. But whilst I see that you are hard hit, I am afraid, your distress is not largely due to India. Conditions have been bad for some years and the boycott came only as the last straw." He said at Springvale Garden Village: "There is not boycott of British cloth, as distinguished from other foreign cloth, since the 5th March when the truce was signed. As a nation we are pledged to boycott all foreign cloth, but in case of an honorable settlement between England and India, i.e., in case of a permanent peace, I should not hesitate to give preference to Lancashire cloth to all other foreign cloth, to the extent that we may need to supplement our cloth and on agreed terms. But how much relief that can give you, I do not know. You must recognize that all the markets of the world are now not open to you. What you have done, all other nations are doing today. Even Indian mills would be producing more and more cloth every day. You, surely, will not want me to restrict Indian enterprise for the sake of Lancashire."

"I am pained," he said, "at the unemployment here. But here is no starvation or semi-starvation. In India we have both. If you went to the villages of India, you would find utter despair in the eyes of the villagers, you would find half-starved skeletons, living corpses. If India could revive them by putting life and food into them in the shape of work, India would help the world. Today India is a curse. There is a party in my country which would sooner see an end to the lives of these half-starved millions in order that the rest may live. I thought of a humane method and that was to give them work with which they were familiar, which they could do in their cottages, which required no great investment in implements and of which the product could be easily sold. This is a task which is worthy of the attention even of Lancashire."

"But look at these mills which were busy hives only the other day lying absolutely idle. In Blackburn, Darwen, Great Harwood and Accrington over a hundred mills have had to close down. In the Great Harwood area nothing less than 17,436 looms are idle. We took special training at College in weaving Indian textiles, we are weaving dhotis [3] exclusively for India, and why should we not make them today and bring about better relations between India and England?" said some of the employers.

"We helped India during the famine of 1897–99. We collected money for the poor and sent it to them. We have always stood for a liberal policy. Why should the boycott be directed against us?" said some of the working people. Some of them placed their individual grievances before Gandhiji. The most pathetic of them all was the following; "I am a cotton operative. I have been a weaver for 40 years and now I am without work. It is not want or distress that worries me. My estimate of myself is gone. I have fallen in my own estimate inasmuch as I am a recipient of unemployment dole. I do not think I am going to finish my life with any self-respect."

At Hayes Farm, which is a rest house in Yorkshire for the employers, and the prosperous among the employees who might care to spend a week-end there, several deputations of unemployed people waited upon Gandhiji with very nearly the same tale and the brethren in the rest house had a special service where they prayed for the will of God to prevail. It was impossible for Gandhiji to disguise his feelings. "I would be untrue to you, I would be a false friend, if I were not frank with you," said Gandhiji and poured out his heart before them for three quarters of an hour—describing how economics and ethics and politics were in his life inextricably mixed up, how he had raised the banner of truth above everything else, how he had refrained from wedding himself to the results, how he was led to place the spinning wheel before the country and how the world conditions had driven them to the present state of things. "I strove with Lord Irwin last March for the liberty to boycott liquor and foreign cloth. He suggested that I might give up this boycott for three months as a gesture and then resume it. I said I could not give it up for three minutes. You have three million unemployed, but we have nearly 300 million unemployed and underemployed for half the year. Your average unemployment dole is 70 shillings. Our average income is seven shillings and six pence a month. That operative was right in saying that he was falling in his own estimation. I do believe it is a debasing thing for a human being to remain idle and to live on doles. Whilst conducting a strike I could not brook the strikers remaining idle for a single day and got them to break stones or carry sand and work in public streets asking my own co-workers to join them in that work. Imagine, therefore, what a calamity it must be to have 300 million unemployed, several millions becoming degraded every day for want of employment, devoid of self-respect, devoid of faith in God. I dare not take before them that message of God. I may as well place before the dog over there the message of God as before those hungry millions who have no lustre in their eyes and whose only God is their bread. I can take before them a message of God only by taking the sacred message of work before them. It is good enough to talk of God whilst we are sitting here after a nice breakfast and looking forward to a nicer luncheon, but how am I to talk of God to the millions who have to go without two meals a day? To them God can only appear as bread and butter. Well, the peasants of India were getting their bread from their soil. I offered them the spinning wheel in order that they may get the butter, and if I appear today before the British public in my loin-cloth, it is because I have come as the sole representative of those half-starved, half-naked, dumb millions. . . ."

. . . The unemployed working men who saw Gandhiji were in no bitter mood. On the contrary, they asked questions about the agricultural conditions in India, why the agriculturist had no work for six months in the year, why the standard of living was so poor and so on and so forth. The question with them, as they frankly put it, was not of starvation but lowered standard of living; where they could spend a shilling they have to be satisfied with six pence, and whilst many of them can save nothing at all, many had to live on their savings. The rate of their present dole is 17/— male, 15/— female (9/— for wife if not a worker) and 2/— for each child per week. "This," said Gandhiji, "is a fortune, and for you, a resourceful race, it should not be difficult to hit upon other industries and occupations. For my starving crores, I have no other occupation. If some of you experts can find it, I am prepared to substitute it for the spinning wheel. In the meanwhile, I can hold out to you no more hope than this, that an independent India, as an equal partner of Great Britain, will give preference to Lancashire cloth, which India needs and which Lancashire alone can produce, over all foreign cloth."

Poor comfort this, but as they left I found no bitterness in them. One of them said: "Something good cannot but come out of this. And, if nothing good, no evil can come out, and good-will certainly is the immediate result. We understand each other now. It is a privilege to have seen Mr. Gandhi, a mighty force thrown up by the awakening East." Another said: "I am one of the unemployed, but if I was in India, I would say the same thing that Mr. Gandhi is saying."

TO THE PLENARY SESSION
• by M. K. Gandhi

At the second Round Table Conference Gandhi was one of 112 delegates, of whom 20 represented the British government, 22 the Indian States (ruled by princes under British suzerainty), and 65 British India (provinces under direct British rule). The central issue was the Congress Party's demand for complete independence, which the British were unwilling to concede. No less difficult was the communal question, i.e., the demands of various Indian minorities—Moslems, untouchables, etc.—for special protection of their rights, which led to disagreement among the Indian delegates. Gandhi was representing the Congress, which claimed to speak for all Indians regardless of religion or caste, and he refused to countenance measures which he felt would intensify communal dissension. There were several conference committees and Gandhi spoke before those on federal structure and on minorities. During a plenary session chaired by Prime Minister J. Ramsay MacDonald, Gandhi made a historic speech which summed up his attitude, after listening to many weeks of debate, on British rule and Indian independence.

I DO NOT THINK that anything that I can say this evening can possibly influence the decision of the Cabinet. Probably the decision

• Reprinted with permission from C. Rajagopalachari and J. C. Kumarappa, editors, *The Nation's Voice* (Ahmedabad: Navajivan, 1932), pp. 74-8 (abridged).

has been already taken. Matters of the liberty of practically a whole Continent can hardly be decided by mere argumentation, or even negotiation. Negotiation has its purpose and has its play, but only under certain conditions. Without those conditions negotiations are a fruitless task. But I do not want to go into all these matters. I want as far as possible to confine myself within the four corners of the conditions that you, Prime Minister, read to this Conference at its opening meeting. . . .

Although you have invited the Congress, you distrust the Congress. Although you have invited the Congress, you reject its claim to represent the whole of India. Of course it is possible at this end of the world to dispute that claim, and it is not possible for me to prove this claim; but, all the same, if you find me asserting that claim, I do so because a tremendous responsibility rests upon my shoulders.

The Congress represents the spirit of rebellion. I know that the word "rebellion" must not be whispered at a Conference which has been summoned in order to arrive at an agreed solution of India's troubles through negotiation. Speaker after speaker has got up and said that India should achieve her liberty through negotiation, by argument, and that it will be the greatest glory of Great Britain if Great Britain yields to India's demands by argument. But the Congress does not hold quite that view. The Congress has an alternative which is unpleasant to you.

I heard several speakers—I have tried to follow every speaker with utmost attention and with all the respect that I could possibly give to these speakers—saying what a dire calamity it would be if India was fired with the spirit of lawlessness, rebellion, terrorism and so on. I do not pretend to have read history, but as a schoolboy I had to pass a paper in history also, and I read that the page of history is soiled red with the blood of those who have fought for freedom. I do not know an instance in which nations have attained their own without having to go through an incredible measure of travail. The dagger of the assassin, the poison bowl, the bullet of the rifleman, the spear and all these weapons and methods of destruction have been up to now used by, what

I consider, blind lovers of liberty and freedom. And the historian has not condemned them. I hold no brief for the terrorists. . . . For the sake of liberty people have fought, people have lost their lives, people have killed and have sought death at the hands of those whom they have sought to oust.

The Congress then comes upon the scene and devises a new method not known to history, namely, that of civil disobedience, and the Congress has been following up that method. But again, I am up against a stone wall and I am told that is a method that no Government in the world will tolerate. Well, of course, the Government may not tolerate, no Government has tolerated open rebellion. No Government may tolerate civil disobedience, but Governments have to succumb even to these forces, as the British Government has done before now, even as the great Dutch Government after eight years of trial had to yield to the logic of facts. General Smuts is a brave General, a great statesman, and a very hard taskmaster also, but he himself recoiled with horror from even the contemplation of doing to death innocent men and women who were merely fighting for the preservation of their self-respect. Things which he had vowed he would never yield in the year 1908, reinforced as he was by General Botha, he had to do in the year 1914, after having tried these civil resisters through and through. And in India, Lord Chelmsford had to do the same thing; the Governor of Bombay had to do the same thing in Borsad and Bardoli. I suggest to you, Prime Minister, it is too late today to resist this, and it is this thing which weighs me down, this choice that lies before them, the parting of the ways probably. I shall hope against hope, I shall strain every nerve to achieve an honorable settlement for my country, if I can do so without having to put the millions of my countrymen and countrywomen, and even children, through this ordeal of fire. It can be a matter of no joy and comfort to me to lead them again to a fight of that character, but, if a further ordeal of fire has to be our lot, I shall approach that with the greatest joy and with the greatest consolation that I was doing what I felt to be right, the country was doing what it felt to be right, and the country will have the additional satisfaction of knowing that it was not at least taking lives, it was giving lives: it was not making the British people directly suffer, it was suffering. Professor Gilbert Murray told me—I shall never forget that, I am paraphrasing his inimitable language—"Do you not consider for one moment that we Englishmen do not suffer when thousands of your countrymen suffer, that we are so heartless?" I do not think so. I do know that you will suffer; but I want you to suffer because I want to touch your hearts; and when your hearts have been touched then will come the psychological moment for negotiation. . . .

Whilst there is yet a little sand left in the glass, I want you to understand what this Congress stands for. My life is at your disposal. The lives of all the members of the Working Committee, the All-India Congress Committee, are at your disposal. But remember that you have at your disposal the lives of all these dumb millions. I do not want to sacrifice those lives if I can possibly help it. Therefore, please remember, that I will count no sacrifice too great if, by chance, I can pull through an honorable settlement. You will find me always having the greatest spirit of compromise if I can but fire you with the spirit that is working in the Congress, namely, that India must have real liberty. Call it by any name you like; a rose will smell as sweet by any other name, but it must be the rose of liberty that I want and not the artificial product. If your mind and the Congress mind, the mind of this Conference and the mind of the British people, means the same thing by the same word, then you will find the amplest room for compromise, and you will find the Congress itself always in a compromising spirit. But so long as there is not that one mind, that one definition, not one implication for the same word that you and I and we may be using, there is no compromise possible. . . .

. . . It is for friendship I crave. My business is not to throw overboard the slave-holder and tyrant. My philosophy forbids me to do so, and today the Congress has accepted that philosophy, not as a creed, as it is to me, but as a policy, because the Congress believes that is the right and the best thing for India, a nation of 350 millions, to do. . . .

But what is it that that nation does? To summarily, or at all, dismiss Englishmen? No. Its mission is today to convert Englishmen. I do not want to break the bond between England and India, but I do want to transform that bond. I want to transform that slavery into complete freedom for my country. Call it complete independence or whatever you like. I will not quarrel about that word, and even though my countrymen may dispute with me for having taken some other word, I shall be able to bear down that opposition so long as the content of the word that you may suggest to me bears the same meaning. Hence, I have times without number to urge upon your attention that the safeguards⁴ that have been suggested are completely unsatisfactory. They are not in the interests of India.

. . . I will not be baffled. I shall be here as long as I am required because I do not want to revive civil disobedience. I want to turn the truce that was arrived at in Delhi into a permanent settlement. But for heaven's sake give me, a frail man 62 years gone, a little bit of a chance. Find a little corner for him and the organization that he represents. You distrust that organization though you may seemingly trust me. Not for one moment differentiate me from the organization of which I am but a drop in the ocean. I am no greater than the organization to which I belong. I am infinitely smaller than that organization; and if you find me a place, if you trust me, I invite you to trust the Congress also. Your trust in me otherwise is a broken reed. I have no authority save what I derive from the Congress. If you will work the Congress for all it is worth, then you will say goodbye to terrorism, then you will not need terrorism. Today you have to fight the school of terrorists which is there with your disciplined and organized terrorism, because you will be blind to the facts or the writing on the wall. Will you not see the writing that these terrorists are writing with their blood? Will you not see that we do not want bread made of wheat, but we want the bread of liberty; and without that liberty there are thousands today who are sworn not to give themselves peace or to give the country peace.

I urge you then to read that writing on the wall. I ask you not to try the patience of a people known to be proverbially patient. We speak of the mild Hindu, and the Musalman also by contact good or evil with the Hindu has himself become mild. And that mention of the Musalman brings me to the baffling problem of minorities. Believe me, that problem exists here, and I repeat what I used to say in India—I have not forgotten those words—that without the problem of minorities being solved there is no Swaraj for India, there is no freedom for India. I know and I realize it; and yet I came here in the hope "perchance" that I might be able to pull through a solution here. But I do not despair of some day or other finding a real and living solution in connection with the minorities problem. I repeat what I have said elsewhere that so long as the wedge in the shape of foreign rule divides community from community and class from class, there will be no real living solution, there will be no living friend-ship between these communities.

It will be after all and at best a paper solution. But immediately you withdraw that wedge, the domestic ties, the domestic affec-tions, the knowledge of common birth—do you suppose that all these will count for nothing?

Were Hindus and Musalmans and Sikhs always at war with one another when there was no British rule, when there was no English face seen there? We have chapter and verse given to us by Hindu historians and by Musalman historians to say that we were living in comparative peace even then. And Hindus and Musalmans in the villages are not even today quarreling. In those days they were not known to quarrel at all. The late Maulana Muhammad Ali often used to tell me, and he was himself a bit of an historian. He said: "If God"—"Allah" as he called God— "gives me life, I propose to write the history of Musalman rule in India; and then I will show, through documents that British people have preserved, that Aurangzeb [5] was not so vile as he has been painted by the British historian; that the Mogul rule was not so bad as it has been shown to us in British history; and so on." And so have Hindu historians written. This quarrel is not old; this quarrel is coeval with this acute shame. I dare to say, it is coeval with the British advent, and immediately this relationship, the unfortunate, artificial, unnatural relationship between Great Britain and India is transformed into a natural relationship, when it becomes, if it does become, a voluntary partnership to be given up, to be dissolved at the will of either party, when it becomes that, you will find that Hindus, Musalmans, Sikhs, Europeans, Anglo-Indians, Christians, Untouchables, will all live together as one man.

. . . Last of all, my last is a pleasant task for me. This is perhaps the last time that I shall be sitting with you at negotiations. It is not that I want that. I want to sit at the same table with you in your closets and to negotiate and to plead with you and to go down on bended knees before I take the final leap and final plunge.

But whether I have the good fortune to continue to tender my cooperation or not does not depend upon me. It largely depends upon you. But it may not even depend upon you. It depends upon so many circumstances over which neither you nor we may have any control whatsoever. Then, let me perform this pleasant task of giving my thanks to all from Their Majesties down to the poorest men in the East End where I have taken up my habitation.

In that settlement, which represents the poor people of the East End of London, I have become one of them. They have accepted me as a member, and as a favored member of their family. It will be one of the richest treasures that I shall carry with me. Here, too, I have found nothing but courtesy and nothing but a genuine affection from all with whom I have come in touch. I have come in touch with so many Englishmen. It has been a priceless privilege to me. They have listened to what must have often appeared to them to be unpleasant, although it was true. Although I have often been obliged to say these things to them they have never shown the slightest impatience or irritation. It is impossible for me to forget these things. No matter what befalls me, no matter what the fortunes may be of this Round Table Conference, one thing I shall certainly carry with me, that is, that from high to low I have found nothing but the utmost courtesy and the utmost affection. I consider that it was well worth my paying this visit to England in order to find this human affection.

It has enhanced, it has deepened my irrepressible faith in human nature that although Englishmen and Englishwomen have been fed upon lies that I see so often disfiguring your press, that although in Lancashire, the Lancashire people had perhaps some reason for becoming irritated against me, I found no irritation and no resentment even in the operatives. The operatives, men and women, hugged me. They treated me as one of their own. I shall never forget that.

I am carrying with me thousands upon thousands of English friendships. I do not know them but I read that affection in their eyes as early in the morning I walk through your streets. All this hospitality, all this kindness will never be effaced from my memory, no matter what befalls my unhappy land. I thank you for your forbearance.

NOTES

1. A small peninsula in western India, northwest of Bombay, divided into a number of small states.

2. The chief minister of the state.

3. The ruler.

4. A period of four months. A vow of fasting and semi-fasting during the four months of the rains. The period is a sort of long Lent.

5. A fast in which the daily quantity of food is increased or diminished according to the moon's waxing or waning.

6. Gandhi no doubt refers here to the occasion when, with his father on his death-bed, he left him and went to his wife's room in a moment of "animal passion." On his return, he found his father had died. Cf. his *Autobiography*, p. 45.

7. A Gujarati poet who lived in the first half of the nineteenth century; he was a disciple of Sahajananda, founder of the Swaminarayan sect.

8. The seven steps a Hindu bride and bridegroom walk together, making at the same time promises of mutual fidelity and devotion, after which the marriage becomes irrevocable.

9. A preparation of wheat which the pair partake of together after the completion of the ceremony.

10. A Hindu sect worshiping Vishnu as the supreme God.

11. A Vaishnava temple.

12. The name of God.

13. The sacred epic of north India.

14. A recitation of sacred texts asking for the protection of Rama.

15. "The Great God"—a name of Siva.

16. Tulsidas (1532–1623), a poet, author of a Hindi version of the Ramayana.

17. Bhagavad Gita, part of the national epic, Mahabharata.

18. Eleventh day of the bright and the dark half of a lunar month.

19. Laws of Manu, a Hindu law-giver. They have the sanction of religion. This is an ancient religious code upholding the caste system and containing accounts of creation.

20. Non-violence.

21. Dalpatram Shulka, one of the four Indians in London to whom he had notes of introduction.

22. He was admitted as a student of the Inner Temple on November 6, 1888.

23. Theosophy is a combination of occult, Indian, and modern spiritualism founded by Madame Helena P. Blavatsky.

24. A seventeenth-century Gujarati poet.

25. I.e., Mohammed.

26. Charles Bradlaugh (1833–1891), English freethinker and politician.

27. A barrister or counselor at law who passed his law examinations in India.

28. The solicitor under English practice does not have the right to plead in a superior court.

29. A Moslem sect, comprising mostly the mercantile community in Bombay, Kathiawar, etc.

CHAPTER 2

1. A Bombay jeweler and poet to whom Gandhi looked in this period for advice.

2. Edward Maitland (1824–1897), an English humanitarian and writer on vegetarianism and anti-vivisection.

3. Gandhi read Count Leo Tolstoy's The Kingdom of God Is Within You and said that it gave his conviction of satyagraha "a permanent form." In 1909 he wrote a long letter to Tolstoy, who noted in his diary that he had received "a pleasant letter from a Hindu of the Transvaal." Gandhi wrote again in April 1910, enclosing a copy of his newly published book, Hind Swaraj. Gandhi's third and last letter was written August 15, 1910. Though ill, Tolstoy replied on the day he received it. In his long letter he admitted that "the longer I live, and especially now, when I vividly feel the nearness of death, I want to tell others what I feel so particularly clearly and what to my mind is of great importance—namely, that which is called passive resistance, but which is in reality nothing else than the teaching of love uncorrupted by false interpretations." Gandhi received the letter several days after Tolstoy's death on November 21, 1910. For further information see Dr. Kalidas Nag, Tolstoy and Gandhi (Patna: Pustak Bhandar, 1950) and "Tolstoy and Gandhi" in Louis Fischer, The Life of Mahatma Gandhi (New York: Harper, 1950).

4. Henry Escombe, Attorney-General of Natal.

5. Gandhi's former client and owner of the S. S. Courland, on which he was detained.

6. In his Autobiography, Gandhi recalls that one song sung by Mr. Alexander at the time was "Hang old Gandhi on the sour apple tree."

7. Joseph Chamberlain.

8. Literally, the fifth caste. Since there are only four castes, the fifth caste means an outcaste or untouchable.

9. Gandhi met Albert West, a partner in a small printing firm, in a vegetarian restaurant and eventually persuaded him to take charge of the Indian Opinion press at Durban.

10. A printer who first proposed to Gandhi the idea of starting *Indian Opinion*.

CHAPTER 3

1. One of the leaders of the *satyagraha* movement. He was a trader, born in Mauritius (the island in the Indian Ocean between Ceylon and Madagascar), where his parents had migrated from Madras.

2. This occurred in Johannesburg.

3. Coconut-husk fiber.

4. Rev. Joseph J. Doke, a missionary and friend of Gandhi.

CHAPTER 4

1. In the Boer War Gandhi organized and led the Indian Ambulance Corps. In the Zulu "Rebellion" of 1906—a one-sided action by the government against the Zulus—Gandhi led a small Indian unit of stretcher-bearers.

2. A small stream.

3. Herman Kallenbach, an architect and close associate of Gandhi in South Africa.

4. A German professional strong man.

5. Henry S. L. Polak, an Englishman closely associated with Gandhi in South Africa.

6. An open plain.

7. Valiamma Moodaly. A memorial to her was unveiled in Johannesburg on July 15, 1914.

8. Swami Nagappan, an eighteen-year-old *satyagrahi* who contracted double pneumonia while doing road work in prison and died after his release on July 7, 1909.

9. General Louis Botha (1863–1919), a Boer leader who became Prime Minister of the Union of South Africa.

10. The Acting Viceroy of India in 1904 (April 30 to December 13) and former Governor of Madras.

11. At the time Lord Crewe was Secretary of State for the Colonies.

12. A law enacted by the Boer Republic. Its object was to prevent any non-white person from obtaining any land rights in the mining areas except in certain areas set apart for them.

CHAPTER 5

1. This is included in most editions of the pamphlet issued after 1921.

2. This is a mistaken recollection on the part of Gandhi. It must have been written in 1909.

3. Seers.

4. Moslem ascetics.

5. Doctors of indigenous medicine.

6. A custom whereby a widow, if she has no male heir, has a child by another man.

7. Using goods made in India.

8. Self-government.

CHAPTER 6

1. Later Gandhi announced that he had adopted Lakshmi as a daughter.

2. A Hindu title of respect.

3. The Indian National Congress.

4. Sir Jagadis Chandra Bose (1858–1937), an Indian scientist who showed the identity of the life mechanisms of plants and those of animals; and Janendra Nath Ray (1898–   ), well-known Indian chemist.

5. A platform or stage; usually an awning formed by grass, leaves, or cloth.

6. The story of the young boy, Prahlad, who suffered for the truth's sake, is one of the most famous in ancient Indian literature. It is well known by every Indian child, as the story of George Washington and the cherry tree is known in America.

7. Bread made without yeast, somewhat like a pancake.

8. The vow of *khaddar* or *khadi* is to spin with one's own hands and to wear nothing but homespun garments.

9. This is an honorific title.

10. Peasants.

11. Residents of the province of Bihar.

12. A kind of milk soup.

13. Split pulse—the seeds of a legume used commonly for food in India.

14. All these are names of Indian social groups.

15. A lunch carrier.

16. Clarified butter.

CHAPTER 7

1. Strike-breakers.

2. The sister of Ambalal Sarabhai, the leading millowner; she was on Gandhi's side in this dispute.

3. The practice of arbitration of labor disputes has continued in the Ahmedabad mills. In 1936, for example, the millowners asked the labor union to accept a 20 per cent cut in wages. The union refused and the dispute went to arbitration, with Gandhi representing the union on a three-man arbitration board. Gandhi suggested, in effect, a closed shop and no wage decrease, and this was accepted by the impartial chairman.

4. A form of non-violent demonstration in which work ceases, shops are closed, etc.

5. Arbitration; originally, a native court of arbitration having five members.

6. The arbitrators.

7. A Sanskrit prayer, correctly called Vishnu Sahasra Nam, which contains 1,000 names of Vishnu.

8. Orthodox.

9. Scriptures.

10. The Bhagavad Gita.

11. The God of Justice, who reputedly descended into hell and then went to heaven, but renounced it because his faithful dog was refused entrance with him. He was finally readmitted because of his compassion.

12. General R. E. H. Dyer was the military leader responsible for the Amritsar massacre. Sir Michael O'Dwyer was the British Acting Governor of the Punjab who approved Dyer's action.

13. A disciple of Ramakrishna and with him one of the leaders of the revival of Hinduism in the nineteenth century.

14. A community north of the city of Madras.

15. Freedom from the cycle of death and rebirth.

16. I.e., not as a member of one of the four castes, but as an untouchable.

17. Street-cleaning and similar work performed by untouchables.

18. Prayers recited by Brahmins thrice daily, at sunrise, noon, and sunset.

19. Non-cooperation movement.

20. Scavengers.

21. An untouchable caste of Gujarat who were originally weavers but were reduced to sweepers of streets.

22. Sacred Hindu legends.

23. Religion of caste.

24. Zoroastrian scripture.

25. Revered teacher; this title was often used for Tagore.

Chapter 8

1. C. Rajagopalachari, a Congress leader at whose home in Madras Gandhi was staying.

2. Mrs. Sarojini Naidu, a Congress leader. Devi is an honorific title for a woman.

3. A part of Gujarat in western India.

4. In March 1918 he had led a *satyagraha* campaign on behalf of peasants who had to pay taxes despite a crop failure.

5. *Satyagraha* Committee.

6. An Indian soldier of the Indian army (under British rule).

7. An incident in eastern Bengal when the workers in the tea gardens of Assam fled and were rounded up at Chandpur.

8. A district on the western coast of India. Here, in 1921, the Moplahs, a Moslem community, revolted against the government and this led to Hindu-Moslem riots.

9. A small community in Bihar.

10. Jawaharlal Nehru's father.

11. Lala Lajpat Rai.

12. Frederick Edwin Smith, Lord Birkenhead (1872–1930), a Tory lawyer who was, at the time, Lord High Chancellor of Britain, and later was Secretary of State for India (1924–1928).

13. Edwin S. Montagu (1879–1924), then Secretary of State for India (1917–1922), co-sponsor of the Montagu-Chelmsford reforms.

14. Indian Civil Service.

15. A South African town which was besieged by the Boers for three months in 1899–1900. Gandhi's ambulance corps assisted General Buller's operations to relieve the town.

16. In Gandhi's native Gujarat district.

17. Perhaps the outstanding Congress leader before Gandhi; he died in 1920.

18. M. R. Jayakar, a leader of the "moderates" in Indian political life.

CHAPTER 9

1. Hinduism; strictly, knowledge of God.
2. Not this.
3. Strength or ability.
4. The spinning wheel.
5. Southeast Bengal, east of Calcutta.
6. A territory under the Madras Presidency in the center of the Indian peninsula, ceded from the Hyderabad State to the British in 1903.
7. Kabir or Kabirpanthis was a weaver who lived in the fifteenth century and tried to effect a reconciliation between Hinduism and Islam.

CHAPTER 10

1. Literally, a university. This name was given to national schools created during the non-cooperation movements in the 1920s.
2. About 200 miles distant.
3. I.e., to obtain spiritual benefit from being near him.
4. A Moslem who, with Patel, had led the satyagraha campaign in Bardoli.
5. J. M. Sengupta, Mayo of Calcutta.
6. Religious sacrifice.
7. The national university founded by Gandhi at Ahmedabad in 1920.
8. A rich member of the Jain sect who was treasurer of the Gujarat Vidyapith for several years.
9. Twice president of the Indian National Congress and former Mayor of Calcutta, who went to Nazi Germany during World War II and was killed in an airplane accident on his way to Japan in 1945
10. The seclusion of women, practiced by Moslems and some Hindus.
11. Long live the revolution!

CHAPTER 11

1. Bishop Frederick B. Fisher, author of a biography of Gandhi entitled *The Strange Little Brown Man* (New York, 1932).
2. Miss Madeleine Slade, a disciple of Gandhi.
3. A kind of lower garment or loincloth worn by men.
4. This presumably refers to powers reserved to the British under the proposed constitution.
5. A Moslem ruler in Delhi from 1660 to 1707.

• CHRONOLOGY OF GANDHI'S LIFE

1869: Oct. 2. Born at Porbandar, Kathiawad, India, son of Karamchand (Kaba) and Putlibai Gandhi.

1876: Attended primary school in Rajkot, where his family moved.
Betrothed to Kasturbai (called Kasturba in her old age), daughter of Gokuldas Makanji, a merchant.

1881: Entered high school in Rajkot.

1883: Married to Kasturbai.

1885: Father died at age of 63.

1887: Passed matriculation examination at Ahmedabad and entered Samaldas College, Bhavnagar, Kathiawad, but found studies difficult and remained only one term.

1888: First of four sons born.
Sept. Sailed from Bombay for England to study law.

HIS TWENTIETH YEAR

1891: Summer. Returned to India after being called to bar. Began practice of law in Bombay and Rajkot.

1893: April. Sailed for South Africa to become lawyer for an Indian firm.
Found himself subjected to all kinds of color discrimination.

1894: Prepared to return to India after completing law case, but was persuaded by Indian colony to remain in South Africa and do public work and earn a living as a lawyer.
Drafted first petition sent by the Indians to a South African legislature.
May. Organized the Natal Indian Congress.

1896: Returned to India for six months to bring back his wife and two children to Natal.
Dec. Sailed for South Africa with family. Was mobbed when he disembarked at Durban for what Europeans thought he wrote about South Africa when he was in India.

HIS THIRTIETH YEAR

1899: Organized Indian Ambulance Corps for British in Boer War.

1901: Embarked with family for India, promising to return to South Africa if Indian community there needed his services again.

1901–1902: Traveled extensively in India, attended Indian National Congress meeting in Calcutta, and opened law office in Bombay.

• Reprinted with permission from Homer A. Jack, editor, *The Wit and Wisdom of Gandhi*. (Boston: Beacon Press, 1951), pp. 205-10.

1902: Returned to South Africa after urgent request from Indian community.

1903: Summer. Opened law office in Johannesburg.

1904: Established the weekly journal, *Indian Opinion.*

Organized Phoenix Farm near Durban, after reading Ruskin's *Unto This Last.*

1906: March. Organized Indian Ambulance Corps for Zulu "Rebellion." Took vow of continence for life.

Sept. First *satyagraha* campaign began with meeting in Johannesburg in protest against proposed Asiatic ordinance directed against Indian immigrants in Transvaal.

Oct. Sailed for England to present Indians' case to Colonial Secretary and started back to South Africa in December.

1907: June. Organized *satyagraha* against compulsory registration of Asians ("The Black Act").

1908: Jan. Stood trial for instigating *satyagraha* and was sentenced to two months' imprisonment in Johannesburg jail (his first imprisonment).

Jan. Was summoned to consult General Smuts at Pretoria; compromise reached; was released from jail.

Feb. Attacked and wounded by Indian extremist, Mir Alam, for reaching settlement with Smuts.

Aug. After Smuts broke agreement, second *satyagraha* campaign began with bonfire of registration certificates.

Oct. Arrested for not having certificate, and sentenced to two months' imprisonment in Volksrust jail.

1909: Feb. Sentenced to three months' imprisonment in Volksrust and Pretoria jails.

June. Sailed for England again to present Indians' case.

HIS FORTIETH YEAR

Nov. Returned to South Africa, writing *Hind Swaraj* en route.

1910: May. Established Tolstoy Farm near Johannesburg.

1913: Began penitential fast (one meal a day for more than four months) because of moral lapse of two members of Phoenix settlement.

Sept. Helped campaign against nullification of marriages not celebrated according to Christian rites, with Kasturbai and other women being sentenced for crossing the Transvaal border without permits.

Nov. Third *satyagraha* campaign begun by leading "great march" of 2,000 Indian miners from Newcastle across Transvaal border in Natal.

Nov. Arrested three times in four days (at Palmford, Standerton, and Teakworth) and sentenced at Dundee to nine months' imprisonment; tried at Volksrust in second trial and sentenced to three months' imprisonment with his European co-workers, Polak and Kallenbach. Imprisoned in Volksrust jail for a few days and then taken to Bloemfontein in Orange Free State.

Dec. Released unconditionally in expectation of a compromise settlement, C. F. Andrews and W. W. Pearson having been sent by Indians in India to negotiate.

1914: Jan. Underwent fourteen days' fast for moral lapse of members of Phoenix Farm.

Jan. *Satyagraha* campaign suspended, with pending agreement between Smuts, C. F. Andrews, and Gandhi, and with ultimate passage of Indian Relief Act.

July. Left South Africa forever, sailing from Capetown for London with Kasturbai and Kallenbach, arriving just at beginning of World War I.

Organized Indian Ambulance Corps in England, but was obliged to sail for India because of pleurisy.

1915: Secured removal of customs harassment of passengers at Viramgam; first incipient *satyagraha* campaign in India.

May. Established *Satyagraha Ashram* at Kochrab, near Ahmedabad, and soon admitted an untouchable family; in 1917 moved *ashram* to new site on Sabarmati River.

1916: Feb. Gave speech at opening of Hindu University at Benares.

1917: Helped secure removal of recruiting of South African indenture workers in India.

Led successful *satyagraha* campaign for rights of peasants on indigo plantations in Champaran. Defied order to leave area in April, was arrested at Motihari and tried, but case was withdrawn. Mahadev Desai joined him at Champaran.

1918: Feb. Led strike of millworkers at Ahmedabad. Millowners agreed to arbitration after his three-day fast (his first fast in India).

March. Led *satyagraha* campaign for peasants in Kheda.

Attended Viceroy's War Conference at Delhi and agreed that Indians should be recruited for World War I.

Began recruiting campaign, but was taken ill and came near death; agreed to drink goat's milk and learned spinning during convalescence.

1919: Spring. Rowlatt Bills (perpetuating withdrawal of civil liberties for seditious crimes) passed, and first all-India *satyagraha* campaign conceived.

April. Organized nation-wide *hartal*—suspension of activity for a day—against Rowlatt Bills.

April. Arrested at Kosi near Delhi on way to Punjab and escorted back to Bombay, but never tried.

April. Fasted at Sabarmati for three days in penitence for violence and suspended *satyagraha* campaign, which he called a "Himalayan miscalculation" because people were not disciplined enough.

Assumed editorship of English weekly, *Young India*, and Gujarati weekly, *Navajivan*.

HIS FIFTIETH YEAR

Oct. After five months' refusal, authorities allowed him to visit scene of April disorders in Punjab. Worked closely with Motilal Nehru. Conducted extensive inquiry into violence in many Punjab villages.

1920: April. Elected president of All-India Home Rule League.

June. Successfully urged resolution for a *satyagraha* campaign of non-cooperation at Moslem Conference at Allahabad and at Congress sessions at Calcutta (Sept.) and Nagpur (Dec.).

Aug. Second all-India *satyagraha* campaign began when he gave up Kaisar-i-Hind medal.

1921: Presided at opening of first shop selling homespun (*khadi*) in Bombay.

Aug. Presided at bonfire of foreign cloth in Bombay.

Sept. Gave up wearing shirt and cap and resolved to wear only a loincloth in devotion to homespun cotton and simplicity.

Nov. Fasted at Bombay for five days because of communal rioting following visit of Prince of Wales (later Edward VIII and Duke of Windsor).

Dec. Mass civil disobedience, with thousands in jail. Gandhi invested with "sole executive authority" on behalf of Congress.

1922: Feb. Suspended mass disobedience because of violence at Chauri Chaura and undertook five-day fast of penance at Bardoli.

March. Arrested at Sabarmati on charge of sedition in *Young India*. Pleaded guilty in famous statement at the "great trial" in Ahmedabad before Judge Broomfield. Sentenced to six years' imprisonment in Yeravda jail.

1923: Wrote *Satyagraha in South Africa* and part of his autobiography in prison.

1924: Jan. Was operated on for appendicitis and unconditionally released from prison in February.

Sept. Began 21-day "great fast" at Mohammed Ali's home near Delhi as penance for communal rioting (between Hindus and Moslems), especially at Kohat.

Dec. Presided over Congress session at Belgaum as president.

1925: Nov. Fasted at Sabarmati for seven days because of misbehavior of members of *ashram*.

Dec. Announced one-year political silence and immobility at Congress session at Cawnpore.

1927: No-tax *satyagraha* campaign launched at Bardoli, led by Sardar Patel.

1928: Dec. Moved compromise resolution at Congress session at Calcutta, calling for complete independence within one year, or else the beginning of another all-Indian *satyagraha* campaign.

1929: March. Arrested for burning foreign cloth in Calcutta and fined one rupee.

HIS SIXTIETH YEAR

Dec. Congress session at Lahore declared complete independence and a boycott of the legislature and fixed January 26 as National Independence Day. Third all-Indian *satyagraha* campaign began.

1930: March 12. Set out from Sabarmati with 79 volunteers on historic salt march 200 miles to sea at Dandi.

April 6. Broke salt law by picking salt up at seashore as whole world watched.

May. Arrested by armed policemen at Karadi and imprisoned in Yeravda jail without trial.

One hundred thousand persons arrested. There was no session of Congress in December because all leaders were in jail.

1931: Jan. Released unconditionally with 30 other Congress leaders.

March. Gandhi-Irwin (Viceroy) Pact signed, which ended civil disobedience.

Aug. Sailed from Bombay accompanied by Desai, Naidu, Mira, etc., for the second Round Table Conference, arriving in London via Marseilles, where he was met by C. F. Andrews.

Autumn. Resided at Kingsley Hall in London slums, broadcast to America, visited universities, met celebrities, and attended Round Table Conference sessions.

Dec. Left England for Switzerland, where he met Romain Rolland, and Italy, where he met Mussolini.

Dec. Arrived in India. Was authorized by Congress to renew *satyagraha* campaign (fourth nation-wide effort).

1932: Jan. Arrested in Bombay with Sardar Patel and detained without trial at Yeravda prison.

Sept. 20. Began "perpetual fast unto death" while in prison in protest of British action giving separate electorate to untouchables.

Sept. 26. Concluded "epic fast" with historic cell scene in presence of Tagore after British accepted "Yeravda Pact."

Dec. Joined fast initiated by another prisoner, Appasaheb Patwardhan, against untouchability; but fast ended in two days.

1933: Began weekly publication of *Harijan* in place of *Young India*.

May 8. Began self-purification fast of 21 days against untouchability and was released from prison by government on first day. Fast concluded after 21 days at Poona.

July. Disbanded Sabarmati *ashram*, which became center for removal of untouchability.

Aug. Arrested and imprisoned at Yeravda for four days with 34 members of his *ashram*. When he refused to leave Yeravda village for Poona, he was sentenced to one year's imprisonment at Yeravda.

Aug. 16. Began fast against refusal of government to grant him permission to work against untouchability while in prison; on fifth day of fast he was removed to Sassoon Hospital; his health was precarious; he was unconditionally released on eighth day.

Nov. Began ten-month tour of every province in India to help end untouchability.

Nov. Kasturba arrested and imprisoned for sixth time in two years.

1934: Summer. Three separate attempts made on his life.

July. Fasted at Wardha *ashram* for seven days in penance against intolerance of opponents of the movement against untouchability.

Oct. Launched All-India Village Industries Association.

1935: Health declined; moved to Bombay to recover.

1936: Visited Segaon, a village near Wardha in the Central Provinces, and decided to settle there. (This was renamed Sevagram in 1940 and eventually became an *ashram* for his disciples.)

1937: Jan. Visited Travancore for removal of untouchability.

1938: Autumn. Tour of Northwest Frontier Province with the Khan Abdul Ghaffar Khan.

1939: March. Began fast unto death as part of *satyagraha* campaign in Rajkot; fast ended four days later when Viceroy appointed an arbitrator.

HIS SEVENTIETH YEAR

1940: Oct. Launched limited, individual civil-disobedience campaign against Britain's refusal to allow Indians to express their opinions regarding World War II—23,000 persons imprisoned within a year.

1942: *Harijan* resumed publication after being suspended for 15 months.

March. Met Sir Stafford Cripps in New Delhi but called his proposals "a post-dated check"; they were ultimately rejected by Congress.

Aug. Congress passed "Quit India" resolution—the final nation-wide *satyagraha* campaign—with Gandhi as leader.

Aug. 9. Arrested with other Congress leaders and Kasturba and imprisoned in Aga Khan Palace near Poona, with populace revolting in many parts of India. He began correspondence with Viceroy.

Aug. Mahadev Desai, Gandhi's secretary and intimate, died in Palace.

1943: Feb. 10. Began 21-day fast at Aga Khan Palace to end deadlock of negotiations between Viceroy and Indian leaders.

1944: Feb. 22. Kasturba died in detention at Aga Khan Palace at age of seventy-four.

May 6. After decline in health, was released unconditionally from detention (this was his last imprisonment; he had spent 2,338 days in jail during his lifetime).

Sept. Important talks with Jinnah of Moslem League in Bombay on Hindu-Moslem unity.

1946: March. Conferred with British Cabinet Mission in New Delhi.

Nov. Began four-month tour of 49 villages in East Bengal to quell communal rioting over Moslem representation in provisional government.

1947: March. Began tour of Bihar to lessen Hindu-Moslem tensions.

March. Began conferences in New Delhi with Viceroy (Lord Mount-
batten) and Jinnah.

May. Opposed Congress decision to accept division of country into
India and Pakistan.

Aug. 15. Fasted and prayed to combat riots in Calcutta as India was
partitioned and granted independence.

Sept. Fasted for three days to stop communal violence in Calcutta.

Sept. Visited Delhi and environs to stop rioting and to visit camps of
refugees (Hindus and Sikhs from the Punjab).

1948: Jan. 13. Fasted for five days in Delhi for communal unity.

Jan. 20. Bomb exploded in midst of his prayer meeting at Birla House,
Delhi.

Jan. 30. Assassinated in 78th year at Birla House by Vinayak N. Godse.

GROVE PRESS EASTERN LITERATURE AND PHILOSOPHY TITLES

Batchelor, Stephen /ALONE WITH OTHERS: AN EXISTENTIAL APPROACH TO BUDDHISM / $5.95 / 62457-2

Bharti, Ma Satya / DRUNK ON THE DIVINE: AN ACCOUNT OF LIFE IN THE ASHRAM OF BHAGWAN SHREE RAJNEESH / $6.95 / 17656-1

Blofeld, John, tr. / THE ZEN TEACHINGS OF HUANG PO / $9.95 / 17217-5

Briley, John / GANDHI: THE SCREENPLAY / $6.95 / 62471-8

Chang Chung-Yuan, tr. / ORIGINAL TEACHINGS OF CH'AN BUDDHISM / $9.95 / 62417-3

Feuerstein, Georg / THE ESSENCE OF YOGA / $3.95 / 17902-1

Gandhi, Indira / MY TRUTH / $7.95 / 17976-5

Gandhi, Mahatma / THE GANDHI READER: A SOURCEBOOK OF HIS LIFE AND WRITINGS (Homer A. Jack, ed.) / $5.95 / 62472-6

Gelberg, Steven J. / HARE KRISHNA, HARE KRISHNA: FIVE DISTINGUISHED SCHOLARS ON THE KRISHNA MOVEMENT IN THE WEST / $7.95 / 62454-8

Keene, Donald, ed. / ANTHOLOGY OF JAPANESE LITERATURE: FROM THE EARLIEST ERA TO THE MID-NINETEENTH CENTURY / $7.95 / 17221-3

Keene, Donald / MODERN JAPANESE LITERATURE / $12.50 / 17254-X

Linssen, Robert / LIVING ZEN / $3.95 / 17391-0

Luk, Charles, tr. / THE TRANSMISSION OF THE MIND OUTSIDE THE TEACHING (Ku Tsun Su Yu Lu) / $2.95 / 17888-2

Mitchell, Stephen, ed. / DROPPING ASHES ON THE BUDDHA: THE TEACHINGS OF ZEN MASTER SEUNG SAHN / $4.95 / 17910-2

Oe, Kenzaburo / A PERSONAL MATTER / $6.95 / 17650-2

Oe, Kenzaburo / TEACH US TO OUTGROW OUR MADNESS: FOUR NOVELS The Day He Himself Shall Wipe My Tears Away; Prize Stock; Teach Us To Outgrow Our Madness; Aghwee The Sky Monster) / $4.95 / 17002-4

Rahula, Walpola / WHAT THE BUDDHA TAUGHT / $6.95 / 17827-0

Rajneesh, Bhagwan Shree / THE GREAT CHALLENGE: A RAJNEESH READER / $9.95 / 17934-X

Sri Nisargadatta Maharaj / SEEDS OF CONSCIOUSNESS: THE WISDOM OF SRI NISARGADATTA MAHARAJ, edited by Jean Dunn / $9.95 / 17939-0

Stryk, Lucien, and Ikemoto, Takashi, trs. / THE CRANE'S BILL: ZEN POEMS OF CHINA AND JAPAN / $4.95 / 17912-9

Stryk, Lucien, ed. / WORLD OF THE BUDDHA: AN INTRODUCTION TO BUDDHIST LITERATURE / $9.95 / 17974-9

Suzuki, D. T. / INTRODUCTION TO ZEN BUDDHISM / $2.95 / 17474-7

Suzuki, D. T. / MANUAL OF ZEN BUDDHISM / $3.95 / 17224-8

Waley, Arthur / THE WAY AND ITS POWER: A STUDY OF THE TAO TE CHING AND ITS PLACE IN CHINESE THOUGHT / $4.95 / 17207-8

Watts, Alan W. / THE SPIRIT OF ZEN / $2.95 / 17418-6